AN INTRODUCTION TO
THE LAW OF
HEALTH AND SAFETY
AT WORK IN SCOTLAND

AN INTRODUCTION TO THE LAW OF HEALTH AND SAFETY AT WORK IN SCOTLAND

by
Victor Craig
Professor of Employment Law,
Heriot-Watt University

and
Kenneth Miller
Professor of Employment Law,
University of Strathclyde

W. GREEN/Sweet & Maxwell
EDINBURGH
1995

First published 1995

© 1995
W. Green & Son Ltd

ISBN 0 414 01057 4

A catalogue record for this book is
available from the British Library

Typeset by LBJ Enterprises Ltd,
Aldermaston and Chilcompton.
Printed and bound in Great Britain by
The Headway Press, Reading.

PREFACE

It is the purpose of this book to provide a concise and up-to-date introduction to the law of health and safety at work as it applies in Scotland. This approach necessitates us considering the common law, the older regulatory statutes, the Health and Safety at Work, etc. Act 1974 and the regulations made under it, and, of increasing importance, European law. It is true that much of the law is common to all of the United Kingdom. Yet sufficient differences do exist to merit the treatment of the subject in a Scottish context. There can be no doubt that decisions in Scottish cases have made a unique and positive contribution to the development of the common law of health and safety in both Scotland and throughout the English-speaking world. Equally, many of the landmark cases as regards the older regulatory statutes are also Scottish.

This in itself cannot be the sole justification for writing a book from a Scottish perspective. We also wished to produce a book which emphasised the continuing importance of Scots law in this area. Decisions of the Scottish courts continue to play a central role in the development of health and safety law at a United Kingdom level and wherever possible we have sought to rely on Scottish authority where it exists. In other areas where English law is more developed we have speculated on the likely response of the Scottish courts. We also thought it important to write a book which located the law within the legal system of Scotland. For example, there are special features about the award of damages in Scotland and this is reflected in our treatment of the subject in Chapter 7 where we use recent Scottish case law in order to illustrate how damages are calculated here. Nevertheless given the commonality of the current statutory material on health and safety we hope that the book will be useful not only to readers whose interest is primarily Scottish but also to others who may be interested in a text which attempts to treat the general principles of the law of health and safety at work in a contemporary and straightforward way.

The book has been written at a time of great change in health and safety law. As already indicated, European law has started to play a major role in this area and this has necessitated significant alterations to domestic law. Equally, the Government's preference for deregulation is beginning to have an impact on health and safety issues. Thus the recent review of health and safety law conducted by the Health and Safety Commission is likely to lead to the repeal of all the remaining older statutory provisions. Wherever possible we have sought to reflect these developments in the book. Thus a significant portion of the book is devoted to a consideration of European directives and the way in which they have been implemented in domestic law. However, given the pace of development, we do not claim that this book is an exhaustive statement of the law. For one thing, we have had to be selective as regards the health and safety regulations which we discuss. Nonetheless we believe that we have discussed the most important ones.

We would like to thank all our colleagues at Heriot-Watt and Strathclyde Universities for their support and encouragement. In particular, thanks are due to Jenifer Ross for her constructive comments, to Michael Allan and Amanda Cooke for assisting us with the research and to Barbara Syme for her patient transcription of the manuscript. We would also like to thank Greens for agreeing to publish the book and for their sterling editorial support.

Any errors or omissions remain those of the authors and we have sought to state the law as at March 1, 1995.

Vic Craig & Kenny Miller
Edinburgh and Glasgow
March 31, 1995.

Contents

TABLE OF CASES

TABLE OF STATUTES

xxiii

TABLE OF STATUTORY INSTRUMENTS

TABLE OF EC DIRECTIVES

CHAPTER 1

INTRODUCTION

1.1 Few areas of the law can have been transformed, in a relatively short period of time, to the same extent as that area conveniently described as the law of health and safety at work. While there had been a gradual development of the responsibilities of those at work via the common law duty of care as well as occasional but important benchmark-setting legislation in the form of various enactments to regulate factories, mines, offices and certain other premises, radical shifts in the approach of the law to health and safety at work were stimulated first by the Report of the Robens Committee[1] and then by the Council of Ministers approving[2] the First Action Programme on Health and Safety at Work drawn up by the Commission of the European Communities. The former resulted in the passage of the Health and Safety at Work Act 1974 which embraced an entirely new philosophy of enacting general duties supported by Codes of Practice, while the latter saw the adoption of various Directives, most notably the Framework Directive[3] which make express the employer's duty to be proactive by assessing the risks to health and safety and take the necessary implementing measures, thereby equating the area of health and safety with other areas of management.

The common law

1.2 While the early common law recognised that the "master" was, as a general rule, liable for the injuries to the "servant",[4] this was subject to the servant not continuing in the face of a known danger; indeed the

---

[1] *Safety and Health at Work*, Cmnd. 5034 (1972).
[2] Council Resolution 78/C165/1.
[3] Directive on the Introduction of Measures to Improve the Health and Safety of Workers at Work (89/392/EEC).
[4] Fraser, *Master and Servant* (3rd ed.) pp. 177 *et seq.*; and see Chap. 3.

impression might be gained from some of the early decisions that if workmen were properly compensated for injuries sustained in the course of their employment they might be encouraged to omit normal caution and diligence in the exercise of their work.[5] From a moral standpoint the conduct of the employer could be regarded as

> "highly reprehensible as I think they were in the present instance. The workman who depends on his employment for the bread of himself and his family is thus tempted to incur risks to which, as a matter of humanity he ought not to be exposed. But looking at it from a legal point of view if a man for the sake of his employment takes it or continues in it with the knowledge of all the risks he must trust himself to keep clear of injury."[6]

Although this notion of implied consent seems to have had its origins in England, sadly it seems to have been readily accepted in Scots law.[7] Nor was Scots law able to resist the introduction of the cognate doctrine of common employment[8] — a doctrine which required a workman to be regarded as agreeing to accept the risks of working alongside others in whose selection he had not been involved! Of course there were from time to time judicial attempts to temper some common-law rules. Thus the personalisation of the duty of care was to an extent intended to obviate the effects of common employment,[9] and the limitations imposed on the circumstances in which the employer could plead *volenti non fit injuria*[10] were judicial recognitions of the reality of the insecure status of employment, in the absence of any protection against arbitrary dismissal and of any system of welfare benefits. Even the most modest of reforms were the result

---

[5] *Priestly v. Fowler* (1837) M. & W. 1. And see *Seymour v. Maddox* (1851) 20 L.J. Q.B. 327 in which a singer's action failed because she had as good an opportunity of seeing the danger (a hole in the floor) as the employer!

[6] *Woodley v. Metropolitan District Ry. Co. Ltd* (1877) 2 Ex. D. 384 *per* Cockburn C.J.

[7] See, for example, *McNeil v. Wallace* (1853) 15 D. 818; *Robertson v. Adamson* (1862) 24 D. 1231.

[8] See Chap. 3, para. 3.4.

[9] See Chap. 3, para. 3.4.

[10] See Chap. 3, para. 3.49.

of leglislation. Thus the eradication of the doctrine of common employment and the effects of an employee's contribution to his injuries both required legislative intervention[11] and, arguably, in at least one case legislation is still awaited.[12] Further because the common law operates *ex post facto* to compensate an injured employee it is obvious that any generally normative measures which would operate to prevent or reduce injuries at work by setting standards of performance would require legislation. This is not to say that the common law, through the flexible concept of the duty of care, is unable to respond to new risks and dangers. Thus the problems encountered in attempting to recover damages for long-term exposure to noise over periods of employment with different employers were tackled in *Thompson v. Smith Shiprepairers (North Shields) Ltd*[13] while the contemporary dangers of repetitive strain injuries or work-related upper-limb disorders[14] and psychological stress[15] have shown the ability of the common law to respond. Nevertheless the nature of the risks and dangers of modern employment conditions require not merely that remedies are available for those who suffer occupational injury or disease: the public interest is also involved in that those who are rendered incapable of economic activity or whose economic activity is reduced by such injury or disease impose charges on the public health and welfare systems of the State. Thus there is a need for legislation to (1) complement the common law and create

---

[11] See Chap. 3, paras. 3.4 and 3.49.

[12] There still exists the possibility of an insurer requiring, on the basis of a subrogation clause, that an insured employer sue an employee for damages for breach of the implied duty to perform with reasonable care which has resulted in a claim being brought against the employer by a third party. See Chap. 3, para. 3.44.

[13] [1984] I.C.R. 237 (Q.B.D.). And see *McGhee v. National Coal Board* [1973] 1 W.L.R. 1 (H.L.) where the House of Lords treated proof that a breach of duty had increased the risk of dermatitis as proof that the breach had actually caused the disease, which as Lord Wilberforce pointed out (p. 7) was a fiction adopted in the interests of justice to prevent the plaintiff from losing his claim through a failure to prove what in the current state of medical knowledge he had no means of proving.

[14] *Bettany v. Royal Doulton (U.K.) Ltd* (1993, unreported); *cf. Mughal v. Reuters Ltd* (1993, unreported).

[15] See *Johnstone v. Bloomsbury Health Authority* [1991] I.C.R. 269 (C.A.), *Petch v. Commissioners of Customs and Excise* [1993] I.C.R. 789 (C.A.) and *Walker v. Northumberland C.C.* [1995] I.R.L.R. 35.

a framework of provisions which are preventative, applicable to specific dangers where necessary, educative and
mandatory, (2) create the necessary reforming and enforcement agencies and (3) translate into domestic law
requirements of European Union Directives.

Statutory intervention

1.3   Principally because until about the end of the eigh-
teenth century there were in Scotland only "labouring
individuals" in agriculture[16] Acts of the Scots Parliament,
although they gave magistrates of Royal Burghs the
power to fix prices and wages, were not required to deal
with the occupational dangers which accompanied the
post-Union industrial revolution. Many of the early examples of statutory intervention were addressed to the
protection of children (apprentices) and women.[17] As a
result of the extension of the Poor Law of 1601 destitute
children were located in industrial schools and work-
houses. Their exploitation was highlighted by the out-
break of fever in 1784 in the Ratcliffe Cotton Works in
Lancashire, and by 1794 magistrates and justices of the
peace together had powers to prohibit indentures and
fine masters who ill-treated apprentices. In 1802 the
Health and Morals of Apprentices Act was passed and in
1819, in spite of opposition on the grounds that regulation
by the State would inhibit trade and reduce living standards, the Factory Act prohibited employment in a cotton
mill of those under the age of nine, and limited the
working day of those under 16 to 12 hours. The Factory
Act 1833 set up His Majesty's Inspectorate of Factories
and introduced rules regarding provision of fences and
guards for dangerous machines, and by 1901 a rudimen-
tary system of notification of accidents and disease was
set up by the Factory and Workshop Act of that year. In
1959 the Factories Act 1937 was amended to include
provisions dealing with dangerous fumes and substances,
hoists, lifts, floors and stairs. In 1961 the Factories Act
was passed to consolidate many of the earlier provisions
and that legislation, although recently in part repealed by

---

[16] Johnson, *History of the Working Class in Scotland.*
[17] For coverage of early statutory intervention see Hutchins and Harrison, *History of Factory Legislation* (1926).

regulations designed to give effect to European Union Directives,[18] still serves as the basis of health and safety of the many workers engaged in factories. However as the different industries developed, similar and frequently duplicating legislation was enacted to regulate health and safety in mines and quarries, shops, offices and railway premises,[19] but was still typified by legislative reaction to particular disasters or hazards in certain types of work, and by the late 1960s there were over 500 pieces of legislation and regulations in force. Thus until the enactment of the Health and Safety at Work Act 1974 statutory intervention typically took the form of a response to specific dangers and was restricted to particular types of workplace. Thus many people were excluded from the protection of legislation because, for example, the injury was sustained in a type of workplace which was not to be covered — like a school or hospital[20] — or the legislation protected only those who were employed under contracts of employment,[21] or the particular activity was outside the scope of the legislation.[22] Also prior to 1974 legislation was frequently expressed in the form of a prescriptive absolute duty which encouraged the belief that responsibility for safety and health at work was a matter for inspectors and ultimately the criminal courts, with the effect that both employers and employees felt little "ownership" of health and safety issues and there was no guarantee that the different inspectorates applied consistent standards. Finally, but perhaps most important of all, enforcement relied on the criminal law which was concerned only very indirectly with the avoidance of dangers and the minimising of risks. One of the main aims of the Health and Safety at Work Act 1974 was to sweep away many of

[18] See Chap. 5, paras. 6.20–6.37
[19] See Chaps. 4 and 5.
[20] See, for example, *Bromwich v. Ear, Nose and Throat Hospital* [1980] 2 All E.R. 663, in which had it not been held that a workshop, which formed part of a hospital, was in law a "factory" the injured plumber would not have been able to rely on the provision of the Abrasive Wheels Regulations 1970.
[21] *Herbert v. Harold Shaw Ltd*, 1989 2 Q.B. 138.
[22] Consider the issue in *Morganite Crucible Ltd v. Nurse* [1988] I.C.R. 15 (H.L.) namely whether the demolition of structures made partly of asbestos was, for the purpose of the Factories Act 1961 and the Asbestos Regulations 1969, a "process." Had it not been a "process" compliance with the Regulations, which ensured provision of respiratory protective equipment against the escape of asbestos dust, would not have been supported by a criminal sanction.

these illogical and outdated distinctions on which the entire structure of health and safety law had been erected and to replace legislation which targeted specifics and contained narrow, technical definitions with legislation which enacted universally applicable general duties, supplemented where appropriate with guidance and Codes of Practice, while retaining the criminal sanction. However, the 1974 Act's general duties reflect the common-law duty of reasonable care in that they are qualified by the test of reasonable practicability,[23] and in that respect the Act acknowledges that in many cases there is a balance between health and safety on the one hand and cost, administrative convenience and feasibility on the other; and it is open to question the extent to which such a balance is consistent with the relevant Directives.[24]

The effects of European Union

1.4 Much recent and expected health and safety legislation originates in the form of European Union Directives which, in accordance with the Single European Act and Article 118a[25] of the Treaty establishing the European Economic Community, may be adopted by qualified majority. The result is that the interpretation of domestic legislation has to take place against the background of its European origins, and that requires that wherever possible the implementing domestic law has to be given a meaning which comports with its European parent.[26] Furthermore even where the domestic provision is contradictory or absent the provisions of a Directive, if sufficiently precise and unconditional,[27] can be relied on against the State or an "emanation of the State" like a

---

[23] And see the Workplace (Health, Safety and Welfare) Regulations 1992, reg. 12(3).
[24] See Chap. 5.
[25] Art. 118a was added by the Single European Act and provides for the Commission to propose Directives on health and safety for adoption by the Council of Ministers by qualified majority.
[26] *Litster v. Forth Dry Dock and Engineering Co. Ltd,* 1989 S.L.T. 540 (H.L.); *Webb v. EMO Air Cargo (UK) Ltd* [1993] I.R.L.R. 27 (H.L.). Indeed it is probably the case that a U.K. court has to give effect to a Directive unless the domestic statute is directly contradictory (*Marleasing S.A. v. La Commercial Internacional de Alimentacion S.A.* [1992] C.M.L.R. 305 (ECJ); *Faccini Dori v. Recreb Srl, The Times,* Aug. 4, 1994 (ECJ).
[27] See *Faccini,* above.

public health authority,[28] and an employee in the private sector who suffers a loss as a result of his own Member State's failing to implement a Directive may have a right of action against his own government.[29]

What the future holds

1.5 After an exhaustive review of health and safety legislation the Health and Safety Commission has issued a report,[30] and the government has accepted all of its proposals and recommendations. While the report acknowledges that there is room for improvement in certain areas, it proposes no change to the "architecture" of the present system as established by the Health and Safety at Work Act 1974. Nevertheless, in addition to the need generally to rationalise and simplify the many provisions the Commission recognises the need to (1) clarify the respective roles of legislation, Codes of Practice and guidance, (2) update or remove at least 100 sets of regulations and primary legislation and simplify the existing provisions regarding completion of forms and records, and (3) reduce inconsistencies in enforcement. Accordingly, and in keeping with the philosophy of the Deregulation and Contracting-Out Act 1994,[31] a comprehensive system of review is to be undertaken which will result in almost all the pre-1974 legislation being removed. Undoubtedly in this respect the Commission will be constrained by European Directives but, standing the decision in *R. v. Secretary of State for Employment, ex p. NACODS*,[32] there is no requirement to amend or repeal section 1(2)[33] of the 1974 Act because where the Secretary of State believes that the new regulations satisfy the

---

[28] *Marshall v. Southampton etc. Health Authority* [1986] I.C.R. 335. As to what is an emanation of the State, see *Foster v. British Gas* [1991] I.C.R. 84 (ECJ).

[29] *Francovich v. Italy* [1991] I.R.L.R. 84 (ECJ).

[30] *Review of Health and Safety Legislation* (1994).

[31] The Task Force of the Department of Trade and Industry has made several proposals for the amendment of health and safety legislation, and highlights the need to assess whether the administrative and compliance costs are justified by the costs of the risks present.

[32] 1994 H.S.I.B. 222.

[33] s. 1(2) permits the Secretary of State to amend existing provisions by regulations "designed to maintain or improve standards of health, safety and welfare" established by or under those provisions.

statutory criteria, including consultation by the Health and Safety Commission, the court must not review the respective merits of the new proposed legislation.

CHAPTER 2

SOURCES AND INSTITUTIONS

INTRODUCTION

2.1 The legal provisions which operate in the area of health and safety at work have such a variety of sources and qualities that they may fairly be described as kaleidoscopic. The area sees a confluence of common law principles and statutory codes, criminal and civil jurisdictions, contractual and delictual obligations (and civil remedies for breach of statutory duty), private and public law regimes, the intervention of the ordinary courts and specialist industrial tribunals as well as domestic and European Community legislation, both primary and secondary. A proper understanding of health and safety at work law therefore requires an appreciation of these distinctions and how they interact and while a comprehensive treatment of these matters is beyond the scope of this work it is necessary to give at least an indication of the operation of the different provisions in the context of health and safety.

The criminal law

2.2 Many particular risks or dangers have been the subject of express statutory provisions commonly enacted to protect the interests and welfare of women, young persons and children employed in factories or mines. Thus the Factories Act 1833[1] established a 12-hour maximum working day for young persons while for women and children the figure was 10 hours although the effect of this was considerably lessened by the decision in *Ryder v. Mills*[2] construing the statute to permit relay working.

[1] And see the Ten Hours Act 1857.
[2] (1850) 3 Exch. 853.

These modest early statutes however set the pattern for future and contemporary measures by introducing criminal sanctions on employers for infringements.[3] However it was not until the appointment of a Royal Commission in 1875 that there occurred the first attempt at comprehensive factory legislation[4] — a trend continued in later years (and typified by the Mines and Quarries Act 1954, the Factories Act 1961 and the Offices, Shops and Railway Premises Act 1963) but eventually departed from with the enactment of the Health and Safety at Work Act 1974 which, following the recommendation of the Robens Committee on Health and Safety,[5] signalled the commencement of a move away from legislating against specific dangers in particular places of employment to legislating for all places of employment in terms of general duties.[6] However, while undoubtedly the coherent development of the law of health and safety at work has been the province of statutory regulation enforced through the criminal law[7] — a pattern of development which has recently been continued by the passage of delegated legislation to implement the many Directives on health and safety at work made by the European Union Council of Ministers — it is also important to note that while that development remains almost exclusively statutory it has, since the enactment of the Health and Safety at Work Act 1974, taken the form of subordinate legislation and Approved Codes of Practice (ACOPs) under the enabling powers contained in the 1974 Act itself.[8]

2.3 Regulations made in reliance on the powers contained in section 15 of the Health and Safety at Work Act 1974 are known as "health and safety regulations,"[9] and while a

[3] Interestingly the Factories Act 1844 and the Coal Mines Inspection Act 1850 allowed the Home Secretary a power to award part of any fine imposed on an employer to a worker injured as a result of the employer's breach of the statutory provision – a power little used until its eventual abolition in 1959.
[4] Factory and Workshop Act 1878.
[5] Cmnd. 5034.
[6] Contrast for example Factories Act 1961, Pt. II dealing with such specific matters as cleaning of prime movers by women and young persons (s.20) and cranes, ropes and lifting tackles (s. 26) with the general duties in Health and Safety at Work Act 1974, ss. 1–7.
[7] Factories Act 1961, ss. 155, 158, 164, and see Chap. 4.
[8] Health and Safety at Work Act 1974, ss. 15, 16.
[9] HASAWA, s. 15.

government Minister is required to consult the Health and Safety Commission before exercising such enabling powers[10] they may be exercised for any of the purposes contained in Schedule 3 to the 1974 Act.[11] However, whether the legislation be primary or secondary the sanction is invariably, eventually,[12] criminal.[13] Thus it is provided[14] that it is an offence for any person to fail to discharge a duty imposed on the 1974 Act itself or to contravene any of the health and safety regulations or any requirement or prohibition imposed under any such regulations. It is therefore unnecessary for health and safety regulations[15] expressly to provide that their breach is an offence.[16]

2.4 Where an offence is due to the wrongful[17] act or default of some other person that other person may be charged[18] and where the offence is committed by a body corporate is committed with the consent or connivance of or to have been attributable to[19] any neglect on the part of any director, manager,[20] secretary or similar officer he too shall to be guilty of the offence.[21]

The civil law

2.5 Where a person suffers injury at work, compensating such a person for the losses he sustains as a result of

[10] HASAWA, s. 50.

[11] Where the subordinate legislation is to implement a European Union Directive which extends beyond the area of health and safety at work, a Minister may have to rely on the enabling powers contained in the European Communities Act 1972, s. 2; see, for example the Supply of Machinery (Safety) Regulations 1992 (S.I. 1992 No. 3073).

[12] Initially breach of a statutory provision may result in the issuing of an Improvement Notice, but a failure to observe the terms of such a notice is itself an offence (HASAWA), s. 33 (1)(g).

[13] And see the value attributed to administrative sanctions by the report of the Robens Committee on Health and Safety at Work (Cmnd. 5034), Chap. 9.

[14] *Ibid.*, s. 33 (1) (a)–(c).

[15] *Viz.* those regulations made under HASAWA, s. 15.

[16] And see the similar provisions in the Factories Act 1961, s. 155 and the Offices, Shops and Railway Premises Act 1963, s. 63. *Cf.* the Supply of Machinery (Safety) Regulations 1992 (S.I. 3073) Pt. IV.

[17] *Noss Farm Products Ltd v. Lilico* [1946] 2 All E.R. 609.

[18] HASAWA, s. 36.

[19] *Wotherspoon v. H. M. Advocate*, 1928 J.C. 74.

[20] Those who are responsible for deciding corporate policy or strategy are "managers" (*R. v. Boal (Francis)* [1992] Q.B. 591).

[21] *Ibid.*, s. 37.

that injury is of course the province of the civil law which may for present purposes be subdivided into (a) delictual and contractual and (b) breach of statutory duty. It may be said therefore that the principal objective of the current statutory regime is "the suppression of dangers before they arise . . . rather than guarding against risks which have been allowed to occur"[22] whereas the civil law proceeds on the basis that breaches of duty will occur and provides compensation to the victims of such breaches. The relevant principles of the laws of delict and contract are treated in detail later,[23] but it requires to be emphasised here that legislation which imposes a criminal penalty in respect of a failure to comply with the statutory provision may also give rise to a civil law action for breach of statutory duty.[24] Whether a criminal provision also gives rise to an action for breach of statutory duty at the instance of an injured party is a matter of interpretation in order to determine what was the intention of Parliament in enacting the duty concerned,[25] although civil liability will be inferred where the predominant purpose of the statute or the subordinate legislation is the protection of a particular class of workmen by imposing a duty on their employers, the duty of taking special measures to protect their safety.[26] However, the pursuer must prove on the balance of probabilities that it was the breach of statutory duty which caused the injury.[27] In this context it is important to note therefore that while nothing in Part I of the Health and Safety at Work Act 1974 shall be construed as conferring a right of action in any civil proceedings for a failure to comply with any duty imposed by sections 2–8 or as affecting the extent (if any) to which breach of a duty under an existing statutory provision[28] is actionable, breach of a duty imposed by health and safety regu-

---

[22] Redgrave, Fife and Machin, *Health and Safety* (2nd ed.) p. v.

[23] See Chap. 3.

[24] See also Chap. 4.

[25] *Atkinson v. Newcastle Waterworks Co* (1877) 2 Ex. D. 441; *Pullar v. Window Clean Ltd*, 1956 S.C. 13; and see *McArthur v. Strathclyde Regional Council, The Times*, May 20, 1994.

[26] *Black v. Fife Coal Co.*, 1912 S.C. (H.L.) 33; *Bett v. Dalmeny Oil Co.* (1905) 7 F. 787.

[27] *Wardlaw v. Bonnington Castings Ltd*, 1956 S.C. (H.L.) 26. *Cf. Kelly v. Glebe Sugar Refining Co.* (1893) 20 R. 833, where Lord Adam opines that neglect of the criminal duty creates a prima facie case of fault against the employers.

[28] See HASAWA, s. 53(1), Sched. 3.

lations[29] shall, in so far as it causes damage,[30] be actionable except in so far as the regulations provide otherwise.[31]

Approved Codes of Practice (ACOPs)

2.6 In recognition of the difficulty of framing effective statutory regulations and the need to provide "intelligibility and flexibility"[32] the Robens Committee[33] recommended the enactment of the general principles of the responsibilities for health and safety at work supported by regulations and codes of practice, the latter to be used extensively to provide "detailed specifications and guidance on the implementation" of these principles but not to impose legal obligations although to be taken into account where necessary in enforcement proceedings.[34] Effect to that recommendation has been given by sections 16 and 17 of the Health and Safety at Work Act 1974. Thus the Health and Safety Commission may approve and/or issue codes of practice which it regards as suitable for the purpose of providing practical guidance to the requirements of (a) sections 2–7 of the 1974 Act, (b) health and safety regulations.[35] The consent of the Secretary of State for Employment is required before the Health and Safety Commission can approve a code,[36] but many codes of practice have been issued and several British Standards have been approved as codes of practice thereby acquiring the legal characteristics attached to codes of practice by section 17 of the 1974 Act, namely that while a failure on the part of any person to observe the code shall not of

---

[29] *Viz.* regulations made under HASAWA, s. 15.
[30] If this phraseology would exclude interdict from the scope of s. 47(2), where the regulation was passed to implement a European Directive it would offend against the rule that domestic law ensures an effective remedy for breach of provisions contained in a Directive (*Rewe-Handels gesellschaft Nord mbH v. Hauptzollamt Kiel* [1981] E.C.R. 1805).
[31] HASAWA, s. 47 (1), (2). See, for example, the Management of Health and Safety at Work Regulations 1992, reg. 15; however, the amendment of the 1992 regulations to implement the EC Directive (92/85/EEC) for the Protection of Pregnant Workers has removed the exclusion of civil liability for reg. 13A. And see Chap. 7.
[32] Report of Robens Committee (Cmnd. 5034) Chap. 5.
[33] Cmnd. 5034.
[34] *Ibid.*, Chap. 5.
[35] *Viz.* regulations made under HASAWA, s. 15 (HASAWA, s. 53(1)).
[36] *Ibid.*, s. 16(2).

itself render him liable to any civil or criminal proceedings, where in any criminal proceedings a party is alleged to have committed an offence under any provision mentioned in section 16(1) of the 1974 Act[37] in respect of which provision there existed an approved code, any part of such a code as appears relevant to the alleged offence shall be admissible in evidence; further a failure to comply with an approved code results in the accused being required to show that the relevant statutory provision or regulation was complied with otherwise than by observing the provision(s) of the code.[38] Although section 17 makes no provision for the effect of a failure to comply with an approved code of practice in civil proceedings, there would seem to be nothing to prevent it being adduced as evidence of the standard of care to be expected of an employer in an action based on breach of the common law duty of care.[39] Indeed it is well established that guidance and advice in official documents or leaflets may be referred to for showing the proper precautions to be taken or standard of care to be achieved even although, strictly, the guidance does not apply to the circumstances in which the injury occurred.[40] Similarly it has been held that reference may be made to a statutory provision for the purpose of setting the standard of care required for performance of the common law duty of care.[41] However, while compliance with an official document or a code of practice is of evidential value there is no presumption that it demonstrates the defender has performed to the required common law standard of reasonable care[42] and the common law duty of care is not necessarily superseded by a detailed statutory provision.[43]

---

[37] *Viz.* HASAWA, ss. 2–8; health and safety regulations and existing statutory provisions.

[38] HASAWA, s. 17(1), (2); see *West Cumberland By Products Ltd v. D.P.P.* [1988] R.T.R. 391; *Lockhart v. Kevin Oliphant*, 1993 S.L.T. 179.

[39] See Chap. 3.

[40] *Dickson v. Flack* [1953] 2 Q.B. 464; and see *Butt v. Inner London Education Authority* (1968) 66 L.G.R. 379 (C.A.).

[41] *Hewett v. Alf Brown's Transport Ltd* [1991] I.C.R. 471 (Control of Lead at Work Regulations 1980 (S.I. 1980 No. 1248)). Discussed at paras. 6.8–6.9.

[42] *Bux v. Slough Metals Ltd* [1974] 1 All E.R. 262 (strictly by providing goggles the employer had complied with the relevant statutory regulations, but the common law standard required that he encourage their use), and see Chap. 3.

[43] *Matuszczyk v. N.C.B.*, 1953 S.C. 8; and see Chap. 3.

The influence of the European Community[44]

2.7 As noted earlier in this chapter, one of the recommendations of the Robens Committee was to replace the piecemeal approach of legislating for particular industries and places of employment which had produced a "mass of ill-assorted and intricate detail" with a system of comprehensive provisions founded on basic principles which would extend to all employers, employees and the self-employed and would be self-regulating. While the Health and Safety at Work Act 1974 enacted basic principles of responsibility for health and safety at work, it is doubtful whether the system which resulted therefrom was generally self-regulating. Interestingly, however, the principle of self-regulation under the guise of risk assessment is at the heart of the present approach to health and safety embodied in the European Commission's Third Programme on Health and Safety at Work of 1987 and the Social Charter and Action Programme of 1989.

2.8 It is beyond the scope of this work to deal in detail with the European dimension of health and safety at work, but it is necessary here to deal with the major developments.[45] The main reasons for the European Community's interaction into the field of health and safety at work are (a) different safety standards result in price differentials which would inhibit the free flow of products; (b) a reduction in the social and economic costs of accidents results in the enhancement of the quality of life for the whole Community; (c) safe and therefore efficient work practices produce increase in productivity and improved industrial relations; and (d) major industrial incidents can have cross-border effects and their treatment requires to be harmonised. Also the Social Policy provisions of the Treaty of Rome[46] themselves demonstrate that the European Community is not concerned only with economic expansion, and the high number of workplace accidents prompted the Commission relying

---

[44] Technically with effect from Nov. 1, 1993 as a result of the Treaty of Maastricht the European Community has been embraced by the European Union of which it is a "pillar."
[45] For a detailed coverage see *European Community Health and Safety Legislation* (Ed. Neal and Wright) (1992).
[46] Arts. 117–128.

on Article 118 to embark on an initiative to develop, in stages, a preventative policy. Until 1974 the Commission's approach focused on occupational illnesses and diseases. However, in each year there were 100,000 deaths and 12 million injuries resulting from accidents at work and these figures resulted in the Commission, encouraged by the adoption by the Council of Ministers of a resolution,[47] drawing up a series of Action Programmes and the setting up of (a) the Advisory Committee for Safety, Hygiene and Health Protection at Work[48] comprising 72 representatives of governments, trade unions and employers and (b) the Dublin Foundation[49] an autonomous Community body to conduct research into working environment and the impact of new technologies. Until 1978 there were two significant legislative initiatives[50] however in that year the First Action Programme on health and safety at work was drawn up[51] for the period to 1982 to take action to lead to improving the aetiology of accidents and diseases, providing protection against dangerous substances, preventing dangers and harmful effects of machines and bringing about an improvement in attitudes in the workplace. Nineteen eighty saw the adoption of the First Framework Directive[52] dealing with harmonisation of measures for protection against chemical, physical and biological agents at work and its four "daughter" Directives which are early examples of self-assessment operating as a mechanism to trigger more specific provisions. Thus, for example, a daughter Directive[53] provides that where any activity is likely to involve a risk of exposure to dust from asbestos the risk must be assessed to determine the nature and degree of exposure. Where the assessment shows the presence of asbestos fibre below the maximum but above other specified levels, a range of special and detailed provisions is activated. In 1984 the Second Action Programme was set in motion by Council Directive[54] which, when later combined with the amendments to the Treaty of Rome introduced by the Single European Act,

[47] Jan. 21, 1974.
[48] Council Decision 74/325/EEC.
[49] Set up by Council Regulation of May 26, 1976.
[50] Directive 77/576/EEC (safety signs at workplace); Directive 76/610/EEC (exposure to vinyl chloride monomers).
[51] Council Resolution 78/C165/1.
[52] Directive 80/1107/EEC.
[53] 83/477/EEC.
[54] Directive 84/c67/02.

encouraged the Commission to make policy initiatives in reliance of the new Articles 118a and 118b by which the Council was permitted to act by qualified majority.[55] This in turn was followed by the Community Charter of Fundamental Social Rights of Workers[56] the eventual text of which was agreed at Strasbourg in December 1989 by all Member States except the United Kingdom and provided, *inter alia* for social aspects to be given the same importance as economic ones.

2.9 Perhaps the most significant step of all was taken by the adoption of the Framework Directive 89/391 – the first Directive to be introduced under the new Article 118a. Unlike Directive 87/1107 the Framework Directive went beyond self-assessment and imposed certain basic duties on employers and workers. Of particular significance is Article 16 of the Framework Directive which provides that the Council, acting on a proposal of the Commission based on Article 118a of the Treaty of Rome shall adopt *inter alia*[57] individual Directives in the areas listed in the Annex to the Framework Directive, namely, (a) workplaces, (b) work equipment, (c) personal protective equipment, (d) work and visual display units, (e) handling of heavy loads, (f) temporary or mobile worksites and (g) fisheries and agriculture. Individual Directives have been adopted in respect of all areas except (g). However while Articles 100a and 118a of the amended Treaty of Rome allow the Council to act by qualified majority, at the insistence of the United Kingdom, Article 100(2) provides that the power to act by qualified majority shall not apply to any provisions regarding the rights of employed persons and there would now seem to be scope for argument over the application of these articles. Indeed the United Kingdom proposed to challenge the validity of the Pregnant Workers Directive which was made under Article 118a although it deals not just with health and safety but also with the rights of pregnant workers.

2.10 Assuming a Directive is validly made, what is its legal effect in Scots law? Although Directives are

---

[55] Until 1987 only six health and safety Directives had been issued in reliance on Art. 100 which requires unanimity.

[56] Com. (89) 568.

[57] Other directives adopted under the Framework Directive include the Protection of Workers from Risks related to Carcinogens at Work Directive (90/394) and the Protection of Pregnant Workers Directive (92/87).

addressed to Member States and can lead to infraction proceedings at the instance of the Commission or another Member State in the European Court of Justice, in contrast to self-executing Treaty provisions,[58] generally for legal effect they require to be translated into domestic law by Member States.[59] Directives can however effect legal rights within the domestic legal regimes in certain circumstances. Thus where a Member State has failed properly to translate a Directive into domestic law it cannot rely on its own failure to do so in an issue with an individual such as an employee of an emanation of the state[60] on the grounds that it would be incompatible with the binding nature which Article 189 of the EEC Treaty confers on directives to hold that the obligations imposed thereby cannot be relied upon and the European Court of Justice therefore has deduced that a member state which has not adopted the necessary implementing measures may not plead, as against individuals, its own failure to perform the obligations the directive entails.[61] The result is that individuals are entitled, in an issue with an emanation of the state, to rely on a directive which is unconditional and sufficiently precise. Secondly where the Parliament of the United Kingdom has enacted legislation to implement a directive the House of Lords has encouraged domestic courts and tribunals to be prepared to take a progressive attitude to statutory interpretation if necessary to achieve compatibility with Community law.[62] Thus in *Litster v. Forth Dry Dock and Engineering Co.*[63] in order to give effect to Directive 77/187/EEC their Lordships were prepared to write into the implementing domestic regulations[64] words

[58] *e.g.* EEC Treaty, Art. 119 (equal pay).
[59] EEC Treaty, Arts. 169, 170. For a full account of European Community law, see D. Lasok and J. W. Bridge, *Law and Institutions of the European Communities* (5th ed.).
[60] An emanation of the state has been held to include an area health authority (*Marshall v. Southampton and South West Hampshire Area Health Authority (Teaching)* [1986] I.C.R. 335, ECJ), a police authority (*Johnston v. Chief Constable of the Royal Ulster Constabulary* [1987] I.C.R. 83, ECJ) and a nationalised industry (*Foster v. British Gas plc* [1991] I.C.R. 84, (ECJ). *Cf. Doughty v. Rolls-Royce* [1992] I.R.L.R. 126, (C.A.).
[61] *Marshall v. Southampton and S.W. Hampshire Area Health Authority (Teaching)* [1986] I.C.R. 334, ECJ; *Becker v. Finanzamt Münster Innenstadt* [1982] E.C.R. 53, (ECJ).
[62] *Pickstane v. Freeman's plc* [1988] I.C.R. 697 (H.L.).
[63] [1989] I.C.R. 341, (H.L.).
[64] Transfer of Undertakings (Protection of Employment) Regulations 1981 (S.I. 1981 No. 1794).

which had not been in the regulations approved by Parliament and which incidentally have not since been added although the same regulations have in other respects been amended to comply with other provisions of the Directive. Following the decision of the European Court of Justice in *Marleasing v. La Commercial Internacional d'Alimentacion SA*[65] in which it was held that in applying national law, whether it is passed to implement a directive or whether it predates a directive, the domestic court is obliged to do everything possible to achieve the result laid down by the directive it has been argued that the distinction between domestic legislation which predates and postdates a directive is inconsistent with Community law.[66] The House of Lords has now accepted[67] that it is the duty of a United Kingdom court to construe domestic legislation to accord with a directive as interpreted by the European Court of Justice whether the domestic leglislation came before or after the directive subject to two important reservations – (a) that the construction did not distort the meaning of the legislation and (b) only if it is possible for the domestic court to do so. Finally in *R. v. Secretary of State for Transport, ex p. Factortame*[68] the European Court of Justice has held that if a rule of domestic law prevented the enforcement of a Community law that domestic law had to be set aside and in *Francovich v. Halian Republic*[69] it was held that a member state which fails properly to implement a directive could be liable in damages.

2.11 From these principles it follows that where domestic regulations have been introduced to give effect to a directive they have to be construed so far as possible to conform with the directive and it is arguable that in some respects the regulations introduced to give effect to the Framework Directive 89/391/EEC and its daughter directives[70] fall short of doing so. Thus unlike the directives, the domestic regulations and their accompanying codes of

[65] [1990] E.C.R. I 4135 (ECJ).
[66] See, for example, *Porter v. Cannon Hygiene Ltd* [1993] I.R.L.R. 329, (NICA).
[67] *Webb v. EMO Air Cargo U.K. Ltd* [1993] I.R.L.R. 27, (H.L.).
[68] [1990] E.C.R. I 2433 (ECJ).
[69] [1992] I.R.L.R. 84 (ECJ). And see Ross, "Beyond *Francovich*" [1993] M.L.R. 55.
[70] Directive 89/654/EEC; Directive 89/655/EEC; Directive 89/650/EEC; Directive 89/686/EEC; Directive 90/269/EEC and Directive 90/270/EEC.

practice are frequently limited by the insertion of the phrase "as far as reasonably practicable" – a limitation of responsibility not usually found in the directives. The Framework and its daughter directives only permit a reduction of employer's responsibility where occurrences are due to unusual and unforeseeable circumstances, beyond the employer's control, or to exceptional events whose consequences could not have been avoided despite all due care[71] and this seems a more stringent requirement than "not reasonably practicable." However in accordance with the decision of the House of Lords in *Webb v. EMO Air Cargo Ltd*[72] a domestic court may be able to construe the test of reasonable practicability to give effect to the directives. Similarly breach of a provision in a code of practice of itself although probably of evidential value in a civil action certainly does not activate a criminal sanction and it is arguable that where a directive is implemented by a code of practice and not a regulation, the requirement of Community law that for breach of the provisions of a directive there is an effective remedy may not be met. However in *Officier van Justitie v. Kolpinghuis Nijunegen BV*[73] it has been held that because the national court's obligation to interpret domestic law to comply with a directive is limited by the general principles of law – in particular the principles of legal certainty and non-retroactivity – there was not, in the context of criminal proceedings, a duty to comply with a directive which a Member State government itself had not implemented. Finally because the Management of Health and Safety at Work Regulations 1992[74] which purport to complete the implementation of the Framework Directive exclude civil liability[74a] it is arguable that such an exclusion of civil liability offends against the requirement of Community law that legal actions available in the courts of Member States for enforcement of rights which are the product of domestic law should also be available for ensuring observance of Community law.[75] Thus although

---

[71] Directive 89/391/EEC, art. 5(4).

[72] [1993] I.R.L.R. 27 (H.L.).

[73] [1987] E.C.R. 3969 (ECJ).

[74] S.I. 1992 No. 2051.

[74a] *Cf.* reg. 13A inserted by Management of Health and Safety at Work (Amendment) Regulations 1994 (S.I. 1994 No. 2865).

[75] *Rewe Handels–gesellschaft Nord mbH v. Hauptzollamt Kiel* [1981] E.C.R. 1805.

an employer who fails to carry out a risk assessment as required by the Management of Health and Safety at Work Regulations 1992[76] would not be liable for breach of statutory duty it is arguable that the failure to carry out such "a suitable and sufficient assessment"[77] would also be seen to be in breach of the common law requirement to provide a safe system of work.

The institutions of the law of health and safety at work

2.12 As mentioned earlier in this chapter, health and safety law depends on the concentration of different types of legal provisions from different sources and so it is with regard to what may conveniently be called the institutions or agencies of health and safety law. Clearly many of those legal provisions are subject to the jurisdictions of the ordinary civil and criminal courts, or the industrial tribunals.[78] However the effective prosecution of the recommendations of the Robens Committee[79] required the creation of new or the reorganisation of, existing structures. Thus there has been created the Health and Safety Commission and Executive under whose aegis various inspectorates and directorates operate as shown on the organisational diagram contained in schedule 1.

As at 1993

The constitution and powers of the Health and Safety Commission and Executive are dealt with in Chapter 5, but it is necessary here to place these and other agencies in perspective.

2.13 The Health and Safety at Work Act 1974 created a two-tier structure consisting of the Health and Safety Commission (HSC) and its operational arm the Health and Safety Executive (HSE) to which it may give directions.[80] Amongst the HSC's powers is the power to make agreements whereby (1) other agencies can perform

---

[76] S.I. 1992 No. 2051, reg. 5.
[77] *Ibid.*, reg. 5(1).
[78] See, for example, the jurisdiction given to the industrial tribunals to hear appeals against Improvement and Prohibition Notices (HASAWA, 1974, s. 24; and see Chap. 4).
[79] Cmnd. 5034.
[80] HASAWA 1974, s. 11(4).

functions on behalf of the HSC or HSE[81] or (2) the HSE
can perform an appropriate function on behalf of a
minister, government department or public authority.[82]
The HSE is empowered to appoint inspectors[83] and the
former Inspectorates of Factories, Mines and Quarries,
Nuclear Installations, Industrial Pollution and Explosives
have been transferred to the HSE and with effect from
April 1, 1991 the HSE exercises functions previously
conferred on the Secretary of State for Trade and Industry
by the Mineral Workings (Offshore Installations) Act
1971.[84] Since 1898 there had been a medical branch of the
Factories Inspectorate and in 1972 the functions of that
branch were extended and placed on a statutory footing
by the Employment Medical Advisory Service Act 1972
which provided for the establishment, organisation and
function of the Employment Medical Advisory Service
(EMAS) and the abolition of the position and functions of
appointed factory doctors. The purpose of setting up the
EMAS was to ensure that those concerned with the health
of employed persons and those in training for employment would be kept informed of matters concerning the
safeguarding and improvement of the health of such
persons.[85] Part II of the Health and Safety at Work Act
1974 repeals, in part, and re-enacts with some amendments the 1972 Act. The work of EMAS, with its headquarters in London, is carried out on a regional basis, a
Senior Employment Medical Advisor being appointed for
each region.[86]

---

[81] See, for example, the agreements entered into under HASAWA, s. 13
with (a) the National Radiological Protection Board whereby that Board
performs the HSC's function regarding radiation dangers and (b) the
Gas and Oil Measurement Branch of the Department of Trade and
Industry whereby that branch performs functions for the HSE.
[82] See, for example, HSE's acceptance of responsibility for enforcement
of the Employers' Liability (Compulsory Insurance) Act 1969 under S.I.
1975 No. 194.
[83] HASAWA 1974, s. 19.
[84] And see Chap. 6 regarding the change of responsibilities following
the Cullen Report on *Piper Alpha* and the Offshore Safety Act 1992 and
Chap. 5 regarding the inspection of shops, offices, leisure facilities,
hotels, restaurants and places of worship as carried out by the local
authority environmental health officers.
[85] Employment Medical Advisory Service Act 1972, s. 1(1).
[86] The Scottish headquarters are at Belford House, 59 Belford Road,
Edinburgh, EH4 3UE; tel. 0131–247 2000.

CHAPTER 3

THE COMMON LAW

INTRODUCTION

3.1 While the systematic development of health and safety at work is today overwhelmingly the province of statutory regulation (domestic and European) it is important to note that the common law, because of the generality of its principles and their flexibility of application, is still an important source of legal rights and duties. Until very recently Scots health and safety at work law, like its English counterpart, at least in terms of civil liability, consisted of the general principles of delict (or torts in England) supplemented by specific statutory provisions which related to particular workplaces, for example factories,[1] mines and quarries,[2] shops and offices,[3] or to particular operations, for example, the use of particular machines or equipment[4] and substances.[5] While the Health and Safety at Work Act 1974 enacted general duties which would apply irrespective of the nature of the workplace or the operation being undertaken[6] that statute operates only in the field of the criminal law, section 47(1) providing: "[n]othing in . . . Part [I] shall be construed (a) as conferring a right of civil action in any civil proceedings in respect of any failure to comply with any duty imposed by sections 2 to 7; or (b) as affecting the extent (if any) to which breach of a duty imposed by any existing statutory provisions is actionable . . ."

3.2 It is noticeable, however, that since 1974 the statutory regulation of health and safety at work has adopted

[1] Factories Act 1961.
[2] Mines and Quarries Act 1954.
[3] Offices, Shops and Railway Premises Act 1963.
[4] See the Woodworking Machine Regulations 1974.
[5] See, for example, Highly Flammable Liquids and Liquified Petroleum Gases Regulations 1972; Ionising Radiation (Unsealed Radioactive Substances) Regulations 1968.
[6] See, for example, Health and Safety at Work Act 1974, ss. 2–7.

the "generalist" approach of the 1974 Act. Thus the regulations made under the Health and Safety at Work Act 1974 which, in accordance with section 47(2),[7] create civil liability unless they provide otherwise, apply to risk-creating work operations and are couched in the flexible terminology of "reasonable practicability." Examples of this current approach can be seen in (a) the Manual Handling Operations Regulations 1992[8] which may apply in circumstances as different as a nurse lifting a patient in a hospital and a factory worker carrying a box from one part of the factory to another and (b) the Workplace Health and Safety Regulations 1992[9] which may apply equally to the provision of sanitary facilities for agricultural field-workers[10] and the arrangement of work-stations in a college or university.[11] One result of this approach to statutory regulation of health and safety at work has been, at least in some respects,[12] the convergence of the approach of common law and statute in that in each case the concepts of "reasonableness" and "practicability" form the basis of legal rules which apply generally to risks and dangers at work. A by-product of this convergence has been a cross-fertilisation of the statutory and common law systems which has come about in two ways — first, the decision of a court dealing with an employee's common law claim based as it is on an employer's duty to take "reasonable care" is capable of influencing a court entertaining an employee's claim based on breach of statutory duty which will frequently turn on whether an employer took such steps as were "reasonably practicable"; secondly, there can be no doubt that a court when faced with a question as to whether an employer has acted reasonably whether dealing with an

---

[7] s. 47(2) provides that "breach of a duty imposed by health and safety regulations . . . shall so far as it causes damage be actionable except in so far as the regulations provide otherwise."

[8] reg. 2(1) defines "load" to include any person or animal. But note that the accompanying Guidance provides that an implement, tool or machine is not considered a load while in use for its intended purpose; see paras. 6.30–6.31.

[9] S.I. 1992 No. 3004; see paras. 4.66–4.76.

[10] *Ibid.*, regs. 3, 22.

[11] *Ibid.*, reg. 11.

[12] Clearly in many areas statutory regulations prescribe absolute standards where necessary because of special risks which a particular operation may involve: see, for example, the Mines and Quarries Act 1954 and the Agriculture (Threshers and Balers) Regulations 1960.

action based on common law or for breach of statutory duty will be much influenced by formal, normative documents like approved codes of practice[13] as well as informal guidance given by the Health and Safety Executive.[14]

DEVELOPMENT OF THE EMPLOYER'S OBLIGATION BEFORE BARTONSHILL

3.3 Until the infamous *Bartonshill Coal Company* cases[15] the essential principle of an employer's duty to his employee was not in doubt and is comprehensively stated by Lord Justice-Clerk Hope in *Dixon v. Rankin*[16]:

> "The master's primary obligation in every contract of service in which his workmen are employed in a hazardous and dangerous occupation for his interest and profit, is to provide for, and attend to the safety of the men. That is . . . paramount even to that of paying for their labour. This obligation includes the duty of furnishing good and sufficient machinery and apparatus to enable them, with safety to their lives, to perform the work they are employed in for his profit, and to keep the same in reasonable and good condition . . . In this obligation is equally included — as he cannot do everything himself — the duty to have all acts, by others whom he employs, done properly and carefully, in order to avoid risk. The obligation to provide for the safety of the lives of his servants by fit machinery, is not greater, or more inherent in the contract, than the obligation to provide for their safety from the acts done by others whom he also employs."

This approach therefore prevented an employer escaping liability by showing that the injury was caused by the

---

[13] Under the Health and Safety at Work Act 1974, s. 16(1), the Health and Safety Commission may, with the consent of the Secretary of State for Employment, approve codes of practice with certain practical guidance with respect to the requirements of various statutory provisions.

[14] The interrelationships between the common law, statutory regulation and a code of practice is well illustrated by *Hewett v. Alf Brown's Transport Ltd* [1992] I.C.R. 530 (C.A.). And see *Balfour v. William Beardmore & Co. Ltd*, 1956 S.L.T.(Notes) 205, O.H.

[15] *Reid v. Bartonshill Coal Co.* (1858) 17 D. 1017; *Bartonshill Coal Co. v McGuire* (1858) 3 Macq. 300.

[16] (1852) 14 D. 420 at p. 424; and see *Sword v. Cameron* (1839) 1 D. 493.

negligence of another employee and in the same year in *Nisbett v. Dixon & Co.*[17] the First Division thwarted an early attempt to avoid liability by interposing an independent contractor. Dixon & Co., having entered into a lease of ironstone workings engaged Nimmo and Watson to extract the ironstone. Due to the negligence of Watson an adjacent coal mine was damaged by fire (and the necessary steps taken to extinguish it) and the issue arose of whether Dixon & Co. could, by employing contractors, get rid of their responsibility to the landlord. Although the case did not involve an employer's duty of safety the reluctance of the court to allow the avoidance of responsibility by engaging third parties — unless they are truly contractors exercising an independent calling — is clearly illustrated by the judgments and, as Fraser points out,[18] the cases supported the principle that where a person is legally bound to do a thing he cannot delegate his responsibility to a contractor. The non-delegability of the employer's duty is beyond doubt by 1854 when the First Division upheld the decision in *Baird v. Addie*[19] in which the Lord Ordinary had opined:

> "Assuming that the law imposes upon a coalmaster the duty of looking to the safety of the workmen employed in his service, it would be subversive of the whole benefit of the principle, to hold that he could exonerate himself by merely changing the mode of his operations, and by engaging one person to undertake the whole service, instead of himself employing the men. The primary obligation being imposed on the coalmaster, it is clear that if he employs another to fulfil it, he is liable for any failure or neglect in its fulfilment; he must be answerable for anything left undone, if it were his duty to see it done by himself or others in his employment. The contractor is, with reference to parties in the position of the pursuer . . . to be regarded in the light of a servant, for whose neglect or fault he is responsible."

[17] (1852) 14 D. 971.

[18] *Master and Servant* (3rd ed.), pp. 291 *et seq.*

[19] (1854) 14 D. 420. Contrast the approach adopted in *Baird* with the English decision in *Wigmore v. Jay* [1850] 19 L.R. Ex. 300, in which a builder was held not liable for the death of a bricklayer killed as a result of a defect in a scaffold erected under supervision of the builder's foreman.

Similarly, in *Macdonald v. Wyllie & Son*,[20] a new trial was granted when Macdonald's employer escaped liability for his (Macdonald's) injury following a direction by the trial judge:

> "That if the jury are satisfied that the defender, not having the knowledge and skill to erect the scaffolding in question, selected a tradesman having skill and experience of such work, and contracted with him to provide such a scaffold, he would not be liable as for fault if the scaffolding fell in consequence of it not having been erected in a skilful manner through the fault of the skilled person who contracted to erect it."

COMMON EMPLOYMENT

3.4 However, a major development occurred in 1858 when in *Reid v. Bartonshill Coal Co*,[21] the House of Lords imposed on Scots law "the fatuous rule"[22] that there was implied into the contract of employment a term that the employee took the risk of injury by the negligence of a fellow employee or one in "common employment" with himself. Having been applied in America in *Farwell v. Boston and Worcester Railroad Corporation*[23] the rule was adopted in England in *Hutchison v. York, Newcastle and Berwick Railway Co.*[24] where it was stated that: "[t]he principle is that a servant, when he engages to serve a master, undertakes as between himself and his master, to run all the ordinary risks of the service; and this includes the risk of negligence upon the part of a fellow servant, when he is acting in the discharge of his duty as servant of him who is the common master of both." Whether any other implied term could have such far-reaching consequences is difficult to imagine and, of course, it resulted in those who needed the protection most being deprived of it. Thus Alderson B. in *Hutchison* noted that "[i]t may

---

[20] (1898) 1 F. 339; and see *Wilson v. Merry & Co. Ltd* (1867) 5 M. 807.
[21] (1858) 17 D. 1017.
[22] Gow, *Mercantile and Industrial Law of Scotland*, p. 724.
[23] [1842] 4 Metc. 49; the judgment of Shaw C.J. is reproduced at (1858) 3 Macq. 316.
[24] [1850] 19 L.J. Ex. 296.

... be proper ... to add that we do not think that a
master is exempt from responsibility to his servant for an
injury occasioned to him by the act of another servant
where the servant was not at the time of the injury acting
in the service of his master. In such a case the servant
injured is substantially a stranger and entitled to all the
privileges he could have had if he had not been a
servant." In spite of attempts by the Scottish courts to
limit the scope of the doctrine of common employment,[25]
it was not until the passage of the Employers' Liability
Act 1880 that the erosion of the doctrine began. By this
Act an employee had a remedy against his employer
where he was injured by reason of any defect in the
ways, works, machinery or plant or from the negligence
of some person placed in the position of supervisor or
superintendent whose orders the employee had to obey.
Only in 1948 was the doctrine of common employment
abolished by the enactment of the Law Reform (Personal
Injuries) Act. That Act, while repealing the Employers'
Liability Act 1880, provided (i) that it shall not be a
defence to an employer who is sued in respect of personal
injuries caused by the negligence of a person employed
by him, that that person was, at the time the injuries were
caused, in common employment with the person injured,
and (ii) that any provision in a contract of employment or
apprenticeship or any collateral agreement is void in so
far as it would have the effect of excluding or limiting any
liability of the employer in respect of personal injuries
caused to the person employed by the negligence of
persons in common employment with him. *Lindsay v.
Connell & Co. Ltd*,[26] adopting a firm purposive approach to
the interpretation of the statute, rejected the argument
that it did not make an employer liable for what were
"merely casual acts which emerged in the course of the
day's work, . . . which the master could not guard
against." The effect of the 1948 Act was to "replace the
doctrine of common employment by the old maxims and
by what before 1858 was the law of Scotland."[27] However,
as has been remarked elsewhere[28] the development of the
law after 1858 took place in order to avoid the defence of
common employment.

[25] See the interesting discussion in Miller, *Industrial Law in Scotland*,
pp. 158–163.
[26] 1951 S.C. 281.
[27] *per* Lord Blades, 1951 S.C. 281 at p. 285.
[28] Gow, *Mercantile and Industrial Law of Scotland*, p. 724.

THE NATURE OF THE EMPLOYER'S DUTY
CONTRACT OR DELICT?

3.5 Before addressing this issue it is necessary to spend some time considering the nature of the contract of employment. A more detailed discussion of judicial identification of the contract of employment may be found elsewhere.[29] For present purposes it is important to note that the test currently applied[30] is nothing if not flexible and may be fairly described as the "multiple and variable test" in that it requires the tribunal of fact to consider and evaluate a wide range of factors. It is therefore capable of application where the underlying issue involves whether the "worker" benefits from a statutory protection limited to those employed under a contract of employment[31] or whether the "employer" owes a duty of care for the "worker's" safety[32]; its flexibility also allows particular significance or weight to be attached to one or more factors. Thus in a case dealing with casual staff or homeworkers, greater weight will be attached to the factor of "mutuality of obligation."[33] Similarly where the question is the existence of the duty of care, while the English courts have doubted the ability of a worker to have the benefit of being self-employed for purposes of taxation while claiming the status of being employed for claiming compensation for injuries,[34] the recent approach by Scottish courts when considering the existence of a duty of care is to emphasise the factor of control.[35]

3.6 In England it has been accepted for some time that the employer's duty to take reasonable care for the safety

[29] For a more detailed account of the concept of the employment contract and the judicial attempts to promulgate definitive tests reference may be made to Craig, V. and Miller, K., *Employment Law in Scotland*, Chap. 2.

[30] See, for example, *Short v. J. & W. Henderson*, 1946 S.C. (H.L.) 24; *Market Investigations Ltd v. Minister of Social Security* [1969] 2 Q.B. 173.

[31] See, for example, *Massey v. Crown Life Insurance Co.* [1978] I.R.L.R. 31.

[32] See, for example, *Ferguson v. Dawson and Partners Ltd* [1976] I.R.L.R. 346.

[33] See, for example, *Nethermere (St Neots) Ltd v. Taverna and Gardiner* [1984] I.R.L.R. 240; *O'Kelly v. Trusthouse Forte plc* [1983] I.R.L.R. 369.

[34] See *Ferguson v. Dawson and Partners Ltd* [1976] 1 W.L.R. 1213; *Lee Ting Sang v. Chung Chi-Keung* [1990] 1 W.L.R. 1173 (PC).

[35] See *Rennie v. Dorans*, 1991 S.L.T. 443; *Marshall v. W. Sharp & Sons Ltd*, 1991 S.L.T. 114 (IH) and *United Wholesale Grocers v. Sher*, 1993 S.L.T. 284.

of his employees may be based on tort or by a term to that effect being implied into the contract of employment[36] and the employee may elect whether to sue in contract or in tort.[37] While in some fields of law there has been a declared unwillingness to develop liability in tort where the parties are in a contractual relationship,[38] it has been stated[39] that such an approach is not in point when considering the employer's duty of safety. Nevertheless although the substance of the employer's duty has been developed in the context of litigation based on tort, English law now clearly recognises that a failure to take care for the safety of the employee will give rise to contract-law remedies.[40] Although there is no similarly unequivocal judicial statement, Scots law does recognise that the employer's duty of safety may be expressed as a matter of contractual or delictual liability and there would appear to be no reason for Scots law to accept the approach advocated by Lord Scarman in that there is nothing to the advantage of the law's development "in searching for a liability in tort where the parties are in a contractual relationship."[41] Although all of the early Scots decisions are the result of actions of reparation for the death or personal injury of a workman, these same

---

[36] *Matthews v. Kuwait Bechtel Corporation* [1959] 2 Q.B. 57.
[37] And see *Coupland v. Arabian Gulf Oil Co. Ltd, The Times,* June 23, 1983, (C.A.).
[38] See, for example, the dictum of Lord Scarman in *Tai Hing Cotton Mill Ltd v. Liu Chong Hing Bank Ltd* [1986] A.C. 80 at p. 107; *National Bank of Greece S.A. v. Pinios Shipping Co. No. 1* [1990] 1 A.C. 637 at p. 650 and *Banque Keyser Ullman S.A. v. Skandia (U.K.) Insurance Co. Ltd* [1990] 1 Q.B. 665 at p. 799.
[39] *Johnstone v. Bloomsbury Health Authority* [1991] I.C.R. 269 *per* Stuart-Smith L.J. at p. 276. And see the decision of the House of Lords in *Arbuthnott and Others v. Fagan & Feltrim Underwriting Agencies Ltd, The Times,* July 26, 1994 to the effect that a plaintiff who had available to him concurrent remedies in contract and tort could choose the most advantageous remedy.
[40] *Johnstone v. Bloomsbury Health Authority* [1991] I.C.R. 269 (C.A.) (injunction and damages for breach of contract), *Dutton & Clark Ltd v. Daly* [1985] I.C.R. 780 (EAT) (rescission — constructive dismissal); *Jagdeo v. Smith's Industries Ltd* [1982] I.C.R. 47 (EAT) (lawfulness of transfer to work involving unsafe conditions); *British Aircraft Corporation v. Austin* [1978] I.R.L.R. 332m (EAT) (constructive dismissal — employer failing to investigate complaint about provision of safety equipment); *Graham Oxley Tool Steels Ltd v. Firth* [1980] I.R.L.R. 135 (exposure to intolerable cold for several months).
[41] *Tai Hing Cotton Mill Ltd v. Lin Chung Hing Bank Ltd* [1986] A.C. 80 at p. 1078.

decisions recognise that the duty is based on the existence of a contract of service. Thus in *Dixon v. Rankin*[42] the Lord Justice-Clerk opined that "[t]he master's primary obligation in every contract of service in which his workmen are employed in a[n] . . . occupation for his interest and profit, is to provide for, and attend to the safety of the men." Similarly in *Macdonald v. Wyllie & Son*[43] Lord Young observed that "[a]ccording to the law of Scotland in the contract of master and servant . . . it is implied that the employer is responsible to his workmen for the condition of the scaffolding which he has provided for them to work upon"; while more recently still Lord Murray has stated[44] — in the context of a discussion of the standard of the employer's duty of safety — that "contractual obligations which are implied at common law are not absolute." The position in Scots law would appear to be that not just is the contractual relationship of employer and employee one which is sufficiently close to bring the duty of care into play[45] but also there is a parallel implied contractual term which, in the event of its breach, will allow the employee to rescind. Indeed in *Knight v. Barra Shipping Co. Ltd*[46] the EAT has indicated that it is an important term of the contract that the employer will not require an employee to work in conditions which are "intolerable," Lord Coulsfield adding that conditions which present a danger to life can "properly be regarded as intolerable"; although this terminology suggests a development of the existing duty the term could also be expressed as a failure to take reasonable care or to provide a safe system of work. In the result there would appear to be no reason why in Scots law the employee whose employer fails in his duty to take reasonable care for his safety may not raise his legal proceedings on the basis that there has been a breach of an implied term of his contract or that his employer has failed to perform his delictual duty of care, depending on where the advantage might lie. Generally the rules regarding the assessment of damages will

---

[42] (1852) 14 D. 420 at p. 424.
[43] (1898) 1 F. 339 at p. 344.
[44] *Bain v. Fife Coal Co. Ltd*, 1935 S.C. 681 at p. 701.
[45] Cf. *Keatings v. Secretary for Scotland*, 1961 S.L.T. (Sh.Ct.) 63; *K. R. Page v. J. Read* (C.A.), 85/441 (unreported); and see *Rennie v. Doran*, 1991 S.L.T. 443.
[46] Case No. 187/92 (unreported); and see *Graham Oxley Tool Steels Ltd v. Firth* [1980] I.R.L.R. 135 (EAT).

dictate that the employee injured as a result of the breach
or failure (fault) of his employer will sue in delict and not
in contract, and although it might be arguable that an
award of damages for breach of contract would not suffer
a reduction in respect of the pursuer's contributory negligence[47] Lord Davidson has opined[48] that damages for
breach of contract may be reduced for contributory negligence but only if the breach can also be described as a
"fault" within the meaning of section 5 of the Law
Reform (Contributory Negligence) Act 1945, namely a
"wrongful act, breach of statutory duty or negligent act
(or omission) which gives rise to the defence of contributory negligence." In *Lancashire Textiles*, carpet layers had,
sued the carpet suppliers for breach of contract on the
basis that the carpeting was not of merchantable quality
and not reasonably fit for the purpose; while the pursuers
relied on section 14 of the Sale of Goods Act 1979, Lord
Davidson was of the view that that did not mean that
they (the pursuers) sued "in respect of a breach of
statutory duty in the sense in which that expression is
used in section 5."[49] It has to be observed that the history,
terminology and circumstances of the 1945 Act would
seem to suggest that Parliament did not envisage that the
Act would have any bearing on breach of contract claims.

THE PERSONAL ELEMENT

3.7 While the employer's duty may be simply stated as
"Has the employer taken reasonable care for the safety of
the workman?"[51] or, "the basic duty of the employer is to
take reasonable care that the employee is not exposed to

---

[47] See the interesting discussion in A. S. Burrows, *Remedies for Torts and Breach of Contract* (1987), pp. 73–79.

[48] *Lancashire Textiles (Jersey) Ltd v. Thompson, Shepherd & Co. Ltd*, 1986 S.L.T. 41.

[49] Interestingly in England the definition of fault in which "negligence" is substituted for "wrongful act" seems less ambiguous and for this reason the approach of English decisions require to be treated with caution and it has been held there that the provisions of the 1945 Act did not entitle a defendant to raise contributory negligence as a defence (*Barclay's Bank plc v. Fairclough Building Ltd, The Times*, May 11, 1993, (C.A.)).

[51] *per* Viscount Simonds, *Davie v. New Merton Board Mills Ltd* [1959] A.C. 604 at p. 618.

unnecessary risk,"[52] frequently the duty is said to be tripartite in that it requires the employer to (a) provide and maintain suitable materials (plant, machinery and equipment), (b) keep premises safe and devise and operate a safe system of working, and (c) exercise care in the selection of competent fellow-employees. A fundamental issue which arises is whether and to what extent the employer can perform his duty by delegation to others — be they his employees or agents, suppliers of materials, or independent contractors; put another way, to what extent is the duty personal to the employer so that where the employee is injured because of the negligence of the delegate the employer cannot escape liability. The issue of delegation has been examined particularly with regard to those aspects of the duty requiring the devising and operating of a safe system of working and the provision of suitable materials.

A safe system of work

3.8 As Gow has remarked,[53] much of the law relating to the safe system of work was developed in order to forestall the defence of common employment in that there became established a critical distinction between defects of a "permanent and continuous" nature and defects of a "transitory kind which may emerge in the course of a day's working." Responsibility for the former resided with the employer and could not be affected by the doctrine of common employment which of course applied only where an employee had been injured by the negligence of a fellow employee. The English attempt in *Fanton v. Denville*[54] to relieve the employer of virtually all responsibility for his employee's safety (by allowing the employer to perform his duty towards the employee by selecting competent persons to whom he would delegate the provision of materials and adequate plant) was emphatically rejected in *Bain v. Fife Coal Company Ltd.*[55] According to Lord Justice-Clerk Aitchison the decision in *Fanton v. Denville*

[52] *Longworth v. Coppas International (U.K.) Ltd*, 1985 S.L.T. 111.
[53] *Mercantile and Industrial Law of Scotland*, p. 724; and see the judgment of Lord Reid in *Davie v. New Merton Board Mills Ltd* [1959] A.C. 604 at p. 637.
[54] [1932] 2 K.B. 309.
[55] 1935 S.C. 681.

> "ignores . . . a fundamental doctrine of the law of
> master and servant, viz., that there are certain duties
> owed by a master to his servant so imperative and
> vital to safety that the master cannot divest himself
> of responsibility by entrusting their performance to
> others, so as to avoid liability in the event of injury
> arising to the servant through neglect of any of these
> duties . . . [I]n the eye of the law they are duties that
> cannot be delegated. If, in fact, they are entrusted by
> the master to others, the maxim applies *qui facit per
> alium facit per se* . . . [I]f the master entrusts the duty
> to someone else instead of performing it himself, he
> is liable for injury caused through the want of care of
> that someone else, as being, in the eye of the law,
> his own negligence."[56]

That the employer's duty to provide a safe system of
working was personal to the employer and non-delegable
was confirmed by the House of Lords in *English v. Wilsons
and Clyde Coal Company Ltd.*[57] English was injured when he
was struck by a train of hutches while he was walking
along the main haulage road from his workplace to the pit
bottom. He sued the owners of the mine, contending that
it was a necessary part of a safe system of working that
the haulage of coal by hutches should be stopped while
the men were making their way to the pit bottom at the
end of their shift. The employers owned several collieries
and had appointed an agent to look after the mining side
of their business and the agent had in turn selected a
manager for each colliery whose appointment had to be
approved by the employers. The employers argued (i)
that if an employer delegates his duty to take care of the
safety to competent subordinates, his responsibility in
respect of his primary common law duty ceases, unless
there is proof of knowledge by him not acted upon, and
(ii) by the Coal Mines Act 1911[58] neither an owner nor his
agent could take part in the technical management of a
mine unless properly qualified — in effect by law the
employers had no alternative but to delegate. The first
argument was rejected because "the negligence . . . lay in
the failure to provide a safe system, not in the working of

---

[56] *Ibid.*, p. 693.
[57] 1937 S.C.(H.L.) 46.
[58] s. 2(4).

the system provided[59]" and as such was non-delegable; the second was rejected because: "There is no reason in principle that a compulsory delegation should displace the . . . responsibility of the employer, if a *de facto* delegation, which is often unavoidable, has not this effect . . . [H]e is answerable either directly for his own negligence or vicariously for his servant's negligence, if the negligence affects the provision of a safe system of working."[60] A more modern application of the principle of non-delegation is seen in *McDermid v. Nash Dredging and Reclamation Co. Ltd*[61] in which McDermid, an employee of Nash Dredging, worked as a deckhand on a tug owned by Steven, a wholly owned subsidiary of Nash Dredging and which employed Sas as the tugboat captain. McDermid's duties included the unhitching of mooring lines between the tug and a dredger working in tandem and, so that Sas would know when the mooring ropes had been unhitched, Sas instructed McDermid to bang twice with his hand on the wheelhouse to indicate that the mooring lines were aboard the tug and that it was safe to move the tug. McDermid was injured when Sas — without receiving the signal from McDermid — put the tug astern with the result that McDermid's leg was trapped by a mooring line. On the personal nature of the duty the Lord Chancellor, Lord Hailsham of Marylebone, stated[62]:

> "the defendants did not and could not dispute the existence of . . . a duty of care, nor that it was 'non-delegable' in the special sense in which that phrase is used in this connection. This special sense does not involve the proposition that the duty cannot be delegated in the sense that it is incapable of being the subject of delegation, but only that the employer cannot escape liability if the duty has been delegated and then not properly performed. . . . There was no double knock because. . . . Sas did not attempt to operate the correct sequence and did operate the engines with the . . . rope still on . . . the dredger.

---

[59] *Ibid., per* Lord Macmillan at p. 58.
[60] *English v. Wilsons and Clyde Coal Company Ltd*, 1936 S.C. 883, *per* Lord President Normand at p. 902, quoted with approval by Lord Thankerton in the House of Lords, 1937 S.C. 46 at p. 57.
[61] [1987] I.C.R. 917 (H.L.).
[62] *Ibid.*, p. 922.

The 'system' was therefore not being operated and was therefore not being 'provided' at all. It matters not whether one says that there was no 'system' in operation at all or whether one says that the system provided was unsafe, or whether one says that the system in fact provided was not in use at the crucial stage. In any event the defendants had delegated their duty to the plaintiff to . . . Sas, the duty had not been performed and the defendants must pay for the breach of their 'non-delegable' obligation."

Lord Brandon of Oakbrook divided

"the relevant legal principle into three parts. First an employer owes to his employee a duty to exercise reasonable care to ensure the system of work provided for him is a safe one. Secondly the provision of a safe system has two aspects: (a) the devising of such a system and (b) the operation of it. Thirdly the duty . . . [is] personal or non-delegable . . . the essential characteristic of the duty is that if the duty is not performed it is no defence for the employer to show that he delegated its performance to a person, whether his servant or not his servant, whom he reasonably believed to be competent to perform it. Despite such delegation the employer is liable for non-performance . . . In the present case . . . the defendants delegated both the devising and the operating of [the] system to . . . Sas, who was not their servant. However . . . Sas did not operate that system . . . and for this failure by . . . Sas to operate the system which he had devised, the defendants, as the plaintiff's employers, are personally, not vicariously liable to him."[63]

Thus where an employee is dispatched to work on a site not under the control of his own employer the latter is liable for any injury the employee may sustain as a result of an unsafe system of work[64] although the standard of performance to be required of an employer may be

---

[63] *Ibid.,* pp. 930–931.
[64] *Morris v. Beaverglen Ltd* [1993] I.R.L.R. 350, (C.A.); *Brown v. Josiah Wedgwood & Sons (Aust.) Pty. Ltd* (1989) 51 S.A.S.R. 81.

affected by the fact that the employer is not in possession or control of the premises.[65]

Plant and materials

3.9 The rule in *English v. Wilsons and Clyde Coal Co. Ltd*[66] was subsequently analysed and explained in *Davie v. New Merton Board Mills Ltd*[67] — a case in which it was sought to apply the "non-delegability" principle so that an employer would be liable to his employee for injury sustained by using a defective tool which the employer had provided but which had been negligently made by a reputable manufacturer.

3.10 Davie, an employee of New Merton Board Mills Ltd, was injured when a piece of metal flew off a metal drift, provided by his employer for his use. The drift although apparently in good condition had been negligently manufactured by reputable makers who had sold it to the firm of suppliers who had sold it to Davie's employers; it was excessively hard and was in the circumstances a dangerous tool. Although the employer's system of maintenance and inspection was not at fault, Davie sued them on the ground that they had negligently supplied him with a defective tool. Viscount Simonds described Davie's case thus:

> "The employer, it was said, was under a duty to take reasonable care to supply his workman with proper plant and machinery including such tools as drifts . . . It was then said that the employer could not escape responsibility by employing a third party, however expert, to do his duty for him. So far so good . . . I agree. But then comes the next step — but I would rather call it a jump, and a jump that would unhorse any rider. Therefore, it was said, the employer is responsible for the defect in goods that

[65] See *McQuilter v. Goulandris Bros. Ltd*, 1951 S.L.T. (Notes) 75 and *Cook v. Square D. Ltd* [1992] I.C.R. 262 (C.A.) which, with respect, may be regarded as unsatisfactory in failing to emphasise the distinction between an employer's non-delegable duty and an isolated act of negligence which could not have been avoided by any "system."
[66] 1937 S.C. (H.L.) 46.
[67] [1959] A.C. 604 (H.L.).

he buys in the market, if it can be shown that the defect was due to the want of skill or care on the part of anyone who was concerned with its manufacture."

However, all of their Lordships rejected this argument because although *English v. Wilsons and Clyde Coal Co. Ltd*[68] had decided that the employer was liable for the acts of himself, his servants and agents and, possibly, independent contractors, a manufacturer could not "by any legitimate use of language be considered the servant or agent of, or an independent contractor with, the employer who buys his manufactures in the market."[69] Lord Reid viewed *English* as a case in which there was no question of the employer being liable for the negligence of some person who was not their servant, noting that "agent" as used in that case was merely the technical name of the chief servant of the coal-mine owner. His Lordship was justified in his opinion that *English* did not decide that the employer's duty was such that he was responsible for the negligence of a manufacturer or supplier by examining the law of Scotland before it was interrupted by the introduction of the rule of common employment.[70] He concluded:

"an employer besides being liable to his servant for injury caused by the negligence of his own servants, is in some cases liable in respect of the negligence of others. Where, then, is the line to be drawn? On the one hand it appears that an employer is liable for the negligence of an independent contractor whom he has engaged to carry out one of . . . his personal duties on his own premises and whose work might normally be done by the employer's own servant — at least if the negligent workmanship is discovered by reasonable inspection. On the other hand . . . I am of opinion that he is not liable for the negligence of the manufacturer of an article which he has bought, provided he has been careful to deal with a seller of repute and has made any inspection which a reasonable employer would make."[71]

[68] 1937 S.C. (H.L.) 46.
[69] *Davie v. New Merton Board Mills Ltd* [1959] A.C. 604, *per* Viscount Simonds at pp. 624–625.
[70] *Ibid.*, pp. 636–645.
[71] *Ibid.*, pp. 645–646.

Clearly delegation, in the sense of being able to escape
liability for the negligence of the supplier or manufacturer, is effective where the employer's duty involves the
provision of safe plant and equipment. However the
effect of the decision in *Davie* has been reversed by the
Employer's Liability (Defective Equipment) Act 1969.[72]

Competent staff

3.11 As earlier indicated, another aspect of the
employer's duty is to take reasonable care to select
competent staff,[73] and the question must arise whether
this aspect may be performed by delegation to someone
other than an employee. If one takes the view that an
employment agency can be equiparated with a "supplier"
the principles enunciated in *English v. Wilsons and Clyde
Coal Co. Ltd*[74] as applied in *Davie* could permit an
employer to escape liability for injury to an employee
caused by the incompetence of another employee who
had been selected through the negligence of an independent employment agency. However such a result would
run counter to the older Scottish decisions which have
held that the duty to select competent employees is
personal to the employer and that if an employee is
injured as a result of the actions of an incompetent
employee the employer is responsible.[75] It has been held
in England that the aspect of the employer's duty relating
to the provision of competent staff is non-delegable and
this personal liability is particularly valuable to employees
who are injured as a result of conduct by fellow
employees who are not at the relevant time acting in the
course of their employment.[76]

TO WHOM IS THE DUTY OWED?

3.12 It is clear that the tripartite duty of safety is owed to
those with whom the employer has entered into contracts

---

[72] See para. 3.38.
[73] *McCarten v. McRobbie*, 1909 S.C. 1022. And see para. 3.38 *post*.
[74] 1937 S.C. (H.L.) 46.
[75] *Donald v. Brand* (1862) 24 D. 295 (inebriate employee); *Wilson v. Merry & Cunningham* (1868) 6 M. (H.L.) 64; *McCarten v. McRobbie*, 1909 S.C. 1020 (incompetent driver).
[76] *Hudson v. Ridge Manufacturing Co. Ltd* [1957] 2 Q.B. 348; *Smith v. Crossley Brothers Ltd* (1951) 95 S.J. 655.

of employment or apprenticeship. However that duty must be circumscribed by the notion of the scope of, or course of the employee's or apprentice's employment.[77] It is long established that the employee who is injured in engaging in activity outwith the scope of his employment cannot recover damages from his employer for his injury[78] unless he took the action to save life or limb.[79] However, some observations require to be made.

3.13 First, many of the older cases[80] take a strict and perhaps unrealistic view of what might be regarded as "in the course of employment." Contrast *Hosie v. Fred M. Walker Ltd*[81] in which an employee employed to use a machine to plane planks of wood was held not to be acting in the course of his employment when he used the machine to cut a piece of wood which he would use to keep his stand clear of cuttings, with *National Coal Board v. England*[82] in which a miner, who was injured while, against instructions and against the Coal Mines Order 1934, he assisted a shotsman to set up for shot-blasting was held by the House of Lords to be acting in the course of his employment.[83] Arguably employees who are injured while engaging in activities which they are not contractually bound to do have benefited from a willingness of the courts to extend the notion of "scope or course of employment" in cases where one employee is injured as a result of the negligence of another in order to fix vicarious liability on the employer.[84] Secondly, as the doctrine of common employment vividly illustrated the older law was more prepared to imply an acceptance of risk by the employee entering into the contract whereas the modern approach emphasises the delictual principle that the greater the danger the higher is the degree of care required. Contrast *Clark v. Caledonian Ry. Co. Ltd*[85] in which the widow of an engine driver who was killed when, his engine having been stopped at a signal, he fell

[77] And see para. 3.44, *post*.
[78] *Morris v. Boase Spinning Co. Ltd* (1895) 22 R. 336.
[79] *Wilkinson v. Kinneil Coal Co. Ltd* (1897) 24 R. 1001.
[80] See the cases referred to in Glegg on *Reparation*, p. 403.
[81] 1907 S.C. 134.
[82] [1954] 1 All E.R. 546 (H.L.).
[83] And see *Davidson v. Handley Page Ltd* [1945] 1 All E.R. 235; *Nancollas v. Insurance Officer* [1985] 1 All E.R. 833.
[84] See para. 3.39.
[85] (1877) 5 R. 273.

over an unfenced bridge while walking ahead to the signal box without a torch to ascertain the reason for the stoppage, was unable to recover damages because "if a servant takes an unusual course and an unusual risk he cannot transfer the risk . . . to his employers,"[86] with *Paris v. Stepney Borough Council*[87] in which it would have been unthinkable to plead that the partially-sighted employee had only himself to blame. Thirdly, the fact that the employee has had to assume responsibility for matters which may, strictly, fall outside his duties itself may indicate that the employer has failed to give sufficient attention to the devising of a safe system of work.[88] Accordingly today only if the evidence clearly demonstrates that the employee has taken himself outside the scope of his employment will the employer's personal duty be inapplicable.

Self-employed workers

3.14 While it cannot be doubted that the employer's duty to devise and operate a reasonably safe system of work extends to those with contracts of employment and apprenticeship — on the grounds that those relationships permit the employer to dictate not merely the work objective but the work method as well — whether the employer owes any duty to other classes of workers also arises. In this respect the source of the obligation becomes of significance in that if the obligation originates purely as an implied term in the contracts of employment and apprenticeship it would follow that those who work under other contractual arrangements or those who might, technically, have exceeded the scope of their own employment would not benefit. If, however, the obligation to employees and apprentices is merely one example of the employer's general duty of care, there is no reason why other classes of worker who in the eyes of the principles of delict the employer should regard as his "neighbour in law," adopting the words of Lord Atkin's

---

[86] *Ibid.*, per Lord Shand at p. 276.
[87] [1951] A.C. 367.
[88] Thus in *Hosie v. Fred M. Walker Ltd*, 1907 S.C. 134, the only reason Hosie attempted to use his machine to make a scraper was because the system of work devised by the employer to keep Hosie's stance level and safe was patently ineffective.

dictum in *Donoghue v. Stevenson*,[89] should not benefit.
Thus in *Calder v. H. Kitson Vickers & Sons (Engineers) Ltd*[90]
the Court of Appeal held that although when Calder was
injured as a result of the negligence of one of the
defendant's employees he was operating as a self-
employed contractor, nevertheless his status and the
financial arrangements between himself and the defendants could not affect the duty of care owed to him which
required that they would not operate the crane in such a
way as to expose Calder to danger. The trial judge, who
was of the view that even if Calder was not an employee
of Kitson the nature of the relations and the degree of
control exercised by Kitson were such that Kitson owed
Calder a duty of care to see that the operation was
reasonably safe and was reasonably safely carried out,
opined that "Kitson . . . supplied a sling or hook which
had no safety chain [and] failed to ensure the 'snatch'
would operate smoothly [and] to see Calder had a suitable safety chain and that it was used." However Ralph
Gibson L.J. opined that, while the duty of care owed by
Kitson was not as extensive as that formulated by the trial
judge, there was at least a duty on Kitson not to operate
the equipment provided by them in a way which, to their
knowledge, exposed Calder to a danger which his team
appeared to be disregarding but to give clear warning to
the team of that danger. "If the risk was severe I think
there was a duty to refuse to operate the gear unless it
was clear that all those affected by the risk were fully
aware of it".[91] However, as the existence of the duty of
care is dependent upon the issue of reasonable foreseeability, different circumstances and facts can have a
major impact on whether a duty was owed, and a more
typical result is seen in *K. R. Page v. J. Read*[92] in which
Page, a self-employed painter, was engaged by the main
contractor on a building site. Page was required to paint
the fascia boards of a house and in the absence of any
scaffolding while sitting on the roof and leaning over to
paint the boards Page fell and was injured. While the
Court of Appeal recognised that everyone must refrain
from doing things which they ought reasonably to know
will harm their neighbour, and this duty would require a

---

[89] 1932 S.C. (H.L.) 31 at p. 44.
[90] [1988] I.C.R. 232 (C.A.).
[91] [1988] I.C.R. 254–255.
[92] (1985) unreported case no. 85/441 (C.A.).

contractor who provides equipment to a sub-contractor to ensure the equipment is safe for the purpose for which it is provided, there is no positive duty of supervision or to offer safety equipment; in that sense the duty to the independent contractor is lower than that owed by an employer to his employee.

Seconded employees, *pro hac vice* and contractors

3.15 It is a common phenomenon for an employer to dispatch one of his own employees to work on the site or premises of another enterprise. Such an occurrence presents two problems. First, which of the two employers is liable to a third party[93] injured by the employee's negligence; and secondly, to what extent, if any, are the responsibilities for the safety of the employee transferred to the secondary or temporary "employer"? Both problems require consideration of whether the employee of the original, or general, employer has at the relevant time — that is, the time a third party sustains injury as a result of the employee's negligence or the time the employee himself is injured as a result of a failure to take reasonable care for his safety — become the employee of the secondary or temporary employer *pro hac vice*. Whether such a transfer has taken place depends principally on whether the secondary employer is authorised to control not merely what the employee does but how he does it[94]; although each case very much depends on its own circumstances which, for there to be a transfer *pro hac vice*, must show that the employee either expressly or impliedly consented to accept the secondary employer.[95] It is clear that where such a transfer has taken place the secondary employer becomes vicariously responsible for the negligent acts and omissions of the employee while acting in the course of his employment.[96] However, it would seem that the primary employer remains respon-

[93] "Third party" would of course include an employee of the employer for whom an employee works *pro hac vice*: *Moir v. Wide Arc Services Ltd*, 1988 H.S.I.B. 146 (O.H.).
[94] *Mersey Docks and Harbour Board v. Coggins and Griffiths* [1947] A.C. 1; and see *McGregor v. J. S. Duthie Ltd*, 1966 S.L.T. 133, *McAllister v. Oban Transport and Trading Co. Ltd*, 1971 S.L.T. (Notes) 71.
[95] *Malley v. L.M.S. Ry. Co.*, 1944 S.C. 129.
[96] *McGregor v. J. S. Duthie Ltd*, 1966 S.L.T. 133.

sible for ensuring that there is provided and operated a reasonably safe system of work for the *pro hac vice* employee on the view that that doctrine is relevant only to the question of vicarious liability.[97] Also it is now doubtful whether there is any difference between the case of an employee hired out as the operator of a piece of complicated machinery and the provision of an unskilled labourer to another person who himself occupied the factory, provided all the tools and equipment and advised on the system of working.[98] Moreover, where the contract of hire provides that the hirer is to be responsible for the negligence of an employee of the owner of the equipment "as if" he (the hirer) were the employer of that employee that will tend to indicate that no transfer has taken place.[99]

3.16 Finally it must be noted that in keeping with the maxim *qui facit per alium facit per se* if an employer who engages a contractor retains sufficient control of the work so as to direct the contractor and his employees as to how the work is to be done the contractor and his employees become *pro hac vice* the employees of the employer.[1] Similarly where a main contractor engages sub-contractors to perform part of the contract, by virtue of his exercising control over the whole site the main contractor may have responsibility for supervising the work of the sub-contractors so that the work is conducted in a reasonably safe manner to make the main contractor liable for injuries sustained by an employee of one sub-contractor who fell through a hole in a roof left by the employees of another sub-contractor.[2] However such a case must be distinguished from that of an occupier of premises such as a building site who has contracted for work to be done

---

[97] *Morris v. Beaverglen Ltd t/a Anzac Construction Co.*, 1993 I.R.L.R. 350 (C.A.) in which the English authorities are extensively reviewed. *Cf. Denham v. Midland Employers Mutual Assurance Ltd* [1955] 2 Q.B. 437 (C.A.); *Gibb v. United Steel Companies Ltd* [1957] 1 W.L.R. 668.

[98] See the suggestion to this effect in *Garrard v. A. E. Southey & Co. Ltd and Standard Telephones and Cables Ltd* [1952] 2 Q.B. 174, *per* Parker J. at p. 179.

[99] *Kerr v. Hailes (Plant) Ltd*, 1974 S.L.T. (Notes) 31. Complicated indemnity provisions in the contract of hire will not influence the question whether there has been a transfer *pro hac vice: ibid.*; and see *McConkey v. Amec plc, The Times*, February 16, 1990 (C.A.).

[1] *Gregory v. Hill* (1869) 8 M. 282; *Stephen v. Thurso Police Commissioners* (1876) 3 R. 535.

[2] *McArdle v. Andmac Roofing* [1967] 1 All E.R. 583.

on the site. While such an occupier may have a duty of care to protect the visitor, a precondition of liability for the condition of the premises and operations carried out there is that the occupier is in control of the premises in the sense of being able to license or forbid entry thereto[3] and in an English case the House of Lords has held that the occupier is not usually liable to an employee of a contractor carrying out work on his (the occupier's) premises because his own employer failed to operate a safe system of work because it would not be reasonable to expect the occupier to supervise the contractor.[4]

GENERAL DELICTUAL ISSUES

3.17 As the existence of the employer's duty to take reasonable care for the health and safety of his employees is merely one facet of general delictual principles, a proper understanding of the duty and liability for breach thereof requires here at least a general treatment of foreseeability, causation and standard of duty. For more detailed coverage of these matters the reader is referred to specialist texts.[5]

Foreseeability

3.18 As pointed out earlier, the relationship between employer and employee, apprentice and independent contractor is such as to make it reasonably foreseeable that the employer's action or inaction would cause harm to the employee, apprentice or contractor. However foreseeability also relates to the kind of harm which may be occasioned; unless the kind of harm was reasonably foreseeable the employer will have no liability even although the injury sustained by his employee was undoubtedly the result of the employer's act or omission.[6]

---

[3] *Murdoch v. A. & R. Scott*, 1956 S.C. 309.
[4] *Ferguson v. Wilson* [1987] 3 All E.R. 777 (H.L.).
[5] See, for example, "The Analysis of Negligence" in *Introductory Essays on Scots Law* (2nd ed.) by W. A. Wilson. *Introduction to the Scots Law of Delict* (2nd ed., 1993) by W. J. Stewart is an excellent but concise statement of the relevant principles; for a different and in some respects more detailed text see D. M. Walker, *Delict*.
[6] *Hughes v. Lord Advocate*, 1963 S.C. (H.L.) 31.

Thus the employers of a deceased employee owed no duty of care to his widow who died of mesothelioma after hand-washing her husband's asbestos-impregnated working clothes from 1948 to 1965 because before 1965 no employer could reasonably have foreseen the risk of physical injury from domestic exposure to asbestos; there was no medical literature on the subject, neither warnings nor guidance in industrial or official publications, and even if the defendants had engaged specialist medical personnel it was unlikely they would have become aware of the risk from domestic exposure to asbestos dust before 1965.[7] On the other hand the employers of a ships' painter were under a duty not to expose him to asbestos dust because the risks of asbestosis had been known since 1947[8]; similarly the employers of a ballistics expert were liable for injury to his hearing when they advised him to combat ringing in his ears by putting cotton wool into them when it was widely known that such a procedure was useless[9] and the test of reasonable foreseeability requires an employer to anticipate an employee using equipment incorrectly although this may raise the issue of contributory negligence.[10] Particularly where statutory regulations have been enacted to eliminate a risk of harm — but for a technicality do not apply — the harm will be something the employer should reasonably have foreseen. Therefore while the lighting provisions of the Construction (Working Places) Regulations 1966 did not apply to power stations the employer owed a duty of care to an

[7] *Gunn v. Wallsend Slipway & Engineering Co. Ltd, The Times,* Jan. 23, 1989 (QBD); and see *Hewett v. Alf Brown's Transport Ltd* [1992] I.C.R. 530 (C.A.), to effect that generally an employer does not owe a duty of care to an employee's family (wife) for lead oxide powder taken home on work clothes and as in the instant case the husband's exposure to lead was below the lowest end of the scale set out in the relevant Code of Practice; it was so insignificant that no duty was owed in the particular circumstances.

[8] *Bryce v. Swan Hunter Group* [1987] 2 Lloyd's Rep. 426; and see *Balfour and Others v. William Beardmore,* 1956 S.L.T. 205 (O.H.) (following interim report of Committee on Dust in Steel Foundries employers could not plead they could not reasonably have foreseen the danger of pneumoconiosis being contracted by employees) and *Douglas Reilly v. Robert Kellie & Son Ltd,* 1990 S.L.T. 78, regarding liability for exposure to isocyanate fumes.

[9] *McCafferty v. Metropolitan Police Receiver* [1977] 2 All E.R. 756; and see *Burgess v. Thorn Consumer Electronics (Newhaven), The Times,* May 16, 1983 (employer previously advised of risk of tenosynovitis by Health and Safety Executive).

[10] *Sampson v. Hunslet Holdings Ltd* (1984) unreported case 84/357 (C.A.).

employee who was injured when he put himself in a dangerous position which he would not have been required to do had adequate lighting been provided.[11]

3.19 However the nature of the work being undertaken clearly affects what harm an employer should reasonably foresee. Thus where "an ordinary piece of furniture [filing cabinet] was being moved by two ordinary men through an ordinary department of an ordinary factory and then through an ordinary door at the end of the department" the employer could not reasonably foresee that the operation would result in one employee injuring his hand when the other employee pushed the cabinet in a particular way,[12] but an employer of an employee who was injured while attempting to lift a large sheet of glass weighing almost 30kg should have foreseen that lifting of the glass would be likely to cause injury to the average employee who had not received any special training.[13] The requirement that the kind of harm be reasonably foreseeable is demonstrated by contrasting *Doughty v. Turner Manufacturing Co. Ltd*[14] with *Rowark v. National Coal Board*.[15] Doughty was injured when along with other employees he stood near a crucible containing molten sodium cyanide which was kept at 800°C whose lid, made of a special asbestos compound, was accidentally knocked into the sodium cyanide. There was a great explosion and Doughty was injured not by splashes of molten cyanide but by exposure to the great heat given off and the ensuing fire. Only later was it discovered that sodium cyanide at over 500°C reacted violently with water and that water was given off by the asbestos compound at high temperature. Doughty's employer escaped liability because although injury by splashing was a foreseeable danger the heat produced by the chemical reaction was of a completely different type. In contrast *Rowark* developed tenosynovitis (inflammation of wrist tendons) after his work over a period of three months required him to haul wagons of waste

---

[11] *Lyons v. Babcock Energy plc and Another* (1992) H.S.I.B. 202 (O.H.).
[12] *McGown v. George McLellan & Co. Ltd,* 1962 S.L.T. (Notes) 30; and see *Forsyth v. Lothian Regional Council,* 1995 G.W.D. 4–204 (I.H.).
[13] *Fotheringham v. Dunfermline District Council,* 1991 S.L.T. 610 (O.H.); and see *Colclough v. Staffordshire County Council* [1994] 10 C.L. 208 (reasonably foreseeable that social worker might have to lift patient).
[14] [1964] 1 All E.R. 98.
[15] 1986, unreported case no. 86/45 (C.A.).

weighing half a ton along a 400-yard track. His employer's
defence that this particular condition could not have been
reasonably foreseen as a result of the type of work involved
was rejected because some kind of strain to the wrist was
foreseeable.[16] The classification of the harm as one type or
another can become very important. Thus if gloves provided by an employer would protect against a glancing
blow but not a piercing injury the fact that the evidence did
not disclose which type of injury was sustained was immaterial because these two types of blow are not entirely
different types of injury but are merely manifestations of
the same type of injury, namely a cutting injury.[17] However,
even where the type of harm is foreseeable it has been held
that for policy reasons senior police officers who are responsible for deploying officers to control serious public disorder
are generally not liable to individual officers under their
command if those officers are injured by attacks from
rioters, because to hold otherwise would be detrimental to
the control of public order because critical decisions should
not be affected by fear of a potential negligence claim.[18]

Causation

3.20   The general principle may be stated that the breach
of duty must have been the predominant or effective
cause of the event or occurrence which resulted in the
injury to the employee; alternatively the breach of duty
must be the *causa causans* and not merely a *causa sine qua
non* of the accident.[19] However, while it is not necessary to
show that the employer's breach of duty was the whole
cause of the harm it must, in order to become the legal
cause, materially increase the risk of the harm. Thus a
workman, whose normal duties were carried out in a pipe
kiln, was required to work in a brick kiln, contracted
dermatitis and sued his employers who, he alleged, failed
to perform their duty of care to him by not providing

---

[16] And see *Bradford v. Robinson Rentals Ltd* [1967] 1 All E.R. 267 (frostbite
not reasonably foreseeable but some injury due to extreme cold was);
Ping v. Esselte-Letraset [1992] C.L.Y.B. 231 (generally upper limb disorders were reasonably foreseeable).

[17] *Muir v. Cumbernauld and Kilsyth District Council*, 1993 S.L.T. 287.

[18] *Hughes v. National Union of Mineworkers and Others* [1991] 4 All E.R. 278
(Q.B.D.).

[19] For a discussion of the policy issues involved in causation see Atiyah,
Accidents Compensation and the Law, Chap. 4.

showering facilities at his place of work. It was held by
the House of Lords that as the employer's breach of duty
had materially increased the risk of the harm that breach
could be regarded as the legal cause, the *causa causans*.[20]
However the application of this rule may only occur
where two (or more) causes could have resulted in the
harm in which case the law should presume, in favour of
the plaintiff, that the breach of duty was responsible for
the damage. Thus in *Kay's Tutor v. Ayrshire and Arran
Health Board*[21] the pursuer's son was admitted to hospital
suffering from meningitis and was negligently given an
overdose of penicillin which caused convulsions and
hemiparesis. As a result of prompt remedial measures he
promptly recovered from the latter and eventually from
the meningitis but was deaf. The evidence that the
penicillin would damage the hearing was rejected and
there was no known case of penicillin overdose causing
deafness but many where deafness had been caused by
meningitis. Although the health board had breached its
duty by administering the overdose the House of Lords
held that it was no cause at all of the deafness. Applying
the principle of *McGhee*[22] was therefore to no avail because
the evidence did not disclose two (or more) competing
causes of the deafness.

Proof

3.21   As a general rule the onus is on the employee to
prove, on the balance of probabilities,[23] that his injuries
have been caused by the employer's breach of duty[24] and

---

[20] *McGhee v. NCB*, 1973 S.C. (H.L.) 37.
[21] 1987 S.L.T. 577.
[22] *McGhee v. NCB*, above.
[23] A pursuer does not have to prove every fact on which his case is
based, however, as it is permissible for a court to draw from the
evidence certain inferences; thus in *Cousins v. Lambeth, Southwark and
Lewisham Health Authority* (1986, unreported case 86/225) the Court of
Appeal has held that though there was no direct evidence of a slippery
floor or a failure to mop it, the first instance judge was entitled to infer
from the evidence that more probably than not the pursuer, a nurse,
slipped on a wet floor, the water must have come from a washbasin, it
was likely that another nurse caused the spillage and the continued
presence of water on the floor was due to the failure of other staff to
mop it up.
[24] *Hendry v. Clan Line Steamers*, 1949 S.C. 320. *Cf. Wilebore v. St
Edmundsbury Borough Council* [1994] 11 C.L. 335 (employee suffering from
osteoarthritis not able to prove injury caused by RSI).

particularly where an employee is working alone the absence of corroboration[25] as to how the injuries occurred have prevented the employee overcoming that onus. An important exception is found in the legal presumption *res ipsa loquitur* (the thing speaks for itself) which applies where the thing is shown to be under the management of the defender and the accident is such that in the ordinary course of things it would not occur if those who have the management use proper care; it affords reasonable evidence in the absence of an explanation of the defenders that the accident arose from want of care. Thus where an employee was injured when an explosion in a hose caused him to leap, in fright, from the platform on which he was working the employers were liable because (i) the most probable cause was the failure of a filter to prevent rust getting into the hose, (ii) at the material time they were in control of the hose and (iii) hosepipes do not usually explode.[26] However the maxim does not apply if there is direct evidence of the cause of the accident, and if the pursuer can reasonably be expected to know the cause of the accident he must prove negligence[27] although in order to do so the House of Lords has held that the pursuer will be entitled to see an employer's internal report into the cause of an accident notwithstanding that one of the purposes of preparing the report was to obtain legal advice in anticipation of litigation.[28]

3.22 The Second Division has pointed out in *Porter v. Strathclyde Regional Council*[29] that *McGhee* is most appropriate to apply "to the case of an industrial disease to which there may have been a number of contributory factors" but "was wholly inappropriate to apply to a fall caused by food on the floor which . . . should not have been there at the time."[30] Thus when Mrs Porter fell after slipping on

---

[25] Strictly, in accordance with the Law Reform (Miscellaneous Provisions) (Scotland) Act 1968, s. 9, in an action for damages for personal injuries corroboration is not necessary: nevertheless an employee's uncorroborated evidence is unlikely to counter other indicators as to how an accident occurred. See, for example, *Hill v. Brian W. Coleman Fumigation Services*, 1993 G.W.D. 9–647 and *Hetherington v. Robertson*, 1993 G.W.D. 2–138.

[26] *Devine v. Colvilles*, 1968 S.C. (H.L.) 67; and see *Davies v. D. Moffat & Son Ltd*, 1995 G.W.D. 2–85 (O.H.).

[27] *Gavin v. Rogers* (1889) 17 R. 206.

[28] *Waugh v. British Railways Board* [1979] I.R.L.R. 364.

[29] 1991 S.L.T. 446.

[30] *Ibid.*, at p. 448.

food which had dropped on to the floor she had to establish whether the system of supervision and removal or covering of the dropped food (which a careful employer would have adopted) would probably have prevented the accident and the Lord Ordinary had been wrong to require merely that such a system would have materially diminished the risk of the accident. Although certain parts of the judgment in *Porter* might suggest that where a pursuer shows there occurred a failure to take a precaution designed to reduce a danger, it inevitably follows that had the precaution been taken the accident would probably have been prevented, the First Division in *Muir v. Cumbernauld and Kilsyth District Council*[31] has emphasised that *Porter* "in no way derogates from the accepted test which is that a pursuer must prove on a balance of probabilities that breach of duty caused or materially contributed to his injury." However, even if it is established that the employer has breached his duty of care by not providing safety equipment the pursuer is still required to prove on a balance of probabilities that he would have used the equipment,[32] and in the absence of medical evidence about the pursuer's mental condition the court is entitled to take account of his evidence that he would not have worn safety goggles even if they had been provided.[33]

Novus actus and contributory negligence

3.23 The chain of causation may begin with the employer's breach of duty but a subsequent event may relieve him of liability for the employee's eventual injury because the chain of causation may be broken by the subsequent event, a sequence of events described by the maxim *novus actus interveniens*. The *novus actus* may be the act of a third party or indeed the pursuer himself. Thus where as a result of his employer's negligence an employee who had sustained minor injuries from which he would have recovered in about two weeks sustained a more serious injury to his right leg when, on experiencing a sudden weakness in his left (injured) leg he jumped

[31] 1993 S.L.T. 287.
[32] *McWilliams v. Sir William Arrol & Co.*, 1962 S.L.T. 121 (H.L.); *Bux v. Slough Metals Ltd* [1973] 1 W.L.R. 1358.
[33] *McKinlay v. British Steel Corporation*, 1988 S.L.T. 810.

down a number of steps to the next landing, his employers were held not liable for the injuries to his right leg because the injury was caused by the pursuer's unreasonable conduct — in putting himself in a position whereby he had to jump downstairs — which was a *novus actus interveniens*.[34]

3.24 More commonly the action of the injured employee will be a co-operating or contributing cause of his injuries rather than a *novus actus*. Until the enactment of the Law Reform (Contributory Negligence) Act 1945 where the negligence of the employee contributed to his injury his employer was relieved of all liability.[35] Since 1945 a finding of contributory negligence merely permits the court to fix liability between the pursuer and the defender(s) in such proportions as reflect their shares of the responsibility,[36] and this is so whether the action lies at common law or for breach of statutory duty.[37] The standard of care required of the pursuer for his own safety is such as is reasonable in the circumstances,[38] and an employee will be contributorily negligent if he ought reasonably to have foreseen that if he did not act prudently he might hurt himself, taking account of the possibility of others being careless[39]; it does not depend on the existence of a legal duty of care for his own safety — "[t]he real question being not whether the [pursuer] was neglecting some legal duty but whether he was acting as a responsible man and with reaonable care,"[40] although where the pursuer is an employee courts have accepted that familiarity with danger breeds contempt and that workmen become careless and take risks.[41]

---

[34] *McKew v. Holland & Hannen & Cubitts (Scotland) Ltd*, 1970 S.L.T. 68, (H.L.).

[35] *Caswell v. Powell and Duffryn Assd. Collieries* [1940] A.C. 152; and see the report of the Law Revision Committee, Cmd. 6032 (1939), that the question is "whose act caused the wrong?"

[36] Law Reform (Contributory Negligence) Act 1945, s. 1(1); note that s. 1(1) does not operate to defeat any defence which arises under a contract and the Act applies to claims brought by dependants of a deceased (s. 1(4)).

[37] *Grant v. Sun Shipping Company*, 1948 S.C. (H.L.) 73; and see Chap. 4 para. 4.15.

[38] *Porter v. Strathclyde Regional Council*, 1991 S.L.T. 446.

[39] *Jones v. Livox Quarries* [1952] 2 Q.B. 608, *per* Denning L. J. at p. 615.

[40] *Davies v. Swan Motor Co.* [1949] 2 K.B. 291.

[41] See, for example, *Flower v. Ebbw Vale Steel Company* [1934] 2 K.B. 132; *Caswell v. Powell Duffryn* [1940] A.C. 152; *Hutchinson v. L.N.E.R.* [1942] 1 K.B. 481.

Unless the trial judge has manifestly gone wrong to a substantial degree the appeal court will not interfere with his apportionment of responsibility.[42] Each case very much depends on its own circumstances but sometimes it is difficult to comprehend the trial judge's apportionment of responsibility. Thus a 50 per cent allocation of responsibility was made and upheld where a nursery assistant had injured herself when she slipped on a small amount of mince and potato which had fallen on to the floor in a room where young children were being fed. She was so intent on carrying a fractious baby at the time that she forgot to look for food on the floor but she ought to have done so because food on the floor was a common occurrence.[43] On the other hand a 30 per cent allocation of responsibility was made and upheld where an experienced factory worker attempted to complete single-handed a task, involving the use of a hydraulic ram, normally performed by two people; his hand was injured when a punch, which he held between thumb and forefinger on the rivet head, slipped while he allowed the ram to come down with some force.[44] It is for the defender(s) to prove contributory negligence.[45]

The standard of the employer's duty

3.25 The duty owed to the employee can be stated in general terms as a duty to take reasonable care for the employee's safety,[46] which involves a question of fact[47]

[42] *McCusker v. Saveheat Cavity Wall Insulation Ltd*, 1987 S.L.T. 24; *McIntosh v. N.C.B.*, 1988 S.L.T. 348. But see *Calder v. H. Kitson Vickers Ltd* [1988] I.C.R. 3232 (C.A.) where Ralph Gibson L.J. felt able to adjust the trial judge's apportionment on the ground that the latter concluded that the contract was one of service, whereas Ralph Gibson L.J. considered the contract between Calder and the defendants to be for services.

[43] *Porter v. Strathclyde Regional Council*, 1991 S.L.T. 446; a similar allocation was made where an employee who knew goggles were available and the risk of working without them was injured when not availing himself of the goggles: *Crouch v. BREL*, 1988 I.R.L.R. 404 (C.A.).

[44] *Jenkinson v. Brook Motors Ltd* (1985) unreported case no. 85/280 (C.A.); and see *McMillan v. Lord Advocate*, 1991 S.L.T. 150 (30 per cent allocation of responsibility to employee who tripped on a door seal which projected not more than one-half inch above the floor because "it was not clearly visible and it would be easy to forget about it").

[45] *Porter v. Strathclyde Regional Council*, 1991 S.L.T. 446.

[46] *Davie v. New Merton Board Mills* [1958] 1 All E.R. 67; *Muir v. Glasgow Corporation*, 1943 S.C. (H.L.) 3.

[47] *Qualcast (Wolverhampton) Ltd v. Haynes* [1959] A.C. 743.

with the result that previous decisions are invariably merely examples of applications of the principles rather than statements of the law. Although it has been author-itatively stated that the standard of foresight of the reasonable man is an impersonal one which is indepen-dent of the idiosyncrasies of the particular person in question, there is to an extent a subjective element in that it is left to the judge to decide what in the circumstances of the particular case the reasonable man would have had in contemplation and what the party sought to be made liable ought to have foreseen.[48] Thus where a man is in a position which requires special skill or knowledge a failure to exercise such skill or knowledge will breach the duty of care, and this applies just as much to doctors and other professions as it does to managements of industrial undertakings, and it has been fairly commented that this is one reason why, in general, a higher standard of care will be expected of employers than of their employees.[49] The fact that the employer is following trade practice is not conclusive proof that he has taken reasonable care[50]; in every case it is a question of whether the circumstances entitle the court to conclude that there has or has not been a failure to exercise reasonable care.[51]

3.26 In *Morton v. Dixon*[52] Lord Dunedin opined that where the negligence consists of a fault of omission proof should be one of two kinds — either that the thing which he did not do was a thing which was commonly done by persons in like circumstances or that it was a thing which was so obviously wanted that it would be folly in anyone to neglect. However, Lord Normand has counselled that Lord Dunedin's opinion did not permit a "facile finding

---

[48] *Muir v. Glasgow Corporation*, 1943 S.C. (H.L.) 3 *per* Lord Macmillan at p. 10; *Forsyth v. Lothian Regional Council*, 1995 G.W.D. 4–204 (I.H.).
[49] Munkman's *Employers' Liability* (11th ed.), p. 36.
[50] "[N]o one can claim to be excused for want of care because others are as careless as himself": *Blenkiron v. Great Central Gas Consumer Co.* (1860) 2 F. & F. 437 *per* Cockburn C.J.
[51] *Cavanagh v. Ulster Weaving Co. Ltd* [1960] A.C. 145 (H.L.), (NI), explaining *Morton v. Wm. Dixon Ltd*, 1909 S.C. 807. And see *Potec v. Edinburgh Corporation*, 1964 S.C. (H.L.) 1 (guard rail not provided at any refuse depot and they would have impeded the operative's activities), *Martin v. Greater Glasgow Health Board*, 1977 S.L.T. (Notes) 66 (banisters in nurses' home same height as in other similar institutions). And see *Marshall v. Wiliam Sharp & Sons Ltd*, 1991 S.L.T. 114 (I.H.) regarding reference to manufacturers' instructions.
[52] 1909 S.C. 807.

that a precaution is necessary when there is no proof that it is one taken by other persons in like circumstances but it does not detract from the test of conduct and judgment of the reasonable and prudent man."[53] Lord President Cooper in a later case[54] adhered to the view that only in the extreme case where it was obvious that some precaution was needed and inexcusable or folly to omit it, was it permissible to ignore current practice and rely on the judgment of the reasonable man. More recent decisions[55] of the House of Lords however have reaffirmed that the correct approach is that long-established practice in a trade, although not necessarily conclusive, is generally regarded as strong evidence of reasonableness and Lord Reid, stressing the need to have regard to what in *Paris v. Stepney Borough Council*[56] amounted to a "folly," namely something unreasonable or imprudent, has opined that Lord Dunedin's statement in *Morton v. Dixon*[57] must be read with Lord Normand's gloss[58]and it is now accepted that where a precaution is shown to be reasonably practicable it is not necessary to prove a practice elsewhere.[59]

3.27 It is clear that where knowledge is developing the employer must keep abreast of it and not be slow to apply it[60]; they must be familiar with codes of practice,[61] pamphlets[62] and other guidance[63] issued by the Health and Safety

---

[53] *Paris v. Stepney Borourgh Council* [1951] A.C. 367.

[54] *Gallagher v. Balfour Beatty & Co. Ltd*, 1951 S.C. 712 at p. 718.

[55] See, for example, *General Cleaning Contractors Ltd v. Christmas* [1953] A.C. 180; *Cavanagh v. Ulster Weaving Co. Ltd* [1960] A.C. 145. *Cf. King v. Smith, The Times,* November 3, 1994 (C.A.) (Standards regarded as reasonable in *Christmas* criticised).

[56] [1951] A.C. 367.

[57] 1909 S.C. 807.

[58] *Morris v. West Hartlepool Steam Navigation Co. Ltd* [1956] A.C. 552, (H.L.); and note the criticism of Lord Dunedin's statement in *Donohue v. Union S.S. Co. of New Zealand* [1951] N.Z.L.R. 862 at p. 879.

[59] *Macdonald v. Scottish Stamping and Engineering Co. Ltd*, 1972 S.L.T. (Notes) 73 (no evidence of practice of safety clamps at other establishments).

[60] *Stokes v. Guest Keen & Nettlefold* [1968] 1 W.L.R. 1776. And see *Lodge & McSherry v. British Telecom* (unreported, 1992).

[61] Codes of practice may be approved by the Health and Safety Commission under s. 16 of the Health and Safety at Work Act 1974 and are declared to be admissible in criminal proceedings, but there would seem to be no reason why they could not be relied on in civil proceedings without the statutory presumption against the employer which is applied by s. 17(2) in criminal proceedings; see Chap. 5, para. 5.71 *et seq.*

[62] *Clifford v. Charles H. Challen & Son* [1951] 1 K.B. 495.

[63] *Burgess v. Thorn Consumer Electronics (Newhaven), The Times,* May 16, 1983.

Executive and other organisations concerned with occupational safety,[64] and a large undertaking will be expected to
attain a higher standard of care in this respect than the
corner shop.[65] Where the evidence discloses that the
employers took all reasonable steps to inform themselves
of the up-to-date position (regarding safe vibration limits
for chain saws) and applied them, the fact that the
technical aspects of the information were not examined in
depth will not prevent the court finding for the employer[66]
and attempts by employers to promulgate their own
limits and standards after collating information about
health risks are frequently accepted as indicators of
reasonableness.[67] Also while it has been stated that "the
law does not expect the employer of bricklayers' labourers
to study and become conversant with the complexities of
dermatology"[68] the decision seems to have turned on the
fact that there was no evidence of a contrary practice in
the building industry or any official or trade publication
on conditions on building sites indicating that labourers
are liable to contract dermatitis; and the rejection of the
pursuer's submission that a careful employer should take
steps to find out if a risk exists and, if it does, take steps
to protect against it, was consistent with neither (a) the
approach in *Sloan v. British Railways Board*[69] in which a
requirement to identify and monitor train drivers at risk
of neurosensory loss was rejected only because it would
not have detected the pursuer's sensitivity before his
injury had become manifest nor (b) the current statutory
philosophy of risk assessment[70]; indeed it is respectfully
suggested that the employer's statutory duty to carry out
a risk assessment will become a prominent feature of
common law claims. Of course the degree of awareness of

---

[64] *Balfour & Others v. William Beardmore & Co. Ltd,* 1956 S.L.T. 205 (O.H.)
(Report of Committee on Dust in Steel Industries).
[65] *Wright v. Dunlop Rubber Co. Ltd and I.C.I. Ltd* (1972) 13 K.I.R. 255
(C.A.); *Cartwright v. G.K.N. Sankey Ltd* (1973) 14 K.I.R. 349.
[66] *Murphy v. Lord Advocate,* 1981 S.L.T. 213, (O.H.).
[67] *Murphy v. Lord Advocate,* above; *Sloan v. British Railways Board,* 1981
S.L.T. 239 (O.H.).
[68] *Riddick v. Weir Housing Corporation Ltd,* 1971 S.L.T. 24, *per* Lord
Thomson at p. 25. Lord Migdale suggested that the employer's duty
varied depending on whether the materials were new or had been in use
for a long time.
[69] 1981 S.L.T. 239 (O.H.).
[70] See Management of Health and Safety at Work Regulations 1992 (S.I.
1992 No. 2051) and their accompanying Code of Practice; and see paras.
5.38–5.41.

the risk will change[71] in which case the issue is from what date would a reasonable employer with proper but not extraordinary solicitude for the welfare of his workers have identified the problem (of excessive noise), recognise that it was capable of solution, weigh up the potential advantages and disadvantages of that solution, decide to adopt it, acquire a supply of protectors, set in train a programme of education, experiment with the sytem and put it into effect.[72]

3.28 Similarly, while an action at common law is distinct from an action for breach of statutory duty[73] the former cannot be considered in complete dissociation from the latter. Thus on the one hand it would be difficult to maintain that an employer who had complied with a cognate statutory provision had failed in his common law duty to take care[74] while compliance with the statutory provision may be of evidential value,[75] while on the other hand the very fact that there has been enacted a statutory provision may be relied on by a pursuer to show that a reasonable employer would have foreseen the risk which the statutory provision was designed to avert and would have taken appropriate action in the performance of his common law duty of care[76] although clearly that does not apply where the facts and circumstances of the case take it outside the statutory provisions in which case the

---

[71] See, for example, *Graham v. C.W.S. Ltd* [1957] 1 All E.R. 654 (not known that mahogany dust could cause cancer); *Tremain v. Pike* [1969] 3 All E.R. 1303 (not at one time known in farming community that Weil's disease could be contracted through contact with rats' urine).

[72] *Thompson v. Smiths Shiprepairers (North Shields) Ltd* [1984] Q.B. 4058.

[73] *Caswell v. Powell Duffryn Associated Collieries* [1940] A.C. 152 (H.L.).

[74] *Franklin v. Gramophone Company Ltd* [1948] 1 K.B. 542 (C.A.).

[75] *Qualcast (Wolverhampton) Ltd v. Haynes* [1959] A.C. 743 (H.L.) *per* Lord Keith of Avonholm at p. 756. Also while the Management of Health and Safety at Work Regulations 1992 generally do not impose civil liability it could be argued that failure to observe the regulations about risk assessment would be evidence of negligence.

[76] *Franklin v. Gramophone Company Ltd* [1948] 1 K.B. 542, *per* Somervell L.J. at p. 558; *National Coal Board v. England* [1954] A.C. 403 (H.L.). And see *Butt v. Inner London Education Authority* (1968) 66 L.G.R. 379; *Hewett v. Alf Brown's Transport Ltd* [1992] I.C.R. 530 (C.A.) in which the standard of the common law duty was determined by reference to the Control of Lead at Work Regulations 1980 on the grounds that they made clear what risks were foreseeable.

common law issue has to be resolved without reference to the statute or regulations.[77]

However an examination of judicial decisions discloses that the concept of reasonable care involves consideration of the following issues — (a) the risk or probability that damage or harm will be done by the conduct or activity; (b) the magnitude of resultant damage or harm; (c) the value or utility of the object to be achieved by the conduct in question; (d) the practicability, cost, time and trouble of taking precautions against the risk of injury.[78]

Probability

3.29 Where an employee was bitten by one of her employer's two West Highland terriers while cleaning the windows of the veterinary surgery where she worked as a receptionist the main issue was whether the injury was reasonably foreseeable and approving the test set out in *Bolton v. Stone*.[79] Lord Weir stated the question was whether the risk of damage to the pursuer was sufficiently probable as to lead the defenders to anticipate it and

> "there is no doubt in my mind that a stranger entering the back garden was at risk of being attacked and at risk of injury, and from the description of the dogs' behaviour I do not consider that the risk was remote or fanciful but a real one. . . . The evidence . . . gives the clear impression that these particular terriers were capable of turning nasty while in the garden and . . . I cannot believe that the defenders could have been unaware prior to the incident of the vicious tendencies of Shona and Dornie. I am satisfied that there was a foreseeable and not remote risk that . . . one or other of [the dogs] would show aggression towards a stranger who for any reason appeared in the garden and that

[77] *Matuszczyk v. National Coal Board*, 1953 S.C. 8; *Chipchase v. British Titan Products Company Ltd* [1956] 1 Q.B. 545; and see *Bux v. Slough Metals Ltd* [1974] 1 All E.R. 262 (C.A.).
[78] *Morris v. West Hartlepool Steam Navigation Co. Ltd* [1956] A.C. 552; and see Atiyah, *Accidents, Compensation and the Law* (3rd ed., 1980), p. 44.
[79] 1951 A.C. 850; *cf. Whitefield v. Barton*, 1987 S.C.L.R. 259, *Lamond v. Glasgow Corporation*, 1968 S.L.T. 291.

this aggression might well take the form of a physical attack".[80]

Similarly where an employee who was carrying a bottle tripped over a metal strip which protruded half an inch above floor level the argument that the hazard was more apparent than real was rejected because "to catch a foot on the rim of this threshold was something which was liable to happen from time to time unless someone was looking where he was going and . . . it was only a matter of time before this would lead to a fall and to injury"[81]; or where an employee slipped on the spillages (from coffee or tea-cups) on a pseudo marble floor the probability test was met because

> "the records had shown that spillages . . . had been common, so that it had been almost inevitable that sooner or later an accident would occur; indeed staff had, several times each year by means of bulletins, been besought to take better care and to put a saucer or tray beneath any cup or mug which they carried from the kitchen."[82]

The magnitude of the risk

3.30 As a general proposition it may be stated that the law exacts a degree of care commensurate with the risk created[83] so that the greater the risk of injury the more rigorous is the standard of care. Thus in the *locus classicus*, *Paris v. Stepney Borough Council*,[84] an employee who was known[85] by the employers to be already blind in one eye was using a hammer to loosen a bolt when a piece of metal flew off into his good eye, rendering him blind; his employers were liable for failing to provide protective goggles even although no goggles were provided to other

[80] *Hill v. Lovett*, 1992 S.L.T. 994 (O.H.).
[81] *McMillan v. Lord Advocate*, 1991 S.L.T. 150 (O.H.); cf. *McClafferty v. British Telecommunications plc*, 1987 S.L.T. 327.
[82] *Bell v. Department of Social Security, The Times*, June 13, 1989 (C.A.); cf. *Latimer v. AEC Ltd* [1953] 2 All E.R. 449, *Hanlon v. British Railways Board*, 1991 S.L.T. 228 (O.H.).
[83] *Henderson v. Carron Co.* (1889) 16 R. 633.
[84] [1951] 1 All E.R. 42 (H.L.); cf. *Sloan v. British Railways Board*, 1981 S.L.T. 239 (O.H.).
[85] See *James v. Hepworth & Grandage* [1968] 1 Q.B. 94.

men engaged in the same type of activity; however the principle of *Pan's* has been restricted to cases about plant and equipment and held not apply to safe systems.[85a] Similarly although an employer by making protective gloves available to his employee, a cleaner, could have avoided or at least reduced the risk of contact dermatitis he failed in his duty of reasonable care by not warning his employee of the risk of contracting this "disease . . . [which] could become quite serious in that it could take a long time to heal and could become a long term problem."[86] On the other hand where the risks of injury are not great and an experienced employee knows the risks it may be sufficient for the employer to make the safety equipment available,[87] and while an employer must warn an employee of the health risks a job involves, where knowledge of the risks would be likely to affect the decision of a sensible, level-headed person about accepting the offer of employment, the duty was not activated by the prospect of the employee suffering from Reynaud's syndrome (a numbing of the fingers) which merely caused minor discomfort and trivial inconvenience with no effect on capacity for work.[88]

Value of activity

3.31 There are few reported cases of courts concluding that the value to attach to the activity or conduct in question outweighs the duty to reduce or eliminate the risk, but it has been held that in wartime the need to make use of all available vehicles could justify the risks involved in using a vehicle with a defective signalling system.[89] However, economic expedience or the inconve-

---

[85a] *Forsyth v. Lothian Regional Council,* 1995 G.W.D. 4–204 (I.H.).

[86] *Campbell v. Lothian Health Board,* 1987 S.L.T. 665 (O.H.). And see *Stokes v. Guest Keen and Nettlefold Ltd* [1968] 1 W.L.R. 1776 (possible risk of developing scrotal cancer not publicised to workforce because of resultant "turmoil's" possible effect on production).

[87] *Qualcast (Wolverhampton) Ltd v. Haynes* [1959] 2 All E.R. 38 (H.L.) (molten metal splashed on to foot of experienced employee to whom spats and boots were available.

[88] *White v. Holbrook Precision Castings Ltd* [1985] I.R.L.R. 215 (C.A.); and see *Condo v. South Australia* [1987] S.A.S.R. 584.

[89] *Daborn v. Bath Tramways Motor Co.* [1946] 2 All E.R. 333.

nience of carrying out repairs during a busy period will probably not justify the risks of postponing repairs.[90]

Practicability, cost, time and trouble

3.32 The extent to which an employer is required to reduce or eliminate a risk is influenced by the difficulty and expense involved in taking such risk-reducing procedures and the effectiveness of protective measures. Thus it has been held that it is not reasonably practicable to prop every part of a mine,[91] to provide a barrier cream as protection against dermatitis where there were doubts about the effectiveness of the protection,[92] or to provide ear defenders to engine drivers where they would reduce the noise but also the driver's ability to hear audio-warning signals.[93] Similarly in *General Cleaning Contractors Ltd v. Christmas*[94] the risk of injury to a window cleaner by the top sash slipping down to cause a "guillotine" effect on his fingers as they held on to the lower sash thereby causing him to lose his grip and fall could have been eliminated by provision of simple wedges; other methods would have been to do all the cleaning from ladders or inserting bolts into the walls at either side of each window but neither of these was practicable.[95] However

---

[90] *Macdonald v. British Transport Commission* [1955] 3 All E.R. 789; and see *Stokes v. Guest Keen and Nettlefold (Bolts and Nuts) Ltd*, above (failure to issue warnings and introduce checks for scrotal cancer for fear that resultant turmoil would interfere with production); *Macdonald v. Scottish Stamping and Engineering Co. Ltd*, 1972 S.L.T. 73 (fitting safety device would slow down production and reduce employees' piece-rate earnings). *Cf. Wood v. Redpath*, 1993 G.W.D. 3–193 (uneconomic to employ winch operator).
[91] *Marshall v. Gotham & Co. Ltd* [1954] A.C. 360.
[92] *Brown v. Rolls Royce Ltd*, 1960 S.C. (H.L.) 22; [1960] 1 All E.R. 577.
[93] *Sloan v. British Railways Board*, 1981 S.L.T. 239 (O.H.).
[94] [1952] 2 All E.R. 1110 (H.L.).
[95] And see *Cook v. Square D Ltd* [1992] I.C.R. 262 (C.A.) in which it was stated unrealistic to require employer of one employee sent abroad to inspect site, but the standard may change where a number of employees are involved or an employee is being sent for considerable period. However in the earlier Scottish case of *McQuilter v. Goulandris Bros. Ltd*, 1951 S.L.T. (Notes) 75 it was made clear that where the employee was working on premises within the possession and control of a third party that does not absolve the employer from exercising reasonable care for the safety of the workmen, although the scope of the duty is circumscribed by the fact that the work is being done on premises not within the possession and control of the employer.

the incidence of accidents will result in the practicability
of preventative measures being reviewed and the measures regarded as acceptable in *Christmas* are, 40 years
later, now inadequate in that some operations are so
inherently dangerous that they should not be performed
at all and an employer would impose an embargo on
employees going on to the window sill where the customer had provided no anchor points for the harness.[95a]
While the transfer of cash between £1,500 and £2,000 did
not require the employment of security specialists provided the employee had received adequate training in
ways of reducing injury to himself[96] the employers of an
employee injured while manually moving a 45-gallon
drum weighing 450lb. were liable for the employee's
injuries when they already had at their disposal a vehicle
and a hoist; there was no extra cost and only minor
inconvenience involved.[97]

THE SUBSTANCE OF THE EMPLOYER'S DUTY

3.33 Although the employer's duty is a general one,
alternatively expressed as a duty to "provide in every way
for the safety of workmen against the risks which their
employment involves," to make "such provision for the
safety of the workman as is reasonable and necessary" or
"to take reasonable care that the employee is not exposed
to unnecessary risks,"[98] which will include the dangers
created by the actions of third parties where such a
danger would have been very likely to occur,[99] it is
frequently considered in relation to particular components
or elements of the duty. However although for convenience it is possible to arrange decisions under particular
headings it must be noted that each decision is very much
related to its own facts and frequently will involve consideration of other relevant issues like foreseeability, causation and standard of care. Decisions relating to the

---

[95a] *King v. Smith, The Times,* November 3, 1994 (C.A.).
[96] *Charlton v. Forrest Printing Ink Co. Ltd* [1980] I.R.L.R. 331 (C.A.).
[97] *Crawford v. Post Office* (1984) unreported case no. 84/85 (C.A.). *Cf.*
Wood v. Redpath, 1993 G.W.D. 3–193.
[98] *McNeill v. Wallace* (1853) 15 D. 818; *Bett v. Dalmeny Oil Company* (1905)
7 F. 787.
[99] *Longworth v. Coppas International (U.K.) Ltd,* 1985 S.L.T. 111.

substance of the employer's duty involve the use of words like "adequate," "maintain," "provide" and "inspect" which are also used in the context of statutory provisions, and decisions dealing with their meanings in such a context may occasionally provide assistance where the words arise in litigation based on common law. However care has to be taken to ensure that the word in its statutory context has not been given a special meaning either by judicial interpretation of the word in its statutory context[1] or by virtue of an interpretation clause in the statute itself.[2]

System

3.34 As indicated earlier,[3] the planning of the work method or the promulgation of a system of work is the personal responsibility of the employer. Just what is a system of work and what is required by way of a system depends on the circumstances and the nature of the work being undertaken but "system" generally denotes that which is permanent as opposed to transitory or casual[4] and may range from the giving of instructions for the safe accomplishment of a work objective[5] to the provision of no or inadequate equipment[6] although it may not include the provision of transport at the end of work.[7]

---

[1] See, for example the meanings ascribed to (a) "maintained" in *Millar v. Galashiels Gas Co. Ltd*, 1949 S.C. (H.L.) 31, and (b) "effective provision" in *Davies v. Massey Ferguson* [1986] I.C.R. 580.

[2] See, for example, Factories Act 1961, s. 176(1) and Personal Protective Equipment Regulations 1992, reg. 7, regarding the meanings of "maintain."

[3] See para. 3.6.

[4] *Marshall v. William Sharp & Sons Ltd*, 1992 S.L.T. 114 (I.H.); and see *Forsyth v. Lothian Regional Council*, 1995 G.W.D. 4–204 (I.H.) (no duty to set up a system to ensure safe lifting for a man with a history of abdominal injury for a particular day on which he had to work with a different workmate).

[5] *Wood v. Redpath*, 1993 G.W.D. 3–193 (failure to instruct marine apprentice to stop winch before attempting to free snagged rope); *Eltringham v. G. B. Papers plc*, 1993 G.W.D. 9–635 (failure to instruct employee to close stopcock when high pressure hosepipe not in use, to prevent formation of airlocks). Cf. *Couper v. Remploy Ltd*, 1993 G.W.D. 27–1715.

[6] *Weir v. Edinburgh Woollen Mill Ltd*, 1993 G.W.D. 1–54 (standing on top of ladder to remove shelving which habitually stuck).

[7] *Ramsay v. Wimpey Ltd*, 1951 S.C. 692, (I.H.).

Place of work

3.35 Ensuring that the employee's place of work is safe
extends not just to tangible physical things like floors,
doors, windows and means of access and egress but also
to environmental conditions like temperature and noise.
By far the most common means by which a workplace can
become unsafe are spillages on or obstruction of floors or
walkways. Generally[8] where spillages are likely to occur
an employer is required to institute and operate a reasonably adequate system of detecting and dealing with them
and what might be an adequate system inspection in one
place (office block) may not be adequate in another
(supermarket).[9] Thus the employers and the rig operator
were jointly liable for the injuries sustained by an oil
platform rigger who slipped while descending a ladder
because his boots were made slippery by an accumulation
of oil and mud on the deck and walkways; the danger of
slipping had been known for several days before the
accident.[10] However a duty of care does not arise if the
pursuer is unable to establish that the employers knew or
ought to have known of the presence of the slippery
substances,[11] and much will depend on the circumstances
of each case so that the employers of a fireman who
slipped in the fire station on a wet floor made of embos-
sed quarry tiles, which were generally satisfactory for
station activities, were held to have taken reasonable
care[12] while the employers of a nurse who slipped on a
small patch of oil on a terrazzo floor which resulted from
the lubrication of the wheels of moveable machinery
should have introduced a system of ensuring that oil did
not get on to the floor in this way.[13] Similarly an employer
may be required to advise or enjoin the evacuation of an
employee where the location of his work might expose

[8] *Cf. Cook v. Square D Ltd* [1992] I.C.R. 262 (C.A.).
[9] Contrast *Bell v. Department of Health and Society Security, The Times,* June
13, 1989, with *Ware v. Tesco Stores Ltd* [1976] 1 W.L.R. 810.
[10] *Breslin v. Britoil plc,* 1992 S.L.T. 414 (O.H.); and see *Bell v. Department
of Health and Social Security,* above.
[11] *Hanlon v. British Railways Board,* 1991 S.L.T. 228 (O.H.).
[12] *Dixon v. London Fire and Civil Defence Authority, The Times,* Feb. 22,
1993 (C.A.).
[13] *Buchanan v. Lanarkshire Health Board,* 1983 S.L.T. 456 (O.H.); and see
Bloxham v. Swan Hunter Shipbuilders Ltd (1985) unreported case 85/208
(C.A.), and *Markwell v. Suffolk Coastal District Council* (1985) unreported
case 85/815 (C.A.) (icy patches on private road and yard).

him to unnecessary risks which could be caused by the intervention of a third party,[14] and in the context of an unfair dismissal case it has been held that an employee could refuse to obey an order to go to Belfast (but not Wexford, Eire) on the grounds that it involved a serious risk not contemplated at the time of the contract.[15] Some decisions are difficult to reconcile and eventually will turn on the court's view of the remoteness of the risk.[16]

3.36 With regard to environmental conditions, these can extend to the provision of washing facilities,[17] lighting,[18] noise,[19] temperature,[20] work and shift patterns[21] and presence of dangerous animals.[22] Exposing employees to the risks of passive smoking may also give rise to breach of duty[23] and while it has been held that an employee had no contractual right to smoke at work,[24] it would seem eminently arguable that the dismissal of an employee for non-compliance with an employer's non-smoking policy would be fair at least on substantive grounds.[25]

[14] *Longworth v. Coppas International (U.K.) Ltd*, 1985 S.L.T. 111.
[15] *Walmsley v. UDEC* [1972] I.R.L.R. 80 (I.T.).
[16] Contrast *Brown v. Redpath Brown & Co. Ltd*, 1963 S.L.T. 219 (I.H.) with *McMillan v. Lord Advocate*, 1991 S.L.T. 150.
[17] *McGhee v. National Coal Board* [1972] 3 All E.R. 1003 (H.L.).
[18] *Garcia v. Harland & Wolff Ltd* [1943] 2 All E.R. 477; *Russell v. Criterion Film Productions Ltd* [1936] 3 All E.R. 627 (injury to eyes by use of abnormally bright lights); *McQuilter v. Goulandris Brothers Ltd*, 1951 S.L.T. (Notes) 75 (falling into open hatch through inadequate lighting); *Lyons v. Babcock Energy plc* (1992) H.S.I.B. 202 (injury by crushing when employee unable to see that heavy pipe might slip because of inadequate lighting).
[19] *Thompson v. Smiths Repairers (North Shields) Ltd* [1984] 1 All E.R. 881; *Baxter v. Harland & Wolff Ltd* [1990] I.R.L.R. 516 (C.A.).
[20] *Bradford v. Robinsons Rentals Ltd* [1967] 1 W.L.R. 337; in *Graham Oxley Tool Steels Ltd v. Firth* [1980] I.R.L.R. 135 (EAT) the duty was expressed as a contractual one to provide a proper working environment.
[21] *Johnstone v. Bloomsbury Health Authority* [1991] I.R.L.R. 118 (C.A.).
[22] *Hill v. Lovett*, 1992 S.L.T. 994 (O.H.) (employer allowing pugnacious dogs into area where employee worked).
[23] The action brought by Veronica Bland against her employers, Stockport Metropolitan Council, was settled by a payment of £15,000 compensation but without admission of liability after Miss Bland was required to share an office with three others who smoked up to 20 cigarettes a day even after the employer's occupational health doctor recommended she be moved to a non-smoking room: *The Times*, Jan. 28, 1993.
[24] *Dryden v. Greater Glasgow Health Board* [1992] I.R.L.R. 469 (EAT).
[25] Contrast *Unkles v. Milanda Bread Ltd* [1973] I.R.L.R. 76.

Equipment, plant and materials

3.37 With regard to these, the employer's duty is to ensure that the employee is provided with such equipment, plant and materials as are adequate for the safe performance of the job and to introduce a system of inspection and maintenance. Thus the employer was liable for the injuries sustained by an employee who was injured while raising piping from the ground to 70 feet up a steel structure; neither a crane nor a chain block and tackle was provided and the employee extemporised by using a rope block and tackle.[26] However an experienced workman may be expected to select the correct equipment for the task where such equipment is available.[27] "Provision" may merely require making available the equipment for the employee's use when required[28] but there may be circumstances which require the employer to ensure that each employee receives a personal issue.[29] However equipment will not be adequate if improper use by the employee which could lead to injury should have been foreseen by the employer.[30] Maintenance of equipment requires not merely repair and renewal as necessary but also the introduction of a system of appropriate inspection. Thus the operators of a bus were liable when the bursting of a tyre caused the bus to crash; the operators should have known of the possibility of undetectable defects in tyres due to unduly harsh treatment and should have introduced a system of reporting heavy blows to the tyres of their vehicles,[31] and where equipment has failed, a failure to produce evidence of any system of inspection being operated may result in the employer being liable.[32] The extent to which an employer

---

[26] *Machray v. Stewarts and Lloyds Ltd* [1964] 3 All E.R. 716; and see *Lovell v. Blundells and T. Albert Crompton & Co. Ltd* [1944] 1 K.B. 502; *General Cleaning Contractors v. Christmas* [1953] A.C. 80.

[27] *Qualcast (Wolverhampton) Ltd v. Haynes* [1959] 2 All E.R. 38 (H.L.); *Johnson v. Croggan Co. Ltd* [1954] 1 All E.R. 121; *Richardson v. S. Clarke Ltd* [1969] 3 All E.R. 705.

[28] *Qualcast (Wolverhampton) Ltd v. Haynes* [1959] 2 All E.R. 38 (H.L.).

[29] Contrast *Crouch v. British Rail Engineering Ltd* [1988] I.R.L.R. 404 (C.A.) with *McKinlay v. British Steel Corporation,* 1987 S.L.T. 522; 1988 S.L.T. 810.

[30] *Sampson v. Hunslet Holdings Ltd* (1984) unreported.

[31] *Barkway v. South Wales Transport* [1950] 1 All E.R. 392; cf. *McDonald v. British Transport Commission* [1955] 3 All E.R. 789.

[32] *Henderson v. Henry E. Jenkins & Sons* [1969] 3 All E.R. 756.

is required to enforce the use of safety equipment depends on all the circumstances including the level of experience of the employee and the type of risk involved.[33] Thus while an employer was required to take very strict measures to enforce the wearing of goggles where employees were sharpening metal tools on a carborundum grinding stone[34] the employer was not liable for the injuries sustained by an experienced fitter who attempted to perform a two-man task in the absence of his mate because in the circumstances the employer, having constituted a safe two-man work method, was not also required expressly to instruct the experienced employees not to devise a short cut or proceed single-handed.[35]

Employers' Liability (Defective Equipment) Act 1969

3.38 Where the plant or equipment is manufactured by a third party the common law rule is subject to a statutory proviso[36] which counteracts the effect of the decision of the House of Lords in *Davie v. New Merton Board Mills Ltd.*[37] The law prior to *Davie* was to the effect that the employers who provided the equipment were as one with the negligent manufacturers and therefore liable for any injuries caused by a latent defect resulting from negligent manufacture.[38] In *Davie* the employer was not liable for the injury sustained by an employee when the drift he was using splintered because although the drift had been negligently manufactured it was apparently in good condition and the employer had obtained it from a reputable

---

[33] *Qualcast (Wolverhampton) Ltd v. Haynes* [1959] 2 All E.R. 38 (H.L.); *Cummings v. Sir William Arrol & Co.* [1962] 1 All E.R. 623 (H.L.).

[34] *Nolan v. Dental Manufacturing Co. Ltd* [1958] 2 All E.R. 449; and see *Bux v. Slough Metals Ltd* [1974] 1 All E.R. 262 (C.A.).

[35] *Rundell v. English Clays Loverin Pochin & Co. Ltd,* unreported case no. 85/649 (C.A.).

[36] Employers' Liability (Defective Equipment) Act 1969. But see the special provisions in the Employment Act 1989, s. 11 regarding the wearing of safety helmets by Sikhs on construction sites: s. 11 provides (i) that any requirement to wear a safety helmet shall not apply to a Sikh wearing a turban and (2) where a person (*e.g.* employer) does not comply with such a requirement no action in reparation shall be brought against him in respect of injury, loss or damage.

[37] [1959] A.C. 604.

[38] See *Donnelly v. Glasgow Corporation,* 1953 S.C. 107.

source.[39] The effect of the decision in *Davie* was that an injured employee would be unable to recover damages for his injuries where the negligent manufacturer had gone out of business, was situated abroad in another jurisdiction or could not be located. The Employers' Liability (Defective Equipment) Act 1969 has reinstated the principle of law enunciated in *Donnelly*[40] by providing that where an employee suffers personal injury in the course of his employment as a result of a defect in equipment provided by his employer for the purpose of his employer's business and the defect is attributable to the fault of a third party, whether identified or not, the injury shall be deemed to be also attributable to negligence on the part of his employer whether or not he is liable for the injury apart from the Act. "Equipment" is widely defined to include "any plant, machinery, vehicle, aircraft and clothing"[41] and has been held to include a bulk carrier,[42] industrial soap issued for cleaning mop heads,[43] and a flagstone to be laid by a road maintenance worker on the grounds that there was no reason to suppose that Parliament had deliberately omitted the word "materials" in juxtaposition to the word "equipment".[44] On the other hand the concept which the Act involves is the "tools for the job" and that actuators which formed part of the braking system of axles which the pursuer was building were not "equipment."[45] However the Act contains some difficulties for the employee,[46] the most serious of which is to demonstrate that the defect is attributable wholly or partly to the fault of a third party, whether identifiable or not; and, as Lang[47] has argued, an employee will invariably fail where there is more than one cause of the accident if he cannot explain the precise nature of the alleged

---

[39] After *Davie*, to succeed the employee injured as a result of a latent defect had to prove either that his employer was not entitled to rely on the skill and care of the manufacturers or that he (the employer) should have discovered the defect by reasonable diligence (*McMillan v. BP Refinery (Grangemouth) Ltd*, 1961 S.L.T. (Notes) 79 (I.H.).

[40] *Donnelly v. Glasgow Corporation*, 1953 S.C. 107.

[41] Employers' Liability (Defective Equipment) Act 1969, s. 1(3).

[42] *Coltman v. Bibby Tankers Ltd (The Derbyshire)* [1988] A.C. 276.

[43] *Ralston v. Greater Glasgow Health Board*, 1987 S.L.T. 386 (O.H.); and see *Yuille v. Daks Simpson Ltd*, 1984 S.L.T. 115.

[44] *Knowles v. Liverpool City Council* [1993] I.R.L.R. 6 (C.A.).

[45] *Loch v. British Leyland U.K. Ltd*, 1975 S.L.T. (Notes) 67.

[46] See for example Lang, (1984) 47 M.L.R. 48.

[47] *Op. cit.*

defect. It has been suggested that an employee injured by a defective product may be better served by an action of damages based on the Consumer Protection Act 1987 on the grounds that in the latter (a) proof of negligence is not required, (b) the definition of product is wider, (c) there is no requirement that the product be provided by the employer or that the employee be injured in the course of his employment, and (c) damages are not limited to personal injury although, in respect of damage to property, they are subject to a limit of £275; on balance the employee will have better prospects of success by raising an action against the employer under the 1969 Act.[48]

Information, instructions and warnings to employees

3.39 Of course the provision of inherently safe plant, materials and safety equipment itself may be insufficient. Although much depends on the circumstances,[49] it will frequently be necessary for the employer to take further steps, for example by instituting regular medical checks,[50] a programme of training,[51] or by providing information[52] about the risks and dangers involved in work activity and how these can, by using appropriate equipment, be reduced or eliminated. Where dangers are obvious it will normally be sufficient to issue simple instructions[53] which the employee can easily follow. Thus an employer was not liable for the injuries sustained by a window cleaner

---

[48] Blaikie, 1993 S.L.T. 153.

[49] *McKinlay v. British Steel Corporation*, 1988 S.L.T. 810 (I.H.).

[50] In *Stokes v. Guest, Keen and Nettlefold* [1968] 1 W.L.R., it was held the employer had been negligent in not instituting a system of periodic medical examinations where it was known that employees who came into regular and prolonged exposure to mineral oil might develop scrotal warts which may become malignant. *Cf. Sorman v. Royal Scottish National Institution Board of Management*, 1961 S.L.T. 217, in which the court seems to have become unnecessarily concerned with compulsory examination and the individual's right to privacy of medical records.

[51] Of course the training must be such as would have prevented the accident or minimised the risk (*McCormick v. City of Aberdeen Council*, 1993 G.W.D. 1–54).

[52] This has been held to include an information system to advise the driver of a fire engine on the likely state of roads (*Spinks v. Strathclyde Regional Council* (1992, unreported)).

[53] Thus the employers were liable for not instructing an employee to switch off a winch before attempting to free a snagged rope (*Wood v. Redpath*, 1993 G.W.D. 3–193).

who fell when the handle on a sash gave way in his hand where the evidence demonstrated the employer had given clear instructions not to clean any window that looked difficult or dangerous and the employee could clearly see that the window was rotting,[54] and it has been held that a foundry labourer who was transferred to grinding work must have known of Raynaud's phenomenon (vibration white finger) so that his employer was not required to warn him of its dangers which were not regarded as serious as it did not cause occupational disability and had not been made a prescribed industrial disease.[55] Where dangers are latent however, clear, regular and more detailed information and advice will be required. Thus the employers were liable where hospital cleaners who contracted dermatitis were given no regular instructions or advice about the effectiveness of wearing rubber gloves which were available for their use[56]; the employers "had a duty to inform their servants . . . that they were exposed to a risk of irritant contact dermatitis and that the risk could be countered by wearing rubber gloves."[57] Similarly where employees engaged on general tasks in the printing industry developed upper limb disorders such as tenosynovitis, tennis-elbow and trigger-thumb, their employers were liable because they failed to give adequate warnings (including an explanation of the reason for, and the importance of reporting any wrist or arm pain immediately) before the work was begun.[58] Thus although it will be sufficient for the employer to warn of the risk of a general type of injury (for example hand

---

[54] *Wilson v. Tyneside Window Cleaning Ltd* [1958] 2 All E.R. 265; and see *Vinnyey v. Star Paper Mills Ltd* [1965] 1 All E.R. 175. In *Woolger v. West Surrey and North East Hampshire Health Authority, The Times,* Nov. 8, 1993 it was held that the method which a trained nurse would use to lift a patient was a matter for the nurse's individual judgment, and a warning against lifting generally may suffice for an experienced employee (*Couper v. Remploy Ltd,* 1993 G.W.D. 27–1715).

[55] *White v. Holbrook Castings Ltd* [1985] I.R.L.R. 215 (C.A.); in fact Raynaud's phenomenon was made a prescribed industrial disease (PDA11(a)–(c)) in 1985. And it has been held that it was not negligent for an employer to fail to warn an employee of the risks of developing "white finger" because a warning could cause unnecessary alarm to all the employees for the sake of the exceptional vulnerable one: *Joseph v. Ministry of Defence (The Times,* March 4, 1980); *sed quaere?*

[56] *Campbell v. Lothian Health Board,* 1987 S.L.T. 665, noted with approval in *Pape v. Cumbria County Council* [1991] I.R.L.R. 463.

[57] *Ibid., per* Lord McCluskey at p. 667.

[58] *Ping v. Esselte-Letraset* [1992] C.L.Y. 3211.

injury caused by repetitive work) without specifying a particular condition which might be contracted (tenosynovitis)[59] recent decisions indicate that Lord Radcliffe's advice in *Qualcast (Wolverhampton) Ltd v. Haynes*[60] that courts be circumspect in filling out the duty to provide adequate equipment with the much vaguer obligation of encouraging, extorting or instructing workmen to make regular use of what is provided may now be regarded as unnecessarily cautious.

3.40 In *Mughal v. Reuters Ltd*[61] Deputy High Court Judge Prosser held that repetitive strain injury (RSI) was not a condition known to medical science because it has no pathology and no clinical symptoms that can be pointed to as confirming that a patient is suffering from it; and did not represent a condition promoted by repetitive work; he therefore rejected the damages claim of the plaintiff (a newspaper sub-editor who operated a VDU); and although "reflex sympathetic dystrophy" (RSD) had clinically observable signs he did not know what the term meant.[62] However *Mughal* contrasts with *Lodge & McSherry v. British Telecom*[63] in which two data processors were awarded damages for RSI as a result of poor posture and prolonged and repetitive keyboard work; the repetitive stereotype movement of unsupported arms and hands, the strain being substantially added to by the strains which arose from the poor working systems in place and the poor posture due to poor ergonomics of the work station, unsuitable chairs and the uncorrected bad habits of the operators, and *Bettany v. Royal Doulton (U.K.) Ltd*,[64]

[59] *Wyeth v. Thames Case Ltd,* unreported case no. 86/533 (C.A.); note that the employers had frequently warned the employees of the need to rotate their individual tasks but they had refused to do so as this affected their work rate. *Cf. Kossiwski v. Chrysler U.K. Ltd,* 1974 K.I.R. 225 (C.A.).

[60] [1959] 2 All E.R. 28 (H.L.).

[61] [1993] I.R.L.R. 571.

[62] Note also that Judge Prosser observed that where employees work with computer keyboards and visual display units each operator has to find by trial and error the position which is comfortable for him/her and that there is little more the employer can do except provide British Standard equipment: this approach seems to shift the responsibility from the employer to the employee. *Cf.* the settlement (£5,500) of unfair dismissal complaint by employee dismissed after RSI rendered her incapable of normal (typing) job: *The Times,* Jan. 30, 1992.

[63] Unreported (1992).

[64] Unreported (1993).

in which, although none of the doctors could detect any physical or demonstrable symptoms and the medical evidence was divided as to the cause of the pain, it was held on the balance of probabilities that Bettany, a crockery painter, had suffered a work-related injury.[65] Interestingly in *Bettany*, while the court accepted that the injury was work-related it did not agree that the employers had been negligent because (a) they had drawn the employee's attention to (i) the risk of upper limb disorder developing and (ii) the need to report promptly any pain or other symptoms, (b) there was in place a system which ensured that Bettany would be seen first by a nurse and then by the work's doctor, (c) the system also involved her being advised to consult her own general practitioner, (d) the system resulted in her being transferred to other work where rapid and repetitive movement was not required and (e) all of these procedures had operated promptly and effectively after Bettany had reported pain. In *Mountenay (Hazard) v. Bernard Matthews plc*[66] the employer was liable for injuries (ganglion, tenosynovitis and trigger-thumb) sustained by poultry processors (including new recruits) who had not received adequate warnings about the risks of contracting upper limb disorders and had not been subject to a proper system of job rotation.

Competent staff

3.41 This facet of the employer's general duty requires reasonable care to be taken to ensure that employees are not exposed to risks by the appointment of fellow-employees, and there would appear to be no reason in principle that this would extend to selection of others, for example independent contractors, with whom an employee may be required to work. Appointment of an inexperienced under-manager and fireman,[67] a drunken wagon-driver,[68] an incompetent driver,[69] an unqualified

---

[65] The employer's defence that the only cause of pain was psychological — possibly induced by the publicity about upper limb disorders circulating in the industry — was rejected.
[66] Unreported (May 4, 1994).
[67] *Black v. Fife Coal Company*, 1912 S.C.(H.L.) 33.
[68] *Donald v. Brand* (1862) 24 D. 295.
[69] *McCarten v. McRobbie*, 1909 S.C. 1020.

fireman[70] and a negligent foreman[71] have all been held to
give rise to claims by employees injured as a result of the
incompetence of the staff.

ECONOMIC LOSS AND NERVOUS SHOCK

3.42 It is clear that if an employee is injured as a result
of his employer not introducing a safe system of work he
is entitled to damages for all his loss which flows from the
employer's delict. Thus an employee who injures his back
will be entitled to damages to cover his pain and suffering
and any reduction in his earning power and in that
respect his economic loss is recoverable. Such economic
loss has been described as "derivative"[72] in that it arises as
a consequence of physical injury to the person or property. In most cases injury sustained as a result of breach
of duty by an employer will be in the form of physical
injury to the person. However in *Reid v. Rush & Tompkins
Group plc*[73] Reid, while acting in the course of his employment in Ethiopia, was injured due to the negligence of a
third party/driver who could not be traced and contended
that his employers were liable for his economic losses in
that (a) they had failed to arrange suitable insurance in
the event of him sustaining injury as a result of the
negligence of a third party or (b) they failed to advise him
to obtain suitable insurance for himself. The first conten-
tion was rejected because it would be inappropriate for
the common law to devise such a duty which Parliament
could have, but had not, imposed[74] and the second
because the employer's duty was, in the absence of a
contractual term, limited to protecting the employee
against physical harm or disease, and such judicial con-
servatism has been endorsed by the English Court of
Appeal which refused the extension of the duty of care to

---

[70] *Ferguson v. N. B. Ry*, 1915 S.C. 566.
[71] *Flynn v. McGaw* (1891) 18 R. 554.
[72] See A. Wilkinson and A. Forte, "Economic Loss," 1985 J.R. 1.
[73] [1990] 1 W.L.R. 212 (C.A.).
[74] Ralph Gibson L.J. noted that "[t]he legislation has not in general
extended the duty of compulsory employer's liability insurance in
respect of employment out of this country [and] it has not been
suggested that the master is required to provide personal accident
insurance where in this country his servant is exposed to the risk of
suffering injury . . . through the fault of a third party who cannot pay."

require a school to advise parents of the dangers of rugby football or by taking out insurance.[75] However in a slightly different context a Scottish court has held that a receiver owed a duty of care to employees of the company not to terminate a pension scheme without first indicating his intention to do so,[76] and it may be that an obligation to advise of the need to take out special insurance or other protection would be more readily introduced through an implied contractual term although this too was rejected in *Reid*.[77]

3.43 It is well established that where a person suffers nervous shock[78] (without also suffering a physical injury) as a result of (a) witnessing an accident, (b) offering physical injury to a third party, or (c) fearing for his own safety, the person whose breach of duty has caused the accident may be liable to compensate the person who suffers the nervous shock.[79] Where an employee suffers a psychiatric illness following nervous shock he may be able to recover damages for his injury. Typically this type of injury occurs as a result of a person being placed in a position in which he fears for his own safety[80] or where he witnesses a physical injury to another. Thus a seaman, although not on board the vessel, who suffered a psychiatric illness as a result of assisting bereaved relatives and identifying colleagues after he volunteered to assist in the *Herald of Free Enterprise* tragedy recovered damages for his injuries.[81] However a person who was aboard a fire-

[75] *Van Oppen v. Clerk to the Bedford Charity Trustees* [1990] 1 W.L.R. 235 (C.A.).

[76] *Larsen's Executrix v. Henderson*, 1990 S.L.T. 498.

[77] But note the willingness of the House of Lords in *Scally v. Southern Health and Social Services Board* [1991] I.R.L.R. 522, to imply a contractual term requiring employer to advise employees of the need to apply for a benefit within a certain time.

[78] It has been said that nervous shock is a medical condition and is not to be confused with simply getting a fright: *Simpson v. I.C.I.*, 1983 S.L.T. 601; and see *Nicholls v. Rushton* (unreported) April 19, 1992 (C.A.). But probably the correct analysis is that in certain cases damages are recoverable for psychiatric illness following nervous shock: *Alcock v. Chief Constable for South Yorkshire Police* [1991] 3 W.L.R. 1057.

[79] *Bourhill v. Young*, 1943 S.L.T. 105; *Robertson v. Forth Road Bridge Joint Board (No. 2)*, 1994 S.L.T. 568.

[80] *Ross v. Glasgow Corporation*, 1919 S.C. 174; *Brown v. Glasgow Corporation*, 1922 S.C. 527; *Walker v. Pitlochry Motor Company*, 1930 S.C. 565; *Simpson v. I.C.I. Ltd*, 1983 S.L.T. 601 (I.H.).

[81] *Dundee Courier*, Oct. 3, 1991, regarding the settlement of Mr Rapley's claim.

fighting ship and witnessed the *Piper-Alpha* disaster was unsuccessful in his claim because the court was of the view that the platform operators could not reasonably have foreseen that someone in the plaintiff's position would suffer psychological injuries.[82] Although not connected with health and safety at work, *Alcock v. Chief Constable of South Yorkshire*[83] must now be regarded as the leading case. The House of Lords held that the victim of a psychiatric illness caused by the shock of witnessing injury to another had to show not only that such injury was reasonably foreseeable but that the relationship between the pursuer and the defender was sufficiently proximate and that the relationship between the victim and the person injured was based on ties of love and affection, the closeness of which would have to be proved in each case; also there had to be propinquity of the pursuer in time and space to the accident or its immediate aftermath. The effect of applying these principles was that two plaintiffs who had been at a football ground at which a section of the crowd was crushed by an inrush of spectators, admitted at the discretion of a police officer, lost their claims because although they had respectively brothers and a brother-in-law in the section of the crowd affected there was no evidence that their relationships with them were "particularly close ties of love and affection."[84] There would seem to be no reason in principle why an employee who witnessed the injury or death of a close work-colleague due to the negligence (personal or vicarious) of his employer could not recover damages for a psychiatric illness suffered as a result of hearing or seeing the accident provided the conditions set out in *Alcock* were met and the First Division has so held in rejecting a claim by two employees who witnessed a workmate being blown over the side of an open pick-up truck while crossing the Forth Road bridge.[84a] Aside from

---

[82] *McFarlane v. E. E. Caledonia Ltd, The Times,* Sept. 30, 1993; *The Scotsman,* Aug. 30, 1993 (C.A.).

[83] [1991] 3 W.L.R. 1057 (H.L.).

[84] *ibid. per* Lord Keith of Kinkel at p. 1101. On the other hand, in the case of a filial relationship or the relationship between fiancés "the closest ties of love and affection fall to be presumed" (*ibid.*).

[84a] *Robertson and Rough v. Forth Road Bridge Joint Board, The Scotsman,* March 8, 1995 (I.H.).

the nervous shock cases, where the employee's injuries are entirely psychological there is no reason in principle why he cannot recover damages from an employer whose breach of duty resulted in the employee developing a psychiatric disorder or a depressive illness.[85] Although in *Petch v. Commissioners of Customs and Excise*[86] the case failed on the facts, it would seem to establish that (a) an employer's duty extends to taking reasonable care for the mental and psychological health of his employee, (b) the employer will be in breach of that duty if through his senior managers he was aware or ought to have been aware that an employee's workload carried the real risk that he would have a breakdown but took no steps to prevent it occurring, and (c) where an employee has already suffered a psychological illness then on his return to work the employer may be in breach of his duty of care if he fails to take appropriate steps to ensure that the workload is adjusted or to arrange a transfer to less demanding work where possible. Indeed an employer has been held to be in breach of his duty of care where an employee suffered a mental breakdown as a result of the stress and anxiety occasioned by his job.[87] Clearly the likelihood or foreseeability of the type of injury is likely to reflect changes in the knowledge of (a) which types of individual and (b) which types of employment are more susceptible to psychological or stress-related disorders. According to the report by the Health and Safety Executive, *"Stress Research and Stress Management: putting theory to work"*[88] both physical and psychosocial factors can have an effect on the incidence of occupational stress and when the knowledge that the presence of hazards and the lack of control over work content and speed of work have been found to induce stress while certain pathologies are associated with stress (heart disease, bronchitis, obesity and peptic ulcers) is placed in the context of risk assessment and health surveillance as required by the Management of Health and Safety at Work Regulations 1992 the test of foreseeability may be more easily overcome.

---

[85] *Johnstone v. Bloomsbury Health Authority* [1991] I.C.R. 269; *Petch v. Commissioners of Customs and Excise* [1993] I.C.R. 789 (C.A.).
[86] [1993] I.C.R. 789 (C.A.).
[87] *Walker v. Northumberland C.C.* [1995] I.R.L.R. 35.
[88] I.S.B.N. 07176 0084 8.

VICARIOUS RESPONSIBILITY

3.44 Vicarious responsibility is of importance to third parties injured as a result of the negligence of employees and to employees themselves whose employer has instituted and operates a safe system of work but which, because of the negligence of another employee, is not followed. Although the employer is not personally liable for any injury in that he has fulfilled his duty by instituting and operating a safe system of work he will be vicariously liable for the injuries caused to an employee by virtue of the casual negligence of a fellow-employee. This form of liability is based on the legal policy[89] enshrined in the maxims *qui facit per alium facit per se* (he who does something by another does it himself) and *respondeat superior* (let the master (or employer) be responsible) and may be seen as cutting across the general proposition that *culpa tenet suos auctores* (blame attaches to its originators). However, the last-mentioned maxim is observed in that although the employer may be vicariously liable for his employee's failure to take reasonable care the employee himself is not released from liability[90] and, at least in the context of the employment contract, may be required to indemnify the employer for any loss the latter sustains as a result of his (the employee's) lack of care.[91]

3.45 The effect of the maxim *respondeat superior* is that an employer is vicariously liable for the injuries sustained by one of his employees through the negligence of another provided the negligent employee was at the relevant time acting in the course of or in the scope of his employment.[92] Whether an employee is acting in the course of his employment is probably a mixed question of fact and law,

[89] For a detailed discussion of the legal policy, see, Atiyah, *Vicarious Liability* (1967), and Williams, "Vicarious Liability and the Master's Indemnity" (1957) 20 M.L.R. 220.
[90] Of course in most cases the action will be against the employer, who in the case of injury to an employee is required to maintain a policy of insurance; see below, para. 7.26.
[91] This is based on the employee's implied obligation to carry out his contractual duties with reasonable care; see Lord Fraser, *Master and Servant* (3rd ed.), pp. 68, 69 and Craig, V. and Miller, K. *Employment Law in Scotland*, para. 3.37.
[92] It has been stated that there is no difference between "scope" and "course" of employment: *McCready v. Securicor Ltd*, I.R.L.I.B. 460, 12 N.I.C.A.

although there are some useful general propositions. In *Kirby v. N.C.B.*[93] Lord President Clyde indicated that there were four situations:

1. where the employer authorises the particular act;
2. where the employee performs an authorised act in an unauthorised way;
3. where the employee exceeds his authority by doing work he is not employed to do; and
4. where the employee uses his employer's time or tools for his own purposes.

In the first two situations the employee will be acting within the scope of his employment, while in the last two situations he will not. Accordingly, when Kirby and several other miners sustained injuries caused by one of them lighting a cigarette during a break, their employer was not vicariously liable as the offending employee was acting in breach of statutory provisions which prohibited possessing matches or cigarettes underground; he was in effect pursuing a purpose of his own. However a deviation from an authorised method or route will not take the employee outside the scope of his employment. Accordingly where a driver deviated from the authorised route he was acting in the course of his employment because he was still carrying out the predominant purpose of the authorised journey, namely, the transport of passengers.[94] Similarly a milkman was acting in the course of his employment when, by driving negligently, he injured a 13-year-old boy whom he had, contrary to his employer's instructions, engaged to assist him in making deliveries because he was merely performing his work in an unauthorised or prohibited way.[95] On the other hand, where the employee does something he is not employed to do (as distinct from merely adopting an unauthorised method), as where a bus conductor drove a bus[96] or a

---

[93] 1958 S.C. 514.
[94] *Williams v. A. W. Hemphill Ltd*, 1966 S.C. (H.L.) 31. *Cf. Century Insurance Co. v Northern Ireland R.T.B.* [1949] A.C. 509 (tanker-driver lighting match when awaiting transfer of petrol from tanker).
[95] *Rose v. Plenty and Co-operative Retail Services* [1976] I.R.L.R. 60 (C.A.). *Cf. Portsea Island Mutual Co-operative Society v. Leyland* [1978] I.R.L.R. 556 (criminal vicarious liability).
[96] *Iqbal v. London Passenger Transport Executive, The Times,* June 6, 1973.

miner did the work of a shot-firer,[97] he will not be acting in the course of his employment.[98]

3.46 Travelling to and from a place of work can present problems, although the modern trend is to view travel and refreshment breaks as in the course of employment.[99] Indeed in *Nancollas v. Insurance Officer*[1] the Court of Appeal has recognised that early cases which concentrate on whether an employee was carrying out his employer's instruction have been overtaken by developments in society and the relationship of employment which is no longer based on orders but on contractual rights and mutual co-operation. Thus where an employee (who had to cover a wide area of the country) travelled from his usual office in Worthing to the Guildford office where it was decided that he should travel the next day to Aldershot, it was held he was acting in the course of his employment that (next) day when he left his home and went directly to Aldershot[2] and in *Smith v. Stages and Darlington Insulation Co. Ltd*[3] Lord Lowry set out the following propositions:

1. Except where the employee is obliged to use transport provided by his employer, an employee travelling to his regular place of work from his ordinary residence is not acting in the course of his employment.
2. Travelling in the employer's time between workplaces or in the course of a peripatetic occupation is in the course of employment.
3. Receipt of wages but not travelling allowance indicates the employee is travelling in the employer's time even where he has discretion as to the mode and time of travel.

[97] *Alford v. N.C.B.*, 1951 S.C. 248.

[98] An employee's authority may be extended by implication: see *Neville v. C. & A. Modes*, 1945 S.C. 175, in which a shop assistant's authority was held to extend to protection of the employer's property so that a defamatory allegation that a customer had stolen a dress was in the course of the assistant's employment. *Cf. Heasmans v. Clarity Cleaning Co. Ltd, The Times,* Jan. 23, 1987 (C.A.) (employee authorised to clean and disinfect telephones, not authorised to use them).

[99] *Harvey v. R. G. O'Dell Ltd* [1958] 1 All E.R. 657. *Cf. Crook v. Derbyshire Stone Ltd* [1956] 1 W.L.R. 432.

[1] [1985] 1 All E.R. 833 (C.A.).

[2] And see *Ball v. Insurance Officer,* unreported, case 85/88 (C.A.).

[3] [1988] I.R.L.R. 177 (H.L.).

Health and Safety

4. Travelling in the employer's time from his ordinary residence to a workplace other than his regular workplace, or in the course of a peripatetic occupation or to the scene of an emergency is in the course of employment.[4]

5. A deviation from or interruption of a journey undertaken in the course of employment (unless merely incidental thereto) will for the time being (including overnight interruption) take the employee out of the course of his employment.

6. Return journeys are to be treated on the same footing as outward journeys.[5]

Thus where an employee (Stages) who nornally worked at Drakelow Power Station was, with a colleague, instructed to work for a week at Pembroke Power Station, he was acting in the course of his employment when driving home, in his own car, immediately after a long spell (from 8.30 a.m. Sunday to 8.30 a.m. on Monday) of work, so that when his colleague was injured when (his) Stages' fatigue caused an accident the employer was liable. Since the employer could have prohibited the employee from travelling immediately after the spell of work and had not done so the homeward journey was an authorised journey in the course of Stages' employment.[6]

3.47 Difficulty may also arise where the employee is engaged on a "frolic of his own" — a phrase which may describe an act of personal vengeance or a prank or workplace horseplay. Thus a bus conductress whose private act of malice or spite caused her to signal the driver to move off when a passenger was in the process of alighting would not be acting in the course of her employment,[7] and the correct test is whether at the relevant time the employee was doing something he was authorised to do although doing it in an unauthorised way, and not

---

[4] This would probably embrace any employee who is called out to perform a task unexpectedly and outside normal hours.
[5] However, averments must be sufficiently precise at least to infer a situation of vicarious liability: *McGowan v. Mein*, 1975 S.L.T. (Sh.Ct.) 10.
[6] And see *Thomson v. British Steel Corporation*, 1977 S.L.T. 26.
[7] *Power v. Central SMT*, 1949 S.C. 367. And see *Keppel Bus Co. Ltd v. Sa'ad Bin Ahman* [1974] 1 W.L.R. 1082 (conductor assaulting passenger who had intervened on behalf of another passenger).

whether the reasonable man would say the act was part and parcel of the employee's employment in the sense of being incidental to it.[8] Thus an apprentice who inserted a high-pressure hose into the rectum of an apprentice, causing internal injuries, was not acting in the course of his employment[9]; nor was an employee who, as a prank, attempted to shut a colleague into a walk-in safe even although the employee was authorised to open and close the safe at night or in an emergency because he was not acting for the employer but for his own purpose entirely,[10] and an employee who is taking industrial action is likely to be regarded as doing something insufficiently related to the authorised acts to be in the course of his employment.[11]

3.48 Generally where a person engages an independent contractor through the medium of a contract *locatio operis* that person is not liable for the negligence of the independent contractor[12] although it has been argued that the increase in the number of atypical workers requires a reassessment of that proposition,[13] and recent cases may suggest that the Scottish courts are aware of the results of applying too rigid a policy where atypical workers are involved.[14] However it has to be emphasised that this general proposition assumes that the contractor is truly independent and not subject to control by the person who instructs him. Thus where a contractor/electrician who was called in by an employer to rectify an electrical fault negligently caused injury to an employee it was held the

[8] In *Aldred v. Naconco* [1987] I.R.L.R. 292 (C.A.) (employee injured in washroom while another employee was trying to startle her), disapproving *Harrison v. Michelin Tyre Co. Ltd* (1985) 1 All E.R. 919.
[9] *Smith v. Crossley Brothers* (1951) 95 S.J. 655.
[10] *McCready v. Securicor Ltd,* 1992 I.R.L.I.B. 460, p. 12 (NICA). *Cf. Bell v. Blackwood Morton & Sons Ltd,* 1960 S.L.T. 145; *Peden v. Strathclyde Regional Council,* 1995 G.W.D. 4–202 (O.H.).
[11] *General Engineering Services Ltd v. Kingston and St Andrew Corporation* [1989] I.C.R. 88 (PC) (firemen on a "go-slow").
[12] *Stephen v. Thurso Police Commissioners* (1876) 3 R. 535 *per* Lord Justice-Clerk Inglis at p. 540. And see *MacLean v. Russell* (1850) 12 D. 887; *Esso Petroleum Company Ltd v. Hall Russell & Co. Ltd,* The Times, Oct. 7, 1988 (H.L.).
[13] See E. McKendrick, "Vicarious Liability and Independent Contractors — a Re-examination" (1990) 53 M.L.R. 770.
[14] See *Rennie v. Dorans,* 1991 S.L.T. 443; *Marshall v. William Sharp & Sons Ltd,* 1991 S.L.T. 114; *United Wholesale Grocers v. Sher,* 1993 S.L.T. 284 (O.H.).

employer who had called him in was vicariously liable for
the injuries to the employee and this was so even
although the electrician was a person with special exper-
tise because he was under the supervision and control of
the employer.[15] In such a case the principal though not
exclusive issue is "personal control or power over the
acting or mode of acting of the subordinate" in the sense
of "control or direction of the person in opposition to the
mere right to object to the quality of the work done."[16]
Additionally the instructor of an independent contractor
may be personally liable for the actings of the contractor
where the instructor has himself been negligent by, for
example, careless selection of an incompetent contractor,[17]
instructing the contractor to carry out dangerous work[18] or
where work is to be done on a public road.[19] Finally an
employer cannot escape liability by delegating the performance of a personal duty to others including a truly
independent contractor and this is of particular importance because such duties would include absolute duties
imposed to protect employees,[20] duties laid on employers
and contractors carrying out certain types of work.[21]

Volenti non fit injuria

3.49 *Volenti non fit injuria*, literally to one who is willing
no legal wrong is done, may operate as a complete
defence against an action based on a failure to take
reasonable care. Thus in *Morris v. Murray*[22] the plaintiff,
having spent the afternoon drinking with a friend, went
for a flight in the friend's light aircraft. The aircraft, which
was piloted by the plaintiff's friend, crashed injuring the
plaintiff who sued his friend's representatives who
pleaded *volenti*. The defence was sustained because the
plaintiff had willingly boarded the plane knowing that the

[15] *Marshall v. William Sharp & Sons Ltd*, 1991 S.L.T. 114 (I.H.).
[16] *Stephen v. Thurso Police Commissioners* (1876) 3 R. 535 at p. 542, *per* Lord
Gifford and adopted by Lord Justice-Clerk Ross in *Marshall v. William
Sharp & Sons Ltd*, 1991 S.L.T. 114.
[17] See, for example, *Pinn v. Rew* (1916) 32 T.L.R. 451.
[18] See, for example, *Boyle v. Glasgow Corporation*, 1949 S.C. 254 and
Honeywill and Stein Ltd v. Larkin Brothers [1934] 1 K.B. 191.
[19] See *Stephen v. Thurso Police Commissioners*, above; *Tarry v. Ashton* (1876)
1 Q.B. 314; *Holliday v. National Telephone Company* [1899] 2 Q.B. 392.
[20] Factories Act 1961, ss. 12, 13, 14.
[21] See, for example, *Donaghey v. O'Brien* [1966] 1 W.L.R. 1170. And see
Riverstone Meat Co. Pty. Ltd v. Lancashire Shipping Co. Ltd [1961] A.C. 807.
[22] [1991] 2 W.L.R. 195 (C.A.).

pilot was so drunk that he could not perform his duty to take reasonable care for the plaintiff's safety, while he, although drunk, was not incapable of appreciating the nature and extent of the risk involved. It may also be successfully pleaded in sporting situations, although it is unlikely that a spectator will be held to have accepted the risk of injury.[23] However the scope for the defence to operate in the field of employment is limited in several ways.[24] First, there must be evidence[25] to the effect that the pursuer freely and voluntarily undertook the risk of the particular harm that in fact he suffered[26]: the very fact of an employment relationship may itself indicate that the employee did not freely accept that risk.[27] Secondly, as the employee must be *volens* (willing) and not merely *sciens* (knowing) it is not enough that the employee continued in the employment with full knowledge and understanding of the dangers involved.[28] Thirdly the maxim only operates as a complete defence where the employer's liability is vicarious and not personal.[29] And too ready an

[23] *Murray v. Haringey Arena* [1951] 2 K.B. 146; *Wooldridge v. Sumner* [1962] 2 All E.R. 978. And see *Stair Memorial Encyclopaedia*, Vol. 19 (Recreation and Sports), para. 1242.

[24] In *Bowater v. Rowley Regis Corporation* [1944] 1 All E.R. 465 (C.A.) Goddard L.J.urged that in the case of employer and employee *volenti* must be applied with extreme caution and "it can hardly ever be applicable where the act to which the servant is said to be 'volens' arises out of his ordinary duty unless the work is one in which danger is necessarily involved . . ." and Scott L.J. opined that a man cannot "be truly willing unless he is in a position to choose freely and freedom of choice predicates not only full knowledge of the circumstances . . . so that he may be able to choose wisely"; there must be absent "from his mind any feeling of constraint so that nothing shall interfere with the freedom of his will."

[25] Whether the pursuer had freely and voluntarily accepted the risk is a question of fact: *Smith v. Baker*, 1891 A.C. 326 (H.L.).

[26] Alternatively it may expressed as agreement by the pursuer; the defender would be discharged from his duty to take reasonable care for his (the pursuer's) safety or a waiver of that duty. For an interesting analysis of the maxim see A. J. E. Jaffey, "Volenti non fit injuria" [1985] C.L.J. 87.

[27] See *Cvetkovic v. Princes Holdings* (1989) 51 S.A.S.R. 365 in which an amusement arcade doorman who was injured while attempting to eject undesirable customers could not be met with the plea of *volenti* when acting on his superior's instructions where the employer had failed to take reasonable care for his safety by refusing to call the police as he (the doorman) had suggested.

[28] *Smith v. Baker* [1981] A.C. 325 (H.L.); *I.C.I. v. Shatwell* [1965] A.C. 656 (H.L.).

[29] *Wheeler v. New Merton Board Mills* [1933] 2 K.B. 669; *I.C.I. v. Shatwell*, above; *Hugh v. National Coal Board*, 1972 S.C. 252.

application of *volenti* could result in the re-introduction of the doctrine of common employment which Parliament has deliberately abolished.[30]

3.50 A realistic appreciation of the employee's position is seen in *Smith v. Baker*[31] in which the House of Lords approved the Scottish decision of *Sword v. Cameron*.[32] Smith had, for a period of several months, been employed to drill holes in a rock face near a crane operated by fellow employees. The crane swung stones over Smith's head without warning and he admitted that he knew of the danger. He sued his employers when he was injured by a stone falling from the crane; their plea of *volenti* was rejected because although he undertook and continued in the employment with full knowledge and understanding of the danger arising from the systematic neglect to give warning, that did not justify the finding that he voluntarily undertook the risk of injury. However, although in more recent cases[33] the plea has been upheld it has to be noted that these are not cases in which the employer has been at fault. Thus in *Shatwell*[34] one of two men in a team of shot-firers was injured when the men combined to disobey their employer's order deliberately and act in contravention of a statutory prohibition even although they knew the risk involved; the plea of *volenti* was sustainable both in respect of an action by the injured man against the other and against the employer on the grounds of vicarious liability.

Consideration has also to be given to express contractual terms which may seek to limit or exclude liability — as in cases where the employee agrees to undertake the work in exchange for an additional premium. Can they operate as substitutes for *volenti*? As the basis for *volenti* is agreement, it follows that an express term in an employment contract which excludes liability is capable of having the same effect. However, while it has to be noted that the Unfair Contract Terms Act 1977 applies to contracts of employment and apprenticeship,[35] a contractual term (or a

---

[30] See above, para. 3.3.
[31] 1891 A.C. 326 (H.L.).
[32] (1839) 1 D. 493.
[33] *I.C.I. v. Shatwell,* above; *Hugh v. National Coal Board,* above.
[34] *Ibid.*
[35] Unfair Contract Terms Act 1977, s. 15(2)(b).

non-contractual notice) which purports to exclude or restrict liability for breach of duty arising in the course of any business in respect of death or personal injury shall be void.[36]

---

[36] *Ibid.*, s. 16 as amended by the Law Reform (Miscellaneous Provisions) (Scotland) Act 1990, s. 68.

CHAPTER 4

THE STATUTORY REGIME

INTRODUCTION

4.1 This chapter concerns the importance of legislation as a mechanism for setting standards and enforcing health and safety law. It will discuss the older health and safety statutes such as the Mines and Quarries Act 1954, the Offices, Shops and Railway Premises Act 1963 and particularly the Factories Act 1961 which were enacted before the Health and Safety at Work Act 1974. One of the purposes of the 1974 Act was to ensure the repeal of these earlier statutes and their replacement by regulations and voluntary codes of practice. By 1992 many of the older provisions had been repealed and replaced and responsibility for enforcement of the legislation had passed to the Health and Safety Executive. The process of repeal has been hastened by regulations[1] made under section 15 of the Health and Safety at Work Act 1974 which are intended to comply with European Directives on this subject. These regulations repeal many of the remaining important provisions of the earlier legislation and they took effect on January 1, 1993. However, in some cases the repeal is not immediately effective so that it will be necessary to consider both the old law and the "European" regulations.[2] Apart

[1] See the Management of Health and Safety at Work Regulations 1992 (S.I. 1992 No. 2051 as amended by S.I. 1994 No. 2865); the Workplace (Health, Safety and Welfare) Regulations 1992 (S.I. 1992 No. 3004); the Provision and Use of Work Equipment Regulations 1992 (S.I. 1992 No. 2932); the Personal Protective Equipment at Work Regulations 1992 (S.I. 1992 No. 2966); the Manual Handling Operations Regulations 1992 (S.I. 1992 No. 2793) and the Health and Safety (Display Screen Equipment) Regulations 1992 (S.I. 1992 No. 2792).
[2] See, for example, the Workplace Regulations which make it clear that the regulations will not apply to existing workplaces until Jan. 1, 1996 (although they do apply immediately to any new workplaces which came into existence after Dec. 31, 1992). Equally, the fencing provisions of the Work Equipment Regulations do not apply to existing machinery until Jan. 1, 1997.

from the Management of Health and Safety at Work Regulations 1992[3] the other five regulations which came into force on January 1, 1993 do give rise to civil liability. Generally, the "European" regulations apply to a much wider category of premises than simply factories or shops.

ROLE OF THE LAW

4.2 In Chapter 3 we saw how the common law regulated health and safety through the implied duties owed by employers to employees under the contract of employment and by the application of the general principles of negligence to compensate victims of accidents at work. The most significant role for the common law is to impose a civil liability on employers to take reasonable care for their employees' health and safety. It is rare for the common law to impinge upon employers in another sense through the application of common law crimes. To be sure there have been occasions when both employees[4] and employers[5] have been prosecuted or threatened with prosecution for culpable homicide for accidents which cause death. However, in the modern era it would be necessary to show that the

---

[3] S.I. 1992 No. 2051. Reg. 15 declares specifically that a breach of duty imposed by the Management Regulations does not confer a right of action in any civil proceedings (except as regards the risk assessment obligations owed to new or expectant mothers).

[4] See, for example, *William Paton and Richard McNab* (1845) 2 Broun 525. In March 1990, a plumber, Ross Fontana, was convicted of culpable homicide for causing the deaths of two people through the improper installation of a gas fire. See *Glasgow Herald,* March 30, 1990.

[5] See, for example, *William Baillie and James McCurrach* (1870) 1 Couper 442. In the modern era the critical issue has been whether it is possible for corporate employers to be prosecuted for culpable homicide. The prosecution of P. & O. European Ferries for manslaughter following the disaster aboard the *Herald of Free Enterprise* in 1987 failed largely because the trial judge was not satisfied that the company's directors and senior managers ought to have known that there was an obvious and serious risk when the ship sailed with its bow doors open. See David Bergman, "Recklessness in the Boardroom" (1990) 140 N.L.J. 1496. The failure of this prosecution undoubtedly influenced the decision of the Lord Advocate not to prosecute Occidental Petroleum for corporate culpable homicide after the *Piper Alpha* disaster. The difficulties of prosecuting companies for crimes are discussed by Jenifer Ross in "Corporate Liability for Crime," 1990 S.L.T. (News) 265.

accused was guilty of gross or wicked negligence.[6] Generally, however, the fact that other crimes which involve
injury to a victim are crimes of intention minimises their
scope in the context of accidents at work.

4.3 None the less, when we turn to examine the statutory
law on health and safety it is clear that both the civil law
and the criminal law have a role to play. This is because
breach of many of the important statutes can give rise to
both a civil damages action and a criminal penalty.[7] As far
as the civil law is concerned statute law not only creates
another basis for legal action by an employee but also
enables a more flexible approach as regards the standard of
care to which employers must adhere. As we have seen,
the common law operates in a way which generally obliges
employers to take reasonable care.[8] In the civil area, the
provisions of a statute can be drafted in such a way that the
duty owed by employers does not have to be based upon
the common law standard of negligence. Statute can adopt
a more positive role by laying down obligations which
employers must fulfil irrespective of the practical difficulties. In such circumstances the liability owed by
employers can be strict with minimal scope for defences.[9]
Moreover, statute can also deal specifically with particularly
dangerous operations or processes of manufacture. It has
been one of the features of British health and safety laws in
the past that there has been much delegated legislation

[6] The development of the law in this area is discussed by G. H. Gordon,
The Criminal Law of Scotland (2nd ed., 1978) at paras. 26–01 to 26–16. He
points out that prosecutions for culpable homicide of this type are now
largely confined to road traffic cases and argues that prosecutions for
accidents at work have dried up because of "the complex nature of
modern factories and mines which makes it very difficult to single out
the negligent party" (para. 26–09). Instead, prosecutions under the
Health and Safety at Work Act 1974 are much more likely. See, for
example, the successful prosecutions of Arco British Ltd and Odeco Ltd
for breaches arising out of the death of a wireless operator aboard the
drilling rig *Ocean Odyssey* in the North Sea: *The Scotsman*, August 11,
1993.
[7] There can be no civil liability for breach of the general duties created
by ss. 2–8 of the Health and Safety at Work Act: see 1974 Act, s. 47(1).
However, s. 47(2) declares that any regulations made under s. 15 of the
1974 Act do give rise to civil liability for breach of statutory duty unless
the regulations provide otherwise.
[8] Although, as we saw in Chap. 3, the extent of this duty will vary
depending upon the circumstances and the proclivities of the employee.
See, for example, *Porteous v. N.C.B.*, 1967 S.L.T. 117.
[9] See, for example *Millar v. Galashiels Gas Co.*, 1949 S.C.(H.L.) 31.

where laws have been made which are directed at specific industries or types of activity. Indeed, until the Health and Safety at Work Act 1974 the major health and safety statutes[10] were themselves aimed at premises where particular forms of work were being carried out.

4.4 It is also true that in the criminal area statutory provisions can move away from the application of *mens rea* principles towards other standards of criminality which reduce the importance of the mental element or avoid it entirely. This enables statutory criminal law to exercise a regulatory role and to fashion offences consistent with the risks. Thus one of the principal reasons for enacting statutory provisions on health and safety has been to create offences which need not necessarily be based on the requirement of intention or *mens rea*. Indeed, the earliest statutes were largely enforced by means of penalties in the criminal courts.[11] In modern times, the Health and Safety at Work Act 1974, s. 47 excludes civil liability for breach of any of the duties specified in ss. 2–7 or any contravention of s. 8. Thus as far as the general duties created by the 1974 Act are concerned the only appropriate means of enforcement through the courts is by criminal prosecution. As regards the earlier health and safety statutes (Mines and Quarries Act 1954, Factories Act 1961 and Offices, Shops and Railway Premises Act 1963) they are capable of enforcement both through criminal prosecution and by civil damages actions. Moreover, as has already been noted, as far as the "European" regulations are concerned, with the exception of the Management of Health and Safety at Work Regulations 1992,[12] the other five sets of regulations which took effect on January 1, 1993 also permit the possibility of dual enforcement.

Statutory criminal law

4.5 It is important, therefore, to consider the nature, role and significance of statutory offences under health and safety legislation before considering those statutory provisions which permit civil actions for breach of statutory

---

[10] Mines and Quarries Act 1954, Factories Act 1961 and Offices, Shops and Railway Premises Act 1963.

[11] J. Munkman, *Employer's Liability* (11th ed., 1990) at p. 17.

[12] S.I. 1992 No. 2051.

duty. This discussion will omit consideration of the role of the criminal law under the Health and Safety at Work Act 1974 since the general duties created by this Act can only be enforced by criminal penalty and, therefore, deserve separate treatment.[13] For present purposes we shall consider those statutes where civil action is also competent and examine the interaction between the civil and criminal law under such provisions.

4.6 The Factories Act 1961, s. 155(1) declares that in the event of the contravention[14] of the provisions of the Act or of any regulation or order made under it the occupier shall be guilty of an offence. The word "occupier" is not defined in the Act and it will be a question of fact to identify the person upon whom the statutory duties are placed. In practice, this will usually be the employer: though it need not always be. The critical question will be to discover who occupies and runs the factory and regulates and controls the work that is done there. Similar provisions are to be found in other health and safety statutes.[15] Thus first and foremost it could be argued that statutes like the Factories Act are primarily penal statutes. This has implications for the way that the provisions of such statutes are interpreted.[16] However, it is also important to establish the ingredients of the offence. One important issue will be to decide whether or not the offence requires *mens rea*. If *mens rea* is not required then there would be no need to establish a mental element for the commission of the offence: it would be enough for conviction that the accused committed the unlawful act regardless of his knowledge or intention.

4.7 In law there is a presumption in favour of the application of *mens rea* in criminal statutes: though this presumption can be rebutted. As Sheriff Gordon points out, this is a matter which is likely to depend upon the terms of the statutory provision. However, there are criteria which the courts have developed for deciding whether or not *mens rea* is required for the commission of a statutory offence. The most important is the wording of the statutory provision

[13] See Chap. 5.
[14] Contravention includes a failure to comply with that provision: Factories Act 1961, s. 176(1).
[15] Mines and Quarries Act 1954, s. 157(1); Offices, Shops and Railway Premises Act 1963, s. 63(1).
[16] See para. 4.21.

creating the offence, the gravity of the offence, the nature of the penalty and the object of the statute.[17] Looking to this final element, the fact that health and safety statutes involve "the regulation for the public welfare of a particular activity"[18] means that offences under them generally do not require *mens rea* unless the particular provision requires it. Thus criminal responsibility is strict, although all the statutes provide for certain defences. This means that under the Factories Act 1961, for example, the occupier is guilty of an offence once it has been proved that there has been a contravention of the provisions of the Act or any regulations made under it. There is no need to prove that the occupier actually intended to contravene the Act or that he even knew that he was breaching it. Despite the strict nature of the statutory offences, it has been held that an occupier can escape conviction for a contravention of the Act where responsibility for the performance of it is imposed solely on an employee.[19]

4.8 It is important, however, to discuss the defences which are available to a person charged with a contravention of a health and safety statute. An occupier has a defence under the Factories Act where the contravention of a regulation or order made under the Act was committed by another person who had a duty expressly imposed upon him by that regulation or order so that the occupier is not guilty of an offence by reason only of a contravention of a provision which imposed the particular duty. However, such a defence will be ineffective where it can be proved that the occupier failed to take all reasonable steps to prevent the contravention.[20] The onus lies with the prosecutor to show that the occupier failed to take all reasonable steps.[21] Equally, the defence will not apply where the contravention by the other person also involves another distinct breach of duty by the occupier under some different statutory provision.[22]

4.9 The Offices, Shops and Railway Premises Act 1963 provides a wider defence to occupiers who are being

---

[17] See generally, G. H. Gordon, *The Criminal Law of Scotland* (2nd ed., 1978) Chap. 8.
[18] *Lim Chin Aik v. The Queen* [1963] A.C. 160 at p. 174.
[19] *Wright v. Ford Motor Co. Ltd* [1967] 1 Q.B. 230.
[20] Factories Act 1961, s. 155(2).
[21] *Carr v. Decca Gramophone Co.* [1947] K.B. 728.
[22] *Wagon Repairers Ltd v. Vosper* (1967) 3 K.I.R. 605; *Davies v. Camerons Industrial Services Ltd* [1980] 2 All E.R. 680.

prosecuted for contraventions. Under section 67 it is defence for persons charged with a contravention to prove that they used all due diligence to secure compliance with the provision. The burden on the occupier in such a case is lower than that required of the prosecution for conviction since the occupier need only satisfy the court as to the probability of what is required.[23] Such a defence is not applicable in civil proceedings.

Breach of statutory duty

4.10 As we have seen, it is arguable that the primary means of enforcing the Factories Act, etc., is by criminal prosecution. The question which is now to be discussed is whether the Acts also give a right of civil action to those who are injured or killed in accidents caused by a contravention of the statutory provisions. The Factories Act is silent on this matter. However, nowadays, a civil action for breach of statutory duty is well-established. The basic requirement for such an action is that where a statute places obligations on an individual in such a way that a particular category of persons is intended to benefit from such a duty, a person who falls within this category and who is injured as a result of a contravention has a right to sue. As Lord Kinnear put it in the context of coal mines legislation in *Black v. Fife Coal Co. Ltd*[24]:

> "There is no reasonable ground for maintaining that a proceeding by way of penalty is the only remedy allowed by the statute. . . . We are to consider the scope and purpose of the statute and in particular for whose benefit it is intended. Now the object of the present statute is plain. It was intended to compel mineowners to make due provision for the safety of the men working in their mines, and the persons for whom all those rules are to be enforced are the

---

[23] *R. v. Dunbar* [1958] 1 Q.B. 1. There used to be a similar sort of defence under s. 161(3) of the Factories Act 1961 where the occupier could satisfy the court that he had used all due diligence to enforce the Act and that the offence was due to some other person who committed it without his consent, connivance or wilful default. This provision was repealed for offences committed after Jan. 1, 1977 by the Factories Act 1961 etc. (Repeals) Regulations 1976 (S.I. 1976 No. 2004).
[24] 1912 S.C.(H.L.) 33.

persons exposed to danger. But when a duty of this kind is imposed for particular persons, there arises at common law a correlative right in those persons who may be injured by its contravention."

4.11 Before an action based on breach of statutory duty will be competent, the following basic elements[25] must be established:

  (1) that the statutory provision, properly construed, imposes upon the defender a duty which is intended to protect a class of persons of which the pursuer was one;
  (2) that the defender has failed to perform this duty;
  (3) that this breach of duty has caused injury to the pursuer of a kind contemplated by the statute.

It is intended to say a few words about each of these elements in the context of health and safety legislation.

4.12 As regards the first element, it is clear that the relevant statutory provision must be examined to ensure that it places a direct obligation on the defender. As we shall see, there may be circumstances where the language of the statute is not sufficiently mandatory to be capable of creating an enforceable duty.[26] If the statute does create a duty it is necessary for that duty to be placed on the defender. In *Gallagher v. Wimpey & Co. Ltd*,[27] for example, the court had to decide whether an obligation to fence machinery which the statute had placed on persons who work or use it gave the pursuer a cause of action against his employer. Finally, under the first element it must be shown that the pursuer is one of the class of persons who is intended to benefit from the provision. In *Hartley v. Mayoh & Co.*,[28] for example, it was held that the widow of a fireman who was electrocuted when fighting a fire in a factory could not sue for breach of statutory duty because the relevant statutory provision was only for the benefit of

[25] For a more detailed and exhaustive analysis see D. M. Walker, *The Law of Delict in Scotland* (2nd ed., 1981), Chap. 9.
[26] See the speech of Lord Kinnear in *Black v. Fife Coal Co. Ltd*, above, and *Harrison v. N.C.B.* [1951] A.C. 639.
[27] 1951 S.C. 515.
[28] [1954] 1 Q.B. 383.

persons employed. In the context of health and safety legislation it has generally been assumed that the class of persons who are intended to benefit are employees. However, much will turn on the construction of the relevant statutory provision and there may be occasions where the intention is to benefit a broader category of person.[29]

4.13 As far as the second element is concerned it is for the pursuer to show two things: first, the standard of the duty imposed upon the defender and, second, the fact that the duty was breached by the required standard not having been satisfied. Under factories legislation the standard placed upon defenders can be strict. In *John Summers & Sons Ltd v. Frost*,[30] for example, a factory owner was held to have breached the fencing provisions of the Factories Act which required that dangerous machinery had to be securely fenced even although to have fenced the dangerous part in this case would have made it impossible to use the machine. In other cases the statutory duty is hedged by requirements that the obligation is to act so far as is reasonably practicable[31] or that it was impracticable[32] to avoid or prevent the contravention. It will be for the court to establish whether or not the defender has breached the relevant standard based upon its interpretation of the

[29] *Wigley v. British Vinegars Ltd* [1964] A.C. 307 (under Factories Act 1961, s. 29, "any person" was construed as to benefit all those who entered the factory in order to work there so that a window cleaner who was employed by the factory owner as an independent contractor was covered).

[30] [1955] A.C. 740.

[31] See, for example, Factories Act 1961, s. 29(1) as regards the provision of safe means of access and the Workplace Regulations 1992, reg. 12 which requires every floor and the surface of every traffic route be kept free from obstructions. Both provisions impose a standard of reasonable practicability. "Practicable" is that which is capable of being carried out in action or feasible: *Lee v. Nursery Furnishings Ltd* [1945] 1 All E.R. 387. The addition of "reasonably" creates a qualification which involves balancing the quantum of risk on the one hand and the measures necessary to avert the risk on the other. See *Sharp v. Coltness Iron Co. Ltd,* 1937 S.C.(H.L.) 68 and *Edwards v. N.C.B.* [1949] 1 K.B. 704 approved by the House of Lords in *Marshall v. Gotham Co. Ltd* [1954] A.C. 360.

[32] See, for example, the Mines and Quarries Act 1954, s. 157 which provides a defence for a contravention of the Act if it was impracticable to avoid or prevent the contravention. This phrase has been interpreted strictly since it relieves a statutory obligation. Thus the fact that compliance with the statutory duty would involve unreasonable time and expense is irrelevant. See generally *Jayne v. N.C.B.* [1963] 2 All E.R. 220.

statutory provision and the facts of the case. In *Latimer v. A.E.C. Ltd*,[33] for example, it was held that there had been no breach of the statutory duty to ensure that floors were properly maintained where it was clear that the lack of safety arose from some transient or exceptional condition.

4.14 Under the third requirement it is necessary to show that the harm that the pursuer suffered was of a type which the statute was intended to protect. A simple example of this arises from the old case of *Gorris v. Scott*[34] where sheep were swept overboard from a ship because of an absence of pens. However, the subsequent damages action failed because the relevant statute required that the pens be provided in order to prevent disease and not to prevent accidents. Clearly everything depends upon the court's interpretation of the purpose of the statute. In *Grant v. N.C.B.*[35] the fact that the House of Lords interpreted the mines and quarries legislation as intending to safeguard miners against accidents generally and not just against the collapse of the roof meant that the pursuer had a cause of action when he was injured by the derailment of a bogey. In the context of the fencing of machines under factories legislation one critical question has been to decide what is the purpose of such fencing. Generally the court's approach has been to require fencing in order to prevent the worker from coming into contact with the machine. This means that workers cannot sue when they are injured when either part of the material being worked or part of the machine flies out.[36]

4.15 Finally, under the third requirement it is necessary to establish a causal link between the breach of duty and the injury. The onus is upon the employee to prove on a balance of probabilities that the breach of duty caused or materially contributed to his injuries.[37] It is significant that the test applies the lesser standard of material contribution. This can be particularly important in industrial disease cases where it would be exceedingly difficult to prove that the

[33] [1954] A.C. 643.
[34] (1874) L.R. 9 Ex. 125.
[35] 1956 S.C.(H.L.) 48.
[36] *Carroll v. Andrew Barclay & Sons Ltd*, 1948 S.C.(H.L.) 100; *Nicholls* v. *Austin (Leyton) Ltd* [1946] A.C. 493.
[37] *Wardlaw v. Bonnington Castings Ltd*, 1956 S.C.(H.L.) 26 at p. 31 *per* Lord Reid.

breach was the sole or exclusive cause of the disease. Usually, prolonged exposure to the disease-creating conditions will suffice[38] and an inference of liability may be created where after a person has been exposed to conditions likely to cause the disease, it starts in a way typical of the way the disease would start in such conditions.[39] On the other hand, it is a potential defence in a case where injuries were alleged to have been caused by a failure to fulfil a statutory duty to provide safety equipment for the employer to show that the employee would not have used that equipment even if it had been provided.[40]

4.16 Unless the above requirements can be established it will not be competent for there to be a civil action for breach of statutory duty. Moreover, it does not follow that simply because some provisions of a statute do give rise to an action for breach of statutory duty that this is true for all the provisions of an Act. There was some doubt, for example, as to whether breaches of the welfare provisions of the Factories Act 1961 (*viz.* ss. 57–60) could give rise to actions for breach of statutory duty. It seemed that whilst breaches of section 58(1) (provisions of washing facilities) and section 59(1) (accommodation for clothing) gave rise to civil liability, the interpretation of the remaining provisions was uncertain.[41] These provisions have been repealed and replaced by regulations 21–25 of the Workplace (Health, Safety and Welfare) Provisions 1992[42] and it will be interesting to see to what extent the courts construe these essentially welfare provisions as giving rise to civil liability for breach of statutory duty.

4.17 It is well-established that an employer cannot argue as a defence in an action for breach of statutory duty that he delegated the duties to other persons such as employees or independent contractors. As Lord Atkin declared in *McMullan v. Lochgelly Iron & Coal Co. Ltd*[43]: "the duty is

---

[38] *Quinn v. Cameron & Roberton Ltd*, 1957 S.C.(H.L.) 22.
[39] *Gardiner v. Motherwell Machinery & Scrap Co. Ltd*, 1961 S.C.(H.L.) 1. *Cf. McGhee v. N.C.B.*, 1973 S.L.T. 14.
[40] *Qualcast (Wolverhampton) Ltd v. Haynes* [1959] A.C. 743; *McWilliams v. Sir Wm. Arrol & Co. Ltd*, 1962 S.C.(H.L.) 70.
[41] See the General Introduction to Redgrave, Fife and Machin, *Health and Safety* (1990). The matter is discussed by the First Division of the Court of Session in *Reid v. Westfield Paper Co. Ltd*, 1957 S.C. 218.
[42] S.I. 1992 No. 3004.
[43] 1933 S.C.(H.L.) 64.

imposed upon the employer, and it is irrelevant whether
his servants had disregarded his instructions or whether he
knew or not of the breach." Generally, therefore, it is no
defence for the employer to argue that he delegated the
duty to others. However, there is certainly one type of case
where it is a defence for the employer to show that the
pursuer was injured as a result of a breach of duty which
had been delegated, so long as the delegation is to the
injured employee himself. In *Smith v. A. Baveystock & Co.
Ltd*,[44] for example, a skilled operator was held to have no
remedy when he was injured by a circular saw when it was
proved that he had not adjusted the guard properly before
use as the regulations required. Essentially, in this type of
case the issue is to decide — whose fault was it?[45]

4.18 An action for breach of statutory duty has been
described as an action for negligence.[46] This is true in the
sense that the pursuer must prove the defender's breach of
duty and establish a causal connection between the breach
and the harm suffered. However, in another sense the
analogy can be somewhat misleading because the standard
of care required of a defender under statute can differ from
that required by the common law. An action for breach of
statutory duty may entail fulfilling the common law standard of reasonable care. Yet, as we have seen, everything
turns on the statutory language, and it is clear that a
statutory provision can impose a higher standard than that
of the common law so that liability can be strict or even
absolute. In *Millar v. Galashiels Gas Co. Ltd*,[47] for example,
the occupiers were held liable for the death of a workman
who was killed by the failure of an automatic braking
system in a lift, despite the fact that the failure was one
which nobody could account for and which could not have
been detected beforehand.

4.19 Given the different basis for the action, therefore,
there is nothing to prevent a pursuer raising both a com-

---

[44] [1945] 1 All E.R. 531.
[45] See Pearson J. in *Ginty v. Belmont Building Supplies Ltd* [1959] 1 All E.R.
414.
[46] *McMullan v. Lochgelly Iron & Coal Co. Ltd*, 1933 S.C.(H.L.) 64.
[47] 1949 S.C.(H.L.) 41. See also the speech of Lord Normand in *Carroll* v.
Andrew Barclay & Sons Ltd, 1948 S.C.(H.L.) 100, who argued that the
duty to fence dangerous machinery under the Factories Act was absolute
because the duty must be actually fulfilled.

mon law action for negligence and an action for breach of statutory duty. Moreover, the competent defences can vary as between the two types of action. For example, although the defence of *volenti non fit injuria* is relevant in common law actions it is not generally available in cases of breach of statutory duty[48] unless employees have breached a statutory duty which is placed upon them for their own safety.[49]

4.20 The above discussion concerned cases where the statute is silent as regards the potential for civil damages actions and the courts have had to construe the statutory provisions in accordance with the above rules in order to discover whether a civil damages action for breach of statutory duty is competent. Obviously, there is nothing to prevent the statute declaring specifically that a breach of one of its provisions will give rise to civil liability. Indeed, this is exactly the position as regards regulations which are made under section 15(1) of the Health and Safety at Work Act 1974. As section 47(2) of the 1974 Act makes clear, breach of a duty imposed by any such regulations is, so far as it causes damage,[50] actionable unless the regulations provide otherwise. As we know, apart from a breach of the Management Regulations, breaches of the other five "European" Regulations do give rise to civil liability.

The interpretation of health and safety statutes

4.21 As we have seen, statutes like the Mines and Quarries Act 1954, the Factories Act 1961 and the Offices, Shops and Railway Premises Act 1963 create criminal offences so that they can be considered as being primarily penal in nature. There is a rule of statutory interpretation in favour of the strict construction of such statutes so that where a provision is ambiguous the benefit of the doubt must be given to the person against whom the penalty is directed.[51] However, it is also the case that health and safety statutes are intended to protect workers so that they could just as easily be construed as being remedial. In this latter case the

---

[48] *Wheeler v. New Merton Board Mills Ltd* [1933] 2 K.B. 669 (C.A.).
[49] *I.C.I. Ltd v. Shatwell* [1965] A.C. 656.
[50] "Damage" includes the death of, or injury to, any person (including any disease and any impairment of a person's physical or mental condition) — s. 47(6).
[51] See *Stair Memorial Encyclopaedia*, Vol. 12, para. 1184.

statute should be read in such a way as to effect its object insofar as the wording fairly and reasonably permits.[52] This entails adopting an interpretation which seeks to prevent accidents at work.[53] Generally it has been this latter approach which has been favoured as regards health and safety statutes.[54] If the Act is intended to protect workers it would be "an illegitimate method of interpretation" to interpret the statute in such a way as to reduce that protection.[55] However, courts must be careful when interpreting statutes like the Factories Act that they do not place a strained meaning on the statutory language simply in order to achieve a social purpose.[56]

The regulatory framework

4.22   It is now time to consider some of the most important statutory provisions which regulate health and safety at work and which enable employees to sue their employers when they are injured at work because of a breach of the statutory provisions. The plan will be to consider first the provisions of the older statutes such as the Factories Act 1961 and then to examine the impact of the new "European" Regulations which provide for civil liability.

A. OLDER STATUTORY ARRANGEMENTS

4.23   As has already been noted, one of the aims of the Health and Safety at Work Act 1974 was to replace the existing statutory provisions as listed in Schedule 1 to the Act and to replace them with a system of regulations and approved codes of practice.[57] The whole of the Factories Act 1961 (with the exception of section 135[58]) is an existing

---

[52] *Harrison v. N.C.B.* [1951] A.C. 639.

[53] *Norris v. Syndic Manufacturing Co. Ltd* [1952] 2 Q.B. 135 (C.A.).

[54] In *McCarthy v. Coldair Ltd* [1951] 2 T.L.R. 1226 Lord Denning argued that the rule in favour of a strict construction was a rule of last resort which should only be applied when other rules fail.

[55] See the speech of Viscount Simonds in *John Summers & Sons Ltd v. Frost* [1955] A.C. 740 at p. 751.

[56] See the speech of Lord Diplock in *Haigh v. Charles W. Ireland Ltd*, 1974 S.L.T. 34.

[57] 1974 Act, s. 1(2).

[58] This provision dealt with particulars of work and wages for pieceworkers. It was repealed by the Wages Act 1986.

statutory provision and so its provisions have been the subject of repeal ever since 1974. After an initial flurry of activity[59] the process of repeal seemed to have become stalled.[60] However, the enactment of the "European" regulations has provided fresh impetus to this process of repeal and it is clear that a great many more provisions of the Factories Act will disappear once the new regulations are fully in place. For the present, we are in a transitional period with a number of the provisions of the Factories Act already repealed, others recently repealed by "European" regulations and others scheduled for total repeal once the transitional period has expired.

4.24 It is obvious that the Factories Act 1961 can only apply as regards safety and health in factories. A factory is defined in section 175 as any premises in which or within the close or curtilage or precincts of which, persons are employed in manual labour[61] in any process for or incidental to any of the following purposes, namely—

(a) the making of any article or of part of any article;

(b) the altering, repairing, ornamenting, finishing, cleaning, or washing or the breaking up or demolition of any article;

(c) the adapting for sale of any article[62];

(d) the slaughtering of cattle, sheep, swine, goats, horses, asses or mules;

(e) the confinement of such animals while awaiting slaughter at other premises—

being premises in which, or within the close or curtilage or precincts of which, the work is carried on by way of trade

---

[59] See, for example, the Factories Act 1961 etc. (Repeals and Modifications) Regulations 1974 (S.I. 1974 No. 1941) which repealed a number of provisions of the 1974 Act as from Jan. 1, 1975.

[60] None the less, there were some important repeals introduced by the Control of Substances Hazardous to Health Regulations 1988 (S.I. 1988 No. 1657). The C.O.S.H.H. Regulations are discussed in more detail in Chap. 6, at paras. 6.11–6.14.

[61] For the meaning of manual labour see *Hoare v. Robert Greene Ltd* [1907] 2 K.B. 315 and *Stone Lighting and Radio Ltd v. Haygarth* [1968] A.C. 157.

[62] It would seem that adapting for sale involves doing something to the article which, in some way, makes it different from what it was before — *per* Lord Dunedin in *Grove v. Lloyd's British Testing Co. Ltd* [1931] A.C. 450 at p. 467. Merely testing the article is not adapting for sale but the preparation, sorting or packaging of the article may be. *Cf. Grove* and *Henderson v. Glasgow Corporation* (1900) 2 F. 1127.

or for the purposes of gain[63] and to or over which the employer of the persons employed there has the right of access or control.

4.25 The most important part of the Factories Act 1961 is Part II (ss. 12–56) which contains the general provisions on safety. Broadly, these provisions deal with two main issues. First, there are provisions on the fencing of machinery and the safety of equipment, and, second, there are provisions concerning the safety of the workplace. With the exception of sections 40–52[64] and 53–55,[65] the provisions of Part II were still in force until the introduction of the "European" Regulations. This picture has now changed considerably. The Provision and Use of Work Equipment Regulations 1992[66] introduce new rules as regards the fencing of machinery and as regards a system of controls for work equipment to replace the fencing provisions of the Factories Act, ss. 12–16. Equally, the Workplace (Health, Safety and Welfare) Regulations 1992[67] introduce much more detailed rules than the Factories Act provided for the safety of workplaces, and in particular repeal ss. 28 and 29. Given that both Regulations specify transitional arrangements, it is necessary to consider the position under the Factories Act and under the Regulations. We will also consider some miscellaneous provisions on safety which continue in force despite the making of the "European" regulations.

(a) The safety of work equipment

(i) The duty to fence

4.26 The fencing provisions of sections 12–16 of the Factories Act 1961 have been considered more often by the judges than any other provisions of the Act. They form a key corpus of rules protecting workers from the dangers

---

[63] The "or" is disjunctive so that it is enough if there is either trade or gain — *Bailey v. Potteries Electric Traction Co. Ltd* [1931] 1 K.B. 385 and *Stanger v. Hendon Borough Council* [1948] 1 K.B. 571.
[64] These sections were repealed from Jan. 1, 1977 by the Factories Act 1961 etc. (Repeals) Regulations 1976 (S.I. 1976 No. 2004).
[65] These provisions were repealed as from Jan. 1, 1975 by the Factories Act 1961 etc. (Repeals and Modifications) Regulations 1974 (S.I. 1974 No. 1941).
[66] S.I. 1992 No. 2932.
[67] S.I. 1992 No. 3004.

inherent in working with machines. It would appear that the provisions are intended to form a single code and should be read together.[68] The machinery which is dealt with by these provisions can be divided into three categories:

(a) prime movers (things which are a source of mechanical power) (s. 12);

(b) transmission machinery (any machinery by which the power of a prime mover is taken to the machine) (s. 13); and

(c) every dangerous part of any other machinery (s.14).

4.27 As far as prime movers are concerned, there is an obligation to fence flywheels connected to prime movers and every moving part, whether the flywheel or prime mover is situated in an engine house or not.[69] Every part of electric generators, motors and rotary converters and flywheels directly connected to them must also be fenced unless the part is in such a position or of such construction as to be as safe to every person employed or working there as it would be fenced.[70] There is a similar obligation as regards the fencing of parts of transmission machinery.[71] In the case of other machinery the duty is to fence those parts of that other machinery which are dangerous unless they are in such a position or of such construction as to be as safe to every person employed or working there as they would be fenced.[72] If, because of the nature of the operation, the safety of a dangerous part of a machine cannot be secured by means of a fixed guard, the fencing obligations will be satisfied when a device is provided which automatically prevents the operator coming into contact with the part.[73]

4.28 The duty to fence only applies in relation to machinery which is completely installed as part of the factory equipment. However, once the installation is complete there is a duty to fence even though the machine is not at

[68] *F. E. Callow (Engineers) Ltd v. Johnson* [1971] A.C. 335.
[69] s. 12(1).
[70] s. 12(3).
[71] s. 13(1).
[72] s. 14(1).
[73] s. 14(2).

the material time being used in the manufacturing process,
so long as it is intended for manufacturing use and is
capable of such use.[74] There is no obligation to fence
machinery which does not form part of the equipment used
in the manufacturing process. In *Parvin v. Morton Machine
Co. Ltd*[75] a machine was manufactured and assembled in the
factory. An apprentice was injured when operating the
machine in order to clean it. The question was whether
there was a duty to fence the dangerous parts of this
machine. The House of Lords decided that the term
"machinery" did not cover machinery which is itself a
product of the factory. Reading sections 12–14 together, it
was concluded that each of these sections limited its protection to machinery which is part of the equipment of the
factory and did not apply to equipment which is actually
manufactured there. Similarly, there appears to be no
obligation to fence machinery which is brought into the
factory for repair — unless that machinery is part of the
factory's own installation.[76]

4.29 Another difficult question is whether there is any
duty to fence mobile machinery. In *Cherry v. International
Alloys Ltd*[77] it was held that the fencing provisions did not
apply to a truck which transported materials produced in
the factory since a truck was a vehicle and not machinery.
This view was overruled by the House of Lords in *Liptrot v.
British Railways Board*[78] where a workman was injured
between the body and wheel of a mobile crane. Here the
House of Lords considered that there were two types of
danger inherent in mobile machinery. First, dangers associated with the movement of the vehicle — it would be
absurd to suggest that the fencing provisions could cover
this type of danger. However, in the case of the second
type of danger — that associated with the mechanism of the
vehicle — the fencing provisions could apply. As Viscount
Dilhorne put it

> "while it would not be right to describe a vehicle as
> machinery, it may contain machinery; and if the

---

[74] *Richard Thomas & Baldwins Ltd v. Cummings* [1955] A.C. 321.
[75] 1952 S.C.(H.L.) 9.
[76] *Thurogood v. Van den Berghs and Jurgens Ltd* [1951] 2 K.B. 537.
[77] [1961] 1 Q.B. 136. See also *Young v. Caterpillar Tractor Co. Ltd*, 1963
S.L.T. (Notes) 63.
[78] [1969] 1 A.C. 136.

vehicle forms part of the equipment of the factory, then, in my opinion, s. 14 imposes an absolute obligation . . . to fence securely every dangerous part of the machinery it contains."[79]

It is clear that even as regards the second type of danger there will only be a duty to fence if the mobile machinery is part of the plant and equipment which is used in the manufacturing process. It is on this basis that it has been held that there was an obligation to fence the dangerous parts of a mobile fire-fighting pump, since it was machinery which was used to facilitate the ordinary and continued operation of the factory itself.[80]

4.30 The obligation is to ensure that prime movers, transmission machinery and dangerous parts of other machinery are "securely fenced". This requirement places an absolute duty on factory occupiers and it is no defence to argue that the best known method was used[81] or that the provision of appropriate fencing will prevent the machinery from being used at all.[82] However, the obligation to fence securely only arises in relation to certain hazards. Generally, the purpose of fencing is to prevent the operator from coming into contact with the machine.[83] Equally, as regards other machinery the duty to provide secure fencing only applies in relation to dangerous parts. There is no requirement that the whole of the machine be fenced.[84] It follows that there is no obligation to fence a machine which is dangerous in itself if it has no dangerous parts which can be properly described as parts of machinery.[85]

4.31 It is also necessary to discover when a part of machinery is dangerous. The thrust of the decisions on this issue has been to apply a test of reasonable foreseeability.[86]

[79] at p. 155.
[80] *McNeill v. Roche Products Ltd*, 1989 S.L.T. 498.
[81] *Dennistoun v. Charles E. Greenhill Ltd* [1944] 2 All E.R. 434.
[82] See, for example, *Mackay v. Ailsa Shipbuilding Co. Ltd*, 1945 S.C. 414.
[83] *Close v. Steel Co. of Wales Ltd* [1962] A.C. 367. This issue is discussed in more detail later.
[84] *B.R.B. v. Liptrot* [1969] 1 A.C. 136.
[85] See the speech of Lord Hailsham L.C. in *F.E. Callow (Engineers) Ltd* v. *Johnson* [1971] A.C. 335.
[86] The older case law is discussed by the House of Lords in *John Summers & Sons Ltd v. Frost* [1955] A.C. 740. The decision does approve the reasonable foreseeability test although it also countenances other approaches. John Munkman argues that the speeches indicate that the question of danger is not to be approached in an elaborate and artificial way, but simply by an examination of the machinery and its working: *Employer's Liability* (11th ed., 1990) at p. 341.

An authoritative statement in support of this approach is to be found in the decision of the House of Lords in *Close v. Steel Co. of Wales Ltd*[87] where their Lordships considered the earlier cases and concluded that the correct approach as to "whether a part of a machine is dangerous [is] whether it might be 'a reasonably foreseeable cause of injury to anybody acting in a way in which a human being might reasonably be expected to act in circumstances which may be reasonably expected to occur.' "[88] The test, therefore, requires the occupier to bear in mind both the conduct of the operator and the behaviour of the machine.

4.32 These are matters which have been discussed by the Scottish courts where the issue has often been viewed as a question of fact and degree.[89] The most authoritative Scottish statement is that of Lord Justice-Clerk Cooper in *Mitchell v. North British Rubber Co. Ltd*[90] where a worker who had to put rubber between two rollers in a machine caught her hand in the "nip" between the rollers. The rollers revolved very slowly and for this reason the company was acquitted at first instance. However, the decision was reversed on appeal on the basis that the nip was a source of danger. Lord Cooper declared[91]:

> "The question is not whether the occupiers of the factory knew that it was dangerous; nor whether a factory inspector had so reported; nor whether previous accidents had occurred; nor whether the victims of these accidents had, or had not, been contributorily negligent. The test is objective and personal. Is the part such in its character, and so circumstanced in its position, exposure, method of operation and the like, that in the ordinary course of human affairs danger may reasonably be anticipated from its use unfenced, not only to the prudent, alert and skilled operative intent upon his task, but also to the careless or inattentive worker whose inadvertent or indolent conduct may expose him to risk of injury or death from the unguarded part?"[92]

---

[87] [1962] A.C. 367.
[88] *per* Lord Guest at p. 412.
[89] See, for example, *Mackay v. Ailsa Shipbuilding Co. Ltd*, 1945 S.C. 414.
[90] 1945 J.C. 69.
[91] at p. 73.
[92] This statement was approved by the House of Lords in *John Summers & Sons Ltd v. Frost* [1955] A.C. 740.

4.33 As has already been noted, the duty under the Factories Act 1961 is to ensure that prime movers, transmission machinery and dangerous parts of other machinery are securely fenced. In this regard it is important to ask against what dangers should secure fencing be provided. The thrust of the authorities has been to hold that the mischief contemplated by the statute is the risk of workers coming into contact with machinery so that it is against this danger that fencing should be provided. The danger may arise through direct contact with the machine or, alternatively, because the worker is drawn into it when his clothing becomes caught in the machine. In such a case there will be liability even although the accident occurred in an entirely unexpected way.[93] However, no liability arises where the worker is using a hand tool and the contact between that tool and the machine causes injury to the worker through contact with a piece of machinery which is not otherwise dangerous.[94]

4.34 More importantly, there is no need to provide fencing against the risk of parts of the machinery flying out. In *Carroll v. Andrew Barclay & Sons Ltd*[95] the House of Lords held that there was no liability when a driving belt broke off transmission machinery and injured a worker standing nearby. Strictly speaking this decision only applied to section 13 (transmission machinery) though it is clear from the speech of Lord Normand that it also applied to prime movers under section 12. In *Close v. Steel Co. of Wales Ltd*[96] the House of Lords made it clear that the same rule also applied to dangerous parts of machinery under section 14. Here a shattered bit flew out from an electric drill and it was held that dangerous parts of machinery need only be fenced to prevent workers coming into contact with them.[97]

[93] *Millard v. Serck Tubes Ltd* [1969] 1 All E.R. 598.
[94] *Sparrow v. Fairey Aviation Co. Ltd* [1964] A.C. 1019 (worker's hand jerked violently by scraper causing it to be thrown against a stationary part of the machine).
[95] 1948 S.C.(H.L.) 100.
[96] [1962] A.C. 367.
[97] This decision was by majority with Lord Denning, in particular, issuing a strong dissent. It also involved overruling a number of English Court of Appeal decisions which had reached a contrary conclusion. See, for example, *Dickson v. Flack* [1953] 2 Q.B. 464. The decision can be criticised for creating an illogical distinction and for limiting the extent of the fencing protections so that obvious perils like parts of the machinery flying off are not covered. See, in particular, the judgment of Holroyd Pearce L.J. in *Eaves v. Morris Motors Ltd* [1961] 2 Q.B. 385 — approved by Lord Hailsham L.C. in *Johnson v. F.E. Callow (Engineers) Ltd* [1971] A.C. 335.

4.35 Since the purpose of fencing is to protect the worker from contact with the machine it is also the case that there is no duty to fence against the dangers of parts of the material being worked upon flying out. In *Nicholls v. Austin Leyton Ltd*[98] a young female worker was working at a circular saw when a small piece of wood flew off and injured her hand. The House of Lords held that the statute was not intended to protect workers from this type of accident. As Viscount Simonds succinctly put it "the fence is intended to keep the worker out, not to keep the machine or its product in." Moreover, employers will even escape liability where the injuries are caused by material being thrown out whilst still attached to the machinery.[99]

4.36 A third situation is where the danger is created by the juxtaposition of the machinery and the material. This issue was considered in *Midland and Low Moor Iron and Steel Co. Ltd v. Cross*[1] where a worker caught his hand whilst feeding metal bars between rollers. The rollers were not dangerous *per se*, but a dangerous "nip" was created between the metal and the rollers. The House of Lords concluded that whether a part of machinery was dangerous had to be determined by looking at the machine in operation doing the actual work which it was designed to perform. If such a danger were created then there is a duty to fence. Thus a part of machinery can become dangerous and require fencing simply through its juxtaposition with the material even although there is no danger when the workpiece is removed.

4.37 In the *Cross* case the House of Lords left unresolved the question whether a stationary part of a machine could become dangerous simply because a moving workpiece is in close proximity to it. This question was answered in the affirmative by the House of Lords in their later decision in *F. E. Callow (Engineers) Ltd v. Johnson.*[2] Here a worker was injured despite the fact that the rollers were almost at rest. Nonetheless, it was concluded that there was a duty to fence if the juxtaposition of the material and the machine creates danger. Thus machinery which is harmless in itself

[98] [1946] A.C. 493.
[99] See, for example, *Walker v. Dick Engineering Co. (Coatbridge) Ltd,* 1985 S.L.T. 465 (sharp metal cuttings emerging from a cutting tool).
[1] [1965] A.C. 343.
[2] Above.

may require to be fenced because of its juxtaposition to material which is being worked upon, and it does not matter whether it is the movement of the machine or of the material which creates the danger.[3]

4.38 As we have seen, fencing is secure when it protects the worker from contact with the machine. The next issue is to consider whether fencing is only necessary in order to protect against foreseeable forms of contact with the machine. In *Burns v. Joseph Terry & Sons Ltd*[4] the Court of Appeal concluded that there was no duty to fence parts of machinery where the approach to or contact with the machine is not reasonably foreseeable. This decision has been heavily criticised[5] and does not appear to represent the law in Scotland. In *Simpson v. Hardie & Smith Ltd*[6] the High Court of Justiciary held that it was an irrelevant defence to a criminal charge under section 13 to argue that an accident was not reasonably foreseeable. In the words of Lord Justice-General Clyde, "the primary question is whether the transmission machinery was securely fenced. The fact that the accident took place demonstrates that it was not securely fenced. . . . The test is not reasonable foreseeability."

(ii) The construction and maintenance of fencing

4.39 Fencing which is required by sections 12–14 must be of substantial construction, and constantly maintained and kept in position while the parts required to be fenced are in motion or use, except when those parts are exposed for examination and for any lubrication or adjustment shown by the examination to be immediately necessary.[7] This

---

[3] Clearly, if no danger is created by the juxtaposition of the moving material and the stationary part of the machine no duty to fence arises — *Hindle v. Joseph Porritt & Sons Ltd* [1970] 1 All E.R. 1142.

[4] [1951] 1 K.B. 454.

[5] See, for example J. Munkman, *Employer's Liability* (11th ed., 1990) at pp. 335–336. Munkman argues that the correct test is to look at the machinery without any fencing at all. In such a state there is nothing unforeseeable about approach from any direction. Secure fencing is therefore required and the only question is whether it precludes contact. This approach is supported by Lord Denning's dissent in *Burns* and by the speech of Lord Keith of Avonholm in *John Summers & Sons Ltd v. Frost* [1955] A.C. 740.

[6] 1968 J.C. 23.

[7] Factories Act 1961, s. 16. This provision does not create a separate offence and any prosecution must be brought under ss. 12–14. Nevertheless in civil proceedings s.16 should be treated as a limitation on the scope and extent of the duty created by s.14. See *McMeehan v. Uniroyal Engelbert Tyres Ltd*, 1994 S.L.T. (Sh.Ct.) 69.

provision fulfils two purposes. First, it indicates how and when the duty to fence arises and second, it provides an exception to the duty to fence for examination, lubrication or adjustment. It is interesting that there is no exception to the fencing requirements for cleaning or repair. As regards the first issue fencing must be in place while the parts of the machinery are "in motion or use."

4.40　The interpretation of "in motion or use" has certainly caused difficulties. One obvious problem is that the two parts of the phrase are capable of different meanings. A part can be in motion but not in use. Equally, it can be in use but not in motion. In *Richard Thomas and Baldwins Ltd v. Cummings*[8] a fitter injured his hand when repairing a machine which he had switched off in order to turn it by hand. The question was whether the machine was in motion or use during this process. The House of Lords formed the view that to be in use the machine had to be running as it was meant to run and doing the work it was meant to do. The machine would be in motion where it was running as it was meant to run but not doing the work it was meant to do. In the present case given that the machine was neither running as it was meant to run (it had been switched off) nor doing the work it was meant to do (it was being repaired[9]) there was no question of it being in motion or in use.

4.41　A machine will not be in use when it is not being used for its normal commercial purpose but during a slack period is being rotated slowly by means of an "inching button."[10] As Holroyd Pearce L.J. put it in this case, "the slow, sporadic rotation or intermittent movement of machinery intended to place it more advantageously for cleaning or repair is not normally motion or use within the section, whether it be produced by manpower or mechanical power."

4.42　More difficult are the cases where the machine is activated for a very short period of time. Everything appears to turn on the speed at which the machine is turning. In *Mitchell v. W. S. Westin Ltd*[11] a machine was

---

[8] [1955] A.C. 321.
[9] The same position would apply if the machine were being cleaned — *Finnie* v. *John Laird & Son Ltd*, 1967 S.L.T. 243.
[10] *Knight v. Leamington Spa Courier Ltd* [1961] 2 Q.B. 253.
[11] [1965] 1 All E.R. 657.

rotated by a fitter switching it on and off almost simultaneously. It was held that the machine was not in motion or in use because the motion was only intermittent, there was no evidence of high speed, and there was no substantial movement comparable to the normal working of the lathe. On the other hand, in *Stanbrook v. Waterlow & Sons Ltd*[12] where the cylinder of a printing machine revolved at high speed for a fraction of a second the court held that the fact the motion was not intended to last for an appreciable time was immaterial. Here it was accepted that there was a vital distinction between a thing which is being moved slowly and a thing which is in motion at high speed. Given the speed at which the cylinder rotated the machine was in motion within section 16. Moreover, even if the machine is turning at its usual speed because of inadvertence it is likely to be in motion; though it will not be in use since it is not being operated for its ordinary commercial purpose.[13] Machines which have been switched off but which are still turning are also still "in motion."[14]

(iii) Unfenced machinery

4.43 In determining whether secure fencing has been provided no account should be taken of any person carrying out, while the part of the machinery is in motion, an examination of it or any lubrication or adjustment shown by the examination to be immediately necessary, if the examination, lubrication or adjustment can only be carried out while the part of the machinery is in motion.[15] There are also special rules for transmission machinery where stopping that machinery would seriously interfere with the carrying on of the manufacturing process. In this case no account should be taken of any person carrying out, by such methods and in such circumstances as may be specified in regulations,[16] any lubrication or any mounting or shipping of belts.[17] This provision only applies where the examination, lubrication or other operation is carried out by

---

[12] [1964] 2 All E.R. 506.

[13] *Horne v. Lec Refrigeration Ltd* [1965] 2 All E.R. 898.

[14] *McLean v. Glenrobert Wood Wool Industries Ltd,* 1969 S.L.T. (Notes) 29.

[15] Factories Act 1961, s. 15(1)(a). Once again this particular defence does not extend to cleaning or repair.

[16] See the Operations at Unfenced Machinery Regulations 1938, S. R. & O. 1938 No. 641 as amended by S. R. & O. 1946 No. 156 and S.I. 1976 No. 955.

[17] Factories Act 1961, s. 15(1)(b).

a person who has attained the age of 18 and all the other conditions of the regulations are complied with.[18]

B. THE PROVISION AND USE OF WORK EQUIPMENT REGULATIONS 1992

4.44 These regulations are intended to implement E.C. Directive 89/655/EEC on the minimum safety and health requirements for the use of work equipment. The regulations are augmented by Guidance Notes published by the Health and Safety Executive and they took effect on January 1, 1993. However, there are transitional arrangements for work equipment first provided for use in the premises or undertaking before January 1, 1993 in that the bulk of the regulations will not be operative in their case until January 1, 1997. Nevertheless, the regulations create obligations as regards the suitability and efficiency of work equipment and information and training even for exisitng equipment as of January 1, 1993. The regulations apply to premises and undertakings except that they do not apply to or in relation to the master or crew of a seagoing ship or to the employer of such persons, in respect of the normal shipboard activities of the ship's crew under the direction of the master.[19]

4.45 The requirements of the regulations which are imposed upon employers apply in respect of work equipment provided for or used by any of their employees who is at work or who is on an offshore installation.[20] The requirements of the regulations also apply to the self-employed, persons in control of non-domestic premises and the occupiers of factories.[21] "Work equipment" covers any machinery, appliance, apparatus or tool and any assembly of components which, in order to achieve a common end, are arranged and controlled so that they function as a whole.[22] "Use" is also broadly defined to mean any activity

---

[18] Factories Act 1961, s. 15(2).

[19] reg. 3.

[20] reg. 4(1).

[21] reg. 4(2).

[22] This is a very wide definition and, as the Guidance Notes make clear, work equipment can include single machines such as power presses and photocopiers, tools such as portable drills and apparatus such as laboratory equipment like Bunsen burners. The definition also includes arrangements for the assembly of components like a bottling plant. For a non-exhaustive list of work equipment see para. 43. Work equipment does not include livestock, substances like acids, structural items and private cars.

involving work equipment and includes starting, stopping, programming, setting, transporting, repairing, modifying, maintaining, servicing and cleaning.[23]

4.46 The regulations contain detailed provisions concerning the suitability of work equipment. Every employer must ensure that work equipment is so constructed or adapted as to be suitable[24] for the purpose for which it is used or provided.[25] In selecting work equipment, employers must have regard to the working conditions and to the risks to the health and safety of persons which exist in the premises or undertaking in which that equipment is to be used and any additional risk posed by its use.[26] Employers must also ensure that work equipment is used only for operations for which, and under conditions for which, it is suitable.[27] These provisions are central and address the safety of work equipment in three ways. They are intended to ensure the initial integrity of work equipment, the place where it will be used and the purpose for which it will be used.

4.47 Work equipment must be maintained in an efficient state, in efficient working order and in good repair and where employers maintain a maintenance log, that log must be kept up-to-date.[28] The Guidance Notes make clear that "efficient" relates to how the condition of the equipment might affect health and safety; it is not concerned with productivity. There is no legal requirement that a maintenance log be kept, though the Guidance Notes certainly recommend this. Where the use of work equipment is likely to involve a specific risk to health and safety, regulation 7 requires employers to restrict its use, repair and maintenance to specific persons. It is the view of the Health and Safety Executive that this particular regulation does not require employers to take any additional measures other than those required by existing legislation.

4.48 There are also requirements as regards information and training. Employees who use work equipment and

---

[23] reg. 2(1).
[24] "Suitable" means suitable in any respect which it is reasonably foreseeable will affect the health and safety of any person — reg. 5(4).
[25] reg. 5(1).
[26] reg. 5(2).
[27] reg. 5(3).
[28] regs. 5(1) and (2).

supervisors and managers of such equipment must have available to them adequate health and safety information and, where appropriate, written instructions about the use of that equipment.[29] In particular such information should include (a) the conditions and the methods for use of the equipment; (b) foreseeable abnormal situations and the action for such situations and (c) any conclusions to be drawn from experience in using the equipment.[30] Any such information must be readily comprehensible to those concerned.[31] There are also requirements for users of work equipment and supervisors and managers to receive adequate training for health and safety purposes, including training in the methods for use of the equipment, any risks which such use may entail and precautions to be taken.[32]

4.49 All the above regulations have immediate effect. The rest of the provisions, which are discussed below, will apply to existing work equipment as from January 1, 1997. These provisions introduce new rules about dangerous parts of machinery, protection against specified hazards, controls and control systems and maintenance requirements.

(a) Dangerous parts

4.50 Regulation 11 replaces section 14 of the Factories Act 1961 and requires employers to ensure that effective measures are taken to prevent access to any dangerous part of machinery or to any rotating stock-bar,[33] or to stop the movement of any dangerous part or rotating stock-bar before any part of a person enters a danger zone.[34] It is clear that this provision follows the approach of section 14 by requiring that measures need only be taken to prevent the contact of employees with the machinery.

4.51 On the other hand, unlike section 14 which placed an absolute obligation on employers to fence dangerous parts

---

[29] regs. 8(1) and (2).
[30] reg. 8(3).
[31] reg. 8(4).
[32] regs. 9(1) and (2).
[33] "Stock-bar" means any part of a stock-bar which projects beyond the head-stock of a lathe — reg. 11(5).
[34] reg. 11(1). "Danger zone" means any zone in or around machinery in which a person is exposed to a risk to health or safety from contact with a dangerous part of machinery or a rotating stock-bar — reg. 11(5).

of machinery, the new regulations introduce a hierarchy of measures based upon the risks and hazards associated with the process and the practicability of the measures. Employers must consider each level of the hierarchy in turn and select measures from that level so far as they are practicable. As important, the selection process must also ensure that the measures which are taken are effective in overcoming the risks and satisfying the requirements of regulation 11(1).[35] The four levels of measure are (a) fixed enclosing guards,[36] (b) other guards[37] and protection devices,[38] (c) protection appliances[39] like jigs, holders and push-sticks and (d) the provision of information, instruction, training and supervision.

4.52 All guards and protection devices must:

(a) be suitable for their purpose;

(b) be of good construction, sound material and adequate strength;

(c) be maintained in an efficient state, in efficient working order and in good repair;

(d) not give rise to any increased risk to health and safety;

(e) not be easily bypassed or disabled;

(f) be situated at sufficient distance from the danger zone;

(g) not unduly restrict the view of the operating cycle of the machinery, where such a view is necessary; and

(h) be so constructed or adapted that they allow operations necessary to fit or replace parts and for maintenance work, restricting access so that

[35] The Guidance Notes suggest that the selection process will often result in a combination of measures being taken.

[36] The Guidance Notes define guards as physical barriers which prevent access to the danger zone and fixed guards should have no moving parts and be fastened in a constant position relative to the danger zone — App. 3, para. 1.

[37] "Other guards" include moveable guards, adjustable guards, automatic guards and fixed guards that are not fully enclosing — App. 3, para. 2.

[38] "Protection devices" are devices which do not prevent access to the danger zone but stop the movement of the dangerous part before contact (*e.g.* photoelectric devices) — App. 3, para. 3.

[39] "Protection appliances" are used to hold or manipulate in a way which allows operators to control and feed a loose workpiece at a machine while keeping their body clear of the danger zone — App. 3, para. 4.

it is allowed only in the area where the work is to be carried out and, if possible, without having to dismantle the guard or protection device.[40]

(b) Protection against specified hazards

4.53 The Regulations place new responsibilities upon employers to take measures to ensure that the exposure of persons using work equipment to any risk to health or safety from specified hazards is either prevented or, where that is not reasonably practicable, adequately[41] controlled.[42] The measures envisaged by this provision are measures other than the provision of personal protective equipment or of information, instruction, training and supervision, so far as reasonably practicable, and include, where appropriate, measures to minimise the effects of the hazard as well as to reduce the likelihood of the hazard occurring.[43] The hazards specified by this provision are

(a) the falling or ejection from work equipment of any article or substance[44];

(b) the rupture or disintegration of parts of work equipment[45];

(c) work equipment catching fire or overheating;

(d) the unintended or premature discharge of any article or of any gas, dust, liquid, vapour or other substance which is produced, used or stored in the work equipment; and

(e) the unintended or premature explosion of any work equipment or any article or substance produced, used or stored in it.[46]

[40] reg. 11(3). If protection appliances are provided, then they must comply with paras. (a) to (d) and para. (g).
[41] "Adequate" means adequate having regard only to the nature of the hazard and the nature and degree of exposure to the risk — reg. 12(4).
[42] reg. 12(1).
[43] reg. 12(2).
[44] In contradistinction to the Factories Act 1961 this provision creates protection against parts of the material flying out.
[45] Again, unlike the Factories Act this provision protects operators from parts of the machinery breaking off and flying out.
[46] reg. 12(3). Examples of the types of hazard which are covered by this regulation are provided in the Guidance Notes, para. 121.

4.54 These protections for specified hazards do not apply where certain other regulations require measures to be taken to prevent or control risks to health and safety. The types of hazard which are excluded from the scope of the Regulations because they are regulated by other provisions are operations involving lead, ionising, and asbestos as well as substances hazardous to health, noise and head protection in the construction industry.[47] The Regulations also require appropriate protection for work equipment and substances kept in work equipment which is at a high or very low temperature so as to prevent burns, scalds or sears.[48]

(c) Controls and control systems

4.55 The Regulations introduce new rules as regards the provision of controls and control systems in work equipment. This is a new departure since in the past requirements for controls only applied in particular areas such as woodworking machines. There are requirements for appropriate controls for starting work equipment (including restarting after a stoppage) or for controlling any change of speed, pressure or other operating conditions of work equipment where the change leads to greater or different risks.[49]
Employers are also required to ensure that, where appropriate, work equipment is provided with readily accessible controls to stop the machinery[50] and there are provisions requiring the installation of readily accessible emergency stop controls which will operate in priority to any other stop control.[51]

4.56 Employers must ensure that all work equipment controls are visible and identifiable and, except where necessary, no control is in a position where persons operating the control are exposed to a risk to their health and safety.[52] All control systems must, so far as reasonably

---

[47] reg. 12(5). For types of hazard regulated by other regulations see Chap. 6.
[48] reg. 13.
[49] reg. 14(1).
[50] reg. 15.
[51] reg. 16.
[52] regs. 17(1) and (2).

practicable, be safe and a control system will not be safe unless (a) its operation does not create any increased risk to health and safety, (b) it ensures, so far as reasonably practicable, that any fault or damage to the system or any loss of energy supply will not result in additional or increased risk to health and safety and (c) it does not impede the operation of stop controls or emergency stop controls.[53]

(d) Maintenance and other requirements

4.57 The Regulations also introduce rules about the isolation of work equipment from all its sources of energy,[54] the stabilisation of work equipment,[55] the provision of suitable and sufficient lighting,[56] markings[57] and warnings and warning devices.[58] Regulation 22 requires employers to take appropriate measures to ensure that work equipment is so constructed or adapted that, so far as reasonably practicable, maintenance operations which involve a risk to health and safety can be carried out while the work equipment is shut down unless maintenance operations can be carried out without a risk to health or safety or appropriate measures can be taken to protect persons carrying out maintenance operations which involve a risk to health and safety. This provision resolves some of the difficulties associated with the construction and maintenance requirements of section 16 of the Factories Act 1961. Moreover, the Guidance Notes provide examples of the sorts of measures which can be taken in order to minimise risks to health and safety when machinery is running or working during maintenance operations.[59]

C. SAFETY AT THE WORKPLACE

4.58 The Factories Act 1961 also contains detailed provisions on the safety of floors, stairs and passages (s. 28)

[53] reg. 18.
[54] reg. 19.
[55] reg. 20.
[56] reg. 21.
[57] reg. 23.
[58] reg. 24.
[59] See para. 213 which recommends that the design of work equipment should ensure that the power, speed or range of movement of dangerous parts be restricted during maintenance.

and as regards safe means of access to places of work (s. 29). These provisions were repealed by the Workplace (Health, Safety and Welfare) Regulations 1992 as from January 1, 1993. However, as regards any workplace or part of a workplace which is not a new workplace or a modification, an extension or a conversion the bulk of the regulations will not take effect until January 1, 1996. Until that date sections 28 and 29 will continue to apply so that it is necessary to consider them given the transitional arrangements for the workplace regulations.

4.59 Under section 28(1) all floors, steps, stairs, passages and gangways shall be of sound construction and properly maintained and shall, so far as reasonably practicable, be kept free from any obstruction and from any substance likely to cause persons to slip. The phrase "floor etc." should be given its ordinary and natural meaning. In *Johnston v. Colvilles Ltd*[60] it was held that "floor" meant the ordinary floor of a factory which was used by those employed in the ordinary course of their employment. On this basis, the base of a furnace could not be a floor, nor the unmade earthen surface of a woodyard.[61] The obligation to keep floors etc. sound is an absolute one so that it is no defence to show that the defect could not have been discovered by reasonable inspection,[62] or that there was a latent defect in the structure of the floor.[63] On the other hand, a minor defect like a shallow depression in the floor is not a breach of the section unless it makes the floor unsafe.[64]

4.60 The second part of section 28(1) is qualified by the phrase "so far as reasonably practicable." [65] It is for the occupier to show that compliance with the statutory duty is not reasonably practicable in the circumstances since he should have knowledge as to what precautions are required.[66] Thus employees need only show that they fell on

[60] 1966 S.L.T. 30.
[61] *Sullivan v. Hall Russell & Co. Ltd*, 1964 S.L.T. 192.
[62] See, for example, *Whitehead v. Stott (James) & Co.* [1949] 1 K.B. 358.
[63] *Latimer v. AEC Ltd* [1952] 2 Q.B. 701.
[64] *Payne v. Weldless Steel Tube Co. Ltd* [1956] 1 Q.B. 196.
[65] This part was added in 1959 in order to reverse the decision of the House of Lords in *Latimer v. A.E.C. Ltd* [1953] A.C. 643 where it was held that the first part only applied to the floor itself and not to temporary conditions affecting it.
[66] *Nimmo v. Alexander Cowan & Sons Ltd*, 1967 S.C.(H.L.) 79.

the floor and were injured. Thereafter, it is for the occupier to prove the he did all that was reasonably practicable to avert the accident. This may entail showing that there was a regular system for ensuring that the floor was kept clean,[67] or by seeking to prevent the danger arising at all through issuing instructions to employees not to litter the floor.[68]

4.61 An obstruction is something which has no business to be on the floor and which ought not reasonably to be there.[69] This means that material or equipment which is properly present for the proper working of the factory is excluded.[70] In *Pengelley v. Bell Punch Co. Ltd*[71] where an employee tripped over heavy reels placed in front of storage stacks it was held that the reels were not obstructions because they were there for a useful purpose. Moreover, the reels were not a source of risk to persons using the place in an ordinary way. In *Marshall v. Ericsson Telephones Ltd*[72] a similar decision was reached as regards a trolley which was being unloaded. However, in this case it was stressed that the trolley was not idle and was there in the ordinary course of business. If the trolley had been left there unnecessarily it could well have constituted an obstruction.[73]

4.62 There are also provisions in section 28 as regards handrails for staircases, openings in floors and ladders. A substantial handrail must be provided for every staircase in a building or affording a means of exit from it and where the staircase has an open side the handrail must be on that side.[74] Where both sides of the staircase are open, or the staircase is one which owing to the nature of its construction or the condition of the surface of the steps or other special circumstances, is specially liable to cause accidents, a handrail must be provided and maintained on both sides.[75]

[67] *Braham v. J. Lyons & Co. Ltd* [1962] 3 All E.R. 281.
[68] *Hall v. Fairfield Shipbuilding & Engineering Co. Ltd*, 1964 S.C.(H.L.) 72.
[69] As Lord Reid put it in *Jenkins v. Allied Ironfounders Ltd* [1969] 3 All E.R. 1609, an obstruction is something whose presence on the floor might cause an accident and whose presence serves no useful purpose.
[70] See, for example, *Lynch v. Babcock Power Ltd*, 1988 S.L.T. 307.
[71] [1964] 1 All E.R. 613.
[72] [1964] 3 All E.R. 609.
[73] In this regard see, for example, *Dorman Long Steel Co. Ltd v. Bell* [1964] 1 All E.R. 617.
[74] Factories Act 1961, s. 28(2).
[75] *Ibid.*, s. 28(2).

All openings in floors must be securely fenced unless the nature of the work renders such fencing impracticable.[76] There is also an absolute duty to ensure that all ladders are soundly constructed and properly maintained.[77]

4.63 Section 29(1) ensures that there shall, so far as reasonably practicable, be provided and maintained safe means of access to every place at which any person has at any time to work, and every such place shall, so far as reasonably practicable, be made and kept safe for any person working there. The duty to provide a safe means of access is very general since it applies to every access to every place of work and it is not confined to access within the factory nor only to conventional forms of access.[78] Place of work is equally broadly defined and undoubtedly covers more than simply the floor space within a factory. The test entails considering the permanently installed machinery and the regular activities of the factory,[79] so that it would include articles which are being worked on in a factory or which have been brought in for repair.[80] On the other hand, it does not cover moveable items of machinery such as trucks.[81]

4.64 The safe means of access has to be provided to any place where a person has to work. This is likely to include any place where employees may be expected to go in order to perform their work.[82] However, it is clear that the protection only applies where the access is to a place where a person has to work. Accordingly, the provision did not apply when molten slag fell on a worker who was going to the toilet,[83] nor when the accident happened when the employee was heading for the canteen.[84] It is not clear whether a particular place can be both a means of access

---

[76] *Ibid.*, s. 28(4).

[77] *Ibid.*, s. 28(5). See also *Cole v. Blackstone & Co. Ltd* [1943] K.B. 615 approved in *Millar v. Galashiels Gas Co. Ltd*, 1949 S.C.(H.L.) 31.

[78] *Lavender v. Diamints Ltd* [1949] 1 K.B. 585; *Hopwood v. Rolls-Royce Ltd* (1947) 176 L.T. 514.

[79] *Yates v. Rockwell Graphics Systems Ltd* [1988] I.C.R. 8.

[80] *Cox v. H.C.B. Angus Ltd* [1981] I.C.R. 683.

[81] *McFaulds v. Reed Corrugated Cases Ltd*, 1993 S.L.T. 670.

[82] *Cf. Smith v. National Coal Board* [1967] 2 All E.R. 593.

[83] *Rose v. Colvilles Ltd*, 1950 S.L.T. (Notes) 72.

[84] *Davies v. De Havilland Aircraft Ltd* [1951] 1 K.B. 50. It is likely that in both this case and the *Rose* case the worker would now have a cause of action under the second part of s. 28(1).

and a place of work. In *Alison v. Henry Bruce & Son Ltd*[85] it was accepted that a person could be at his place of work and yet also be using a means of access. However, a contrary view was adopted by the Second Division in *Morrow v. Enterprise Sheet Metal Works (Aberdeen) Ltd*[86] where it was argued that a particular place in a factory could be a place of work at one time, and a means of access at another. However, it could not, as respects the same person, be both at the same time.

4.65 Under section 29(1) occupiers are also required, so far as reasonably practicable, to make and keep safe places of work. It is for the occupier both to plead and prove that all reasonable and practicable measures have been taken.[87] Beyond this, it would appear that the obligation to keep a place of work safe is absolute. In *Larner v. British Steel plc*[88] the Court of Appeal rejected a test based on reasonable foreseeability and accepted that the test was strict.[89] The obligation to provide a safe place of work undoubtedly applies to structural defects[90] and probably also to obstructions and other temporary dangers.[91] In *Allen v. Avon Rubber Co. Ltd*,[92] for example, it was held that section 29(1) could be infringed by a lack of safety which was temporary and which only arose during stocktaking since the issue of safety is not necessarily lessened by the fact that employees are not frequently exposed to the danger. Occupiers are also required to take reasonably practicable measures by fencing or otherwise for ensuring safety, where any person has to work at a place from which he is liable to fall a distance of

[85] 1951 S.L.T. 399.
[86] 1986 S.L.T. 697 following the decision of the Court of Appeal in *Taylor v. Coalite Oils and Chemicals Ltd* (1967) 3 K.I.R. 315.
[87] *Nimmo v. Alexander Cowan & Sons Ltd*, 1967 S.C.(H.L.) 79; *Gibson v. British Insulated Callenders' Construction Co. Ltd*, 1973 S.L.T. 2; *Bowes v. Sedgefield District Council* [1981] I.C.R. 234.
[88] [1993] I.C.R. 551.
[89] Applying *Robertson v. R. B. Crowe & Co.*, 1970 S.L.T. 122 and doubting *Morrow*, above. *Robertson* and *Larner* were applied by Lord Abernethy in *Neil v. Greater Glasgow Health Board*, 1994 S.C.L.R. 673 who rejected a defence based on reasonable foreseeability.
[90] *Robertson*, above.
[91] But see the decision of the Court of Appeal in *Levesley v. Thomas Firth and John Brown Ltd* [1953] 2 All E.R. 866 which seeks to restrict the dangers to structural ones. This decision is criticised by John Munkman in *Employer's Liability* (11th ed.) at p. 294.
[92] [1986] I.C.R. 695.

more than two metres, unless there are secure footholds and, where necessary, secure handholds.[93]

D. THE WORKPLACE (HEALTH, SAFETY AND WELFARE) REGULATIONS 1992

4.66 These regulations are intended to implement the EC Directive on Minimum Health and Safety Requirements at the Workplace.[94] They took effect for new workplaces used for the first time as a workplace after December 31, 1992 on January 1, 1993 and will apply to workplaces in existence before that date on January 1, 1996. There is also an Approved Code of Practice to accompany the regulations. A workplace is defined as any premises or part of premises which are not domestic premises and are made available to any person as a place of work.[95] The definition includes any place within the premises to which a person has access while at work and any room, lobby, corridor, staircase, road or other place used as a means of access to or egress from that place of work or where facilities are provided for use in connection with that place of work other than a public road.[96] The following workplaces are excluded from the definition:

    (a)   a workplace which is in or on a ship;

    (b)   a workplace where the only activities being undertaken are building operations or engineering construction works;

    (c)   a workplace where the only activities being undertaken are the exploration for or extraction of mineral resources; and

    (d)   a workplace which is situated in the immediate vicinity of another workplace where the only activities being undertaken are the exploration for or extraction of mineral resources.[97]

There are also special rules as regards the application of the regulations to temporary worksites where only the pro-

---

[93] Factories Act, s. 29(2). See also *Wigley v. British Vinegars Ltd* [1964] A.C. 307.

[94] 89/654/EEC.

[95] reg. 2(1).

[96] reg. 2(1)(a) and (b).

[97] reg. 3(1).

visions in regulations 20–25 on sanitary conveniences, washing facilities, drinking water, clothing accommodation, changing facilities and facilities for rest and eating meals apply.[98]

4.67 Employers have a statutory duty to ensure that every workplace which is under their control and where any of their employees works complies with any of the requirements of the Regulations.[99] The Regulations are also specifically applied to the occupiers of factories[1] and to persons who have control of any workplace in connection with trade, business or other undertaking (whether for profit or not).[2] Thus as well as applying the Regulations to persons who already have obligations under the Factories Act 1961, the Regulations also apply to workplaces in institutions such as hospitals, schools and universities which were not previously the subjects of specific statutory regulation.

4.68 The workplace and the equipment, devices and systems (*i.e.* mechanical ventilation systems) must be maintained (including cleaned as appropriate) in an efficient state, in efficient working order and in good repair.[3] It is clear from the Code of Practice that "efficient" in this context means efficient from the view of health, safety and welfare. Such equipment, devices and systems must be subject, where appropriate, to a suitable system of maintenance.[4] The Code of Practice recommends that a suitable system of maintenance should include regular maintenance, remedying potentially dangerous defects, proper remedial work and the keeping of a suitable record to ensure that the maintenance system has been properly implemented.

4.69 There must be effective and suitable provision to ensure that every enclosed workplace is ventilated by a

---

[98] reg. 3(2). Workplaces which are or are in or on aircraft, locomotives or rolling stock, trailers or semi-trailers when stationary in a workplace (but not when on a public road) are generally exempt from the Regulations save for reg. 13 (falls or falling objects) (reg. 3(3)). Also excluded are agricultural or forestry workplaces which are outdoors and away from the undertaking's main buildings save for the requirements on sanitary conveniences, washing facilities and drinking water in regs. 20–22 (reg. 3(4)).

[99] reg. 4(1).
[1] reg. 4(5).
[2] reg. 4(3).
[3] reg. 5(1).
[4] reg. 5(2).

sufficient quantity of fresh and purified air and any plant used for this purpose must include an effective device to give visible and audible warning of any failure of the plant for reasons of health and safety.[5] There are also provisions requiring the temperature in all workplaces during working hours to be reasonable and for the provision of thermometers.[6] The aim here is to provide reasonable comfort without the need for special clothing.[7] However, where, despite the provision of local heating or cooling, workers are exposed to temperatures which do not give reasonable comfort, then suitable protective clothing and rest facilities should be provided. Every workplace must also have suitable and sufficient lighting and, so far as is reasonably practicable, this should be by natural light.[8] Workplaces together with any furniture, furnishings and fittings must be kept sufficiently clean as must the surfaces of floors, walls and ceilings and there are also provisions aimed at preventing the accumulation of waste materials except in suitable receptacles.[9]

4.70 In any room where a person works there must be sufficient floor area, height and unoccupied space for purposes of health, safety and welfare.[10] The Regulations do not provide guidance on the amount of space required. However, the Code of Practice does make recommendations about the minimum amount of space which should be provided. Regulation 11(1) requires that every workstation[11] must be so arranged as to be suitable both for the person required to work there and for the work that is likely to be done there. Suitable seats must also be provided where the work or a substantial part of it must be done sitting.[12] In the case of workstations outdoors there is a requirement that they be so arranged that (a) so far as reasonably practicable,

[5] regs. 6(1) and (2).
[6] regs. 7(1) and (3).
[7] The Code of Practice recommends that the temperature in workplaces should normally be at least 16° Celsius unless much of the work involves severe physical effort where it should be at least 13° Celsius.
[8] regs. 8(1) and (2).
[9] reg. 9(1)–(3).
[10] reg. 10(1).
[11] Workstations where visual display screens etc. are used are also subject to the Health and Safety (Display Screen Equipment) Regulations 1992 and see paras. 6.32–6.37.
[12] reg. 11(3). This can also entail the provision of suitable footrests (reg. 11(4)(b)).

they provide protection from adverse weather; (b) they enable people working there to leave it swiftly; and (c) persons there are not likely to slip or fall.[13] It is interesting that a test of reasonable practicability is introduced for workstations outdoors, whereas the test for other workstations is based solely upon suitability.

4.71 Regulation 12(1) requires that every floor in a workplace and the surface of every traffic route,[14] in a workplace must be of such construction that the floor or surface is suitable for the purpose for which it is used. To some extent this provision echoes some of the language of section 28(1) of the Factories Act 1961. However, regulation 12 also lays down particular requirements that the floor, or surface of the traffic route should have no hole or slope, or be uneven or slippery so as to expose any person to a risk to health or safety and that every floor has effective means of drainage.[15] There are also provisions which seek to avoid obstructions and prevent persons from slipping. Regulation 12(3) requires that, so far as reasonably practicable, every floor in a workplace and every surface of a traffic route are kept free from obstructions and from any article or substance which may cause a person to slip, trip or fall. This provision also echoes section 28(1) of the Factories Act 1961 and it is anticipated that the courts will adopt the same approach to the issue of reasonable practicability in regulation 12(3) as was applied under the older legislation. Finally, there are provisions for suitable and sufficient handrails for staircases except where a handrail could not be provided without obstructing a traffic route.[16]

4.72 Regulation 13 requires that, so far as reasonably practicable, suitable and effective measures are taken to prevent any person falling a distance likely to cause personal injury[17] or being struck by a falling object likely to

[13] reg. 11(2).

[14] "Traffic route" means a route for pedestrian traffic, vehicles or both and includes any stairs, staircase, fixed ladder, doorway, gateway, loading bay or ramp (reg. 2(1)).

[15] reg. 12(2).

[16] reg. 12(5). The Code of Practice recommends that a handrail should be provided on one side of a staircase except where there is a particular risk of falling, where handrails should be provided on both sides.

[17] Unlike the Factories Act 1961, s. 29(2), regs. 13(1) and (3) do not specify any minimum distance. However, the Code of Practice does recommend the provision of secure fencing at any place where a person might fall 2m or more and fencing in other cases where there is an increased likelihood of falling.

cause personal injury. So far as reasonably practicable, the required measures should entail measures other than the provision of personal protective equipment, information, instruction, training or supervision. It is clear, therefore, that the primary obligation is to provide fencing or covers.[18] There is higher obligation where there is a tank, pit or structure and there is a risk of persons falling into a dangerous substance[19] in the tank etc. In such a case the duty is to securely cover or fence, so far as is practicable.[20]

4.73 Windows and transparent and translucent doors, gates and walls must, where necessary for reasons of health and safety, be of safety material or be protected against breakage and be appropriately marked.[21] There are also provisions concerning the safe opening of windows, skylights and ventilators[22] and the safe cleaning of windows and skylights.[23]

4.74 Regulation 17 introduces important new provisions as regards the organisation of traffic routes. Every workplace must be organised in such a way that pedestrians and vehicles can circulate in a safe manner and traffic routes must be suitable for the persons or vehicles using them, sufficient in number, in suitable positions and of sufficient size.[24] Traffic routes do not satisfy the last requirement unless suitable measures have been taken to ensure that (a) pedestrians or vehicles can use them without causing danger to the health and safety of persons at work near it; (b) there is sufficient separation of any traffic route for vehicles from doors or gates or from pedestrian traffic routes which lead into it; and (c) where vehicles and pedestrians use the same traffic route, there is sufficient separation between them.[25]

4.75 Doors and gates must be suitably constructed (including being fitted with any necessary safety devices).[26] In

---

[18] See generally Code of Practice, paras. 108–118.
[19] For the definition of dangerous substance, see reg. 13(7).
[20] reg. 12(5).
[21] reg. 14(1).
[22] reg. 15.
[23] reg. 16.
[24] regs. 17(1) and (2). It should be noted that reg. 17(2) and reg. 17(3) are, so far as is reasonably practicable, to be applied to existing workplaces. See reg. 17(5).
[25] reg. 17(3). Further detailed guidance is provided in the Code of Practice, paras. 159–182. It should be noted that some of the guidance provided in this section of the Code applies to existing workplaces.
[26] reg. 18(1).

particular, sliding doors must have a device to prevent them coming off their tracks during use, upward-opening doors must have a device to prevent them falling back, powered doors or gates must have suitable and effective features to prevent them causing injury by trapping any person and must be capable of being opened manually, and doors and gates which open either way must be constructed in such a way as to provide a clear view of the space close to both sides.[27]

4.76 Escalators and moving walkways must function safely, be equipped with any necessary safety devices and be fitted with one or more emergency stop controls which are easily identifiable and readily accessible.[28] Finally, there are detailed provisions on the provision of suitable and sufficient sanitary facilities, suitable and sufficient washing facilities, an adequate supply of wholesome drinking water, suitable and sufficient accommodation for clothing, suitable and sufficient facilities for changing clothing and suitable and sufficient rest facilities.[29] It should be noted that reg. 25(3) creates a specific obligation to ensure that in the provision of rest facilities suitable arrangements are made to protect non-smokers from tobacco smoke. Suitable facilities must also be provided for pregnant women or nursing mothers to rest.[30]

E.   MISCELLANEOUS GENERAL PROVISIONS ON SAFETY

4.77 There are still a number of the general safety provisions of the Factories Act 1961 which will continue to apply even after the "European" Regulations are implemented in full, though they are likely to be repealed as a result of the HSC review. There continue provisions which protect young persons[31] from cleaning prime movers or transmission machinery while they are in motion or from cleaning other parts of machinery where there is a risk of

---

[27] reg. 18(2).
[28] reg. 19.
[29] regs. 20–25.
[30] reg. 25(4).
[31] A "young person" is defined as a person between school-leaving age and 18 — Factories Act 1961, s. 176.

injury.[32] Young persons should also receive sufficient training and should be adequately supervised when working at dangerous machines which have been prescribed as such by the Minister.[33]

4.78 There are also specific provisions requiring that hoists and lifts be of good mechanical construction, sound material and adequate strength, and that they are properly maintained[34] and there are additional requirements when hoists or lifts are used to carry people.[35] Detailed provisions also exist as regards the use of chains, ropes or lifting tackle for the purpose of raising or lowering persons, goods or materials.[36] All parts and working gear, whether fixed or moveable, including the anchoring and fixing appliances, of every lifting machine[37] must be of good construction, sound materials, adequate strength and free from patent defects, and must be properly maintained.[38]

4.79 The Factories Act 1961, s. 30 contains detailed rules as regards dangerous fumes and lack of oxygen where work has to be done inside confined spaces in which dangerous fumes are liable to be present to such an extent as to involve risk of persons being overcome. Occupiers are also required to take all practicable steps to prevent explosions caused by any grinding, sieving or other process which gives rise to dust which is liable to explode or ignite. The practicable steps which must be taken involve enclosing the plant[39] used in the process, removing or preventing the accumulation of dust that may escape despite enclosure and excluding or effectively enclosing sources of ignition.[40] There is also a series of provisions controlling the construction, use,

---

[32] Factories Act 1961, s. 20. Formerly, this provision also applied to women, but this was repealed by the Employment Act 1989, s. 9(4) and Sched. 7.

[33] *Ibid.*, s. 21(1). See also the Dangerous Machines (Training of Young Persons) Order 1954 (S.I. 1954 No. 921).

[34] *Ibid.*, s. 22(1). The duty under this provision is absolute. See *Millar* v. *Galashiels Gas Co. Ltd*, 1949 S.C.(H.L.) 31.

[35] *Ibid.*, s. 23.

[36] *Ibid.*, s. 26.

[37] "Lifting machine" means a crane, crab, winch, teagle, pulley-block, gin wheel, transporter or runway. It does not include fork-lift trucks — *Walker* v. *Andrew Mitchell & Co. Ltd*, 1982 S.L.T. 266.

[38] *Ibid.*, s. 27.

[39] For guidance as to the meaning of "plant" see *Haigh* v. *Charles W. Ireland Ltd*, 1973 S.L.T. 142.

[40] See generally Factories Act 1961, s. 31.

maintenance and examination of steam boilers, restricting entry into such boilers except in specific circumstances and regulating the construction, maintenance and use of steam receivers, steam containers and air receivers.[41] Finally, section 39 requires that all gasholders must be of sound construction and properly maintained and be subjected to thorough examination.

---

[41] See Factories Act 1961, ss. 32–38.

CHAPTER 5

THE HEALTH AND SAFETY AT WORK ACT 1974

INTRODUCTION

5.1 It was noted in Chapter 4 that the pre-1974 statutory regime was workplace-specific in that the various statutes tended to regulate health and safety at particular places of work or to control specific industrial activities or substances. Each statute possessed its own body of inspectors to enforce its provisions and, as has already been noted, although these statutes made provision for criminal sanction the most likely legal action was a civil damages claim for breach of statutory duty. This regime was the subject of close scrutiny by a Committee of Inquiry chaired by Lord Robens which was appointed in 1970 by the then Secretary of State for Employment. The Committee's report was published on June 9, 1972.[1] It identified a number of weaknesses in the health and safety statutes of that time. It criticised the existing approach to health and safety as being outdated, overcomplex and inadequate and advocated a new approach which gave a far greater emphasis to the idea of self-regulation.

5.2 The Robens Committee believed that the single most important reason for accidents at work was apathy. This was largely because the individual experience of people at work was not conducive to safety awareness. Serious accidents at work were fortunately rare, but even rarer was any personal awareness of the hazards and diseases associated with an unhealthy working environment. For Robens it was vital to foster safety awareness through a variety of ways "through education and training, through the provision of better information and advice, through

---

[1] Cmnd. 5034.

practical, co-operative organisation and action, through legal sanctions where necessary, through research, publicity and so on."[2] One particular reason for the lack of awareness about health and safety was the amount and complexity of the law.[3] Not only was there too much law but the existing provisions were intrinsically unsatisfactory. The legislation was badly drafted, over-elaborate and too detailed and largely unintelligible to those who were most affected by it. In addition, the application of the law was largely negative since it tended to operate only after accidents had happened either through the prosecution of the employer or, more likely, by means of a civil damages action.

5.3 The fact that the legislation was largely dependent upon the type of workplace created another series of problems. First, it meant that many workers fell through the safety net. Robens accepted that something like five million workpeople were employed at premises not subject to any statutory provisions on occupational health and safety. Second, each statute possessed its own separate enforcement agency so that enforcement of health and safety statutes was fragmented and the pattern of control bewilderingly complex.[4] Third, the varying definitions of premises and activities in the various statutes affected the standing and operation of the inspectorates who were required to enforce the statutory provisions. Finally, the fragmentation of administrative responsibility for health and safety had implications for policy-formulation and law-making at national level. It was impossible for any government department with health and safety responsibilities to develop initiatives without close and extensive consultation with several other departments. The Robens Committee believed that such a state of affairs contributed to the obsolescence and inadequacies of many of the existing statutory provisions.

5.4 The Robens Committee believed that there were "severe practical limits on the extent to which progres-

---

[2] Robens, para. 13.

[3] Robens pointed out that there were nine main groups of safety statutes supported by nearly 500 statutory instruments which were being added to every year. See para. 28.

[4] Robens calculated that there were nine separate groups of safety statutes with enforcement bodies administered in England alone by five government departments, together with local authorities. See para. 32.

sively better standards of health and safety at work can be brought about through negative regulation by external agencies."[5] Thus the Committee's most significant recommendation was to argue for a much more effective self-regulating system. In Robens' view the primary responsibility for doing something about the risks of accident or disease must lie with those who create the risks and those who work with them.[6] Moreover, Robens recommended that the existing statutory provisions should be replaced by a comprehensive and orderly set of revised procedures under an enabling Act. The new Act should contain a clear statement of the basic principles of safety responsibility and should be supported by regulations and by non-statutory codes of practice. The basic principles would be enunciated by restating the common-law duties of employers and employees in broad terms. However, it was also necessary to revise, harmonise and update the existing statutory provisions in order to simplify their style and to reduce their number. Any new law should be extended to cover all employers and employees and the self-employed should also be covered where their conduct could affect other workers or the general public.

5.5 Robens also recommended that the existing separate inspectorates should be amalgamated to form a unified service under a new Authority and this new Authority should also have responsibility for the administration of the new Act. It is clear that the Robens Committee preferred administrative enforcement of the law over criminal sanctions, though they did accept that criminal penalties were appropriate where punishment would be generally expected and supported by the public. As far as administrative sanctions were concerned the most significant recommendation was Robens' proposal that inspectors should have the power to issue improvement notices (requiring remedial action with regard to specific faults) and prohibition notices (preventing the use of equipment until faults are remedied) with a right of appeal to industrial tribunals.

THE FRAMEWORK OF THE 1974 ACT

5.6 The framework of the 1974 Act reflects the philosophy of the Robens Committee and the provisions of the

[5] See para. 41.
[6] See para. 28.

Act implement the vast majority of their recommendations. First and foremost it creates a series of general
duties applicable to employers, the self-employed, persons in control of premises, manufacturers, suppliers,
importers and the like and employees. The general duties
are not workplace-based and apply to persons rather than
the occupiers of premises.[7] They are based largely on the
implied duties of the common law. The general duties do
not give rise to civil liability and the only court-based
remedy is by criminal sanction.[8] The 1974 Act, s.33(1)
makes it clear that it is an offence to fail to discharge a
duty under sections 2–7 or to contravene sections 8 and 9.
Additionally, section 15 empowers the Secretary of State
to make regulations consistent with the general purposes
of the Act and for a whole range of purposes which are
listed in Schedule Three. Such regulations are intended to
play a vital role in the repeal of the older provisions and
their progressive replacement by a system of regulations
and codes of practice aimed at improving and maintaining
health, safety and welfare standards. A breach of duty
created by any regulation made under section 15 does
give rise to civil liability except in so far as that regulation
provides otherwise.[9]

5.7 Consistent with the notion of self-regulation, the
1974 Act also grants powers to the Health and Safety
Commission to approve and issue Codes of Practice with
the consent of the Secretary of State and after consulting
any government department and such other bodies as
appears to the Commission to be appropriate.[10] Although
a failure to observe any provision of an approved code of
practice does not create any civil or criminal liability, a
breach of any provision of a code can be used in evidence
in criminal proceedings.[11]

5.8 The Act also ensures the integration of health and
safety law and creates the Health and Safety Commission
(HSC) which has overall responsibility for the general

---

[7] It has been estimated that between 7 and 8 million were brought
within the ambit of protective legislation by the 1974 Act. See Selwyn,
Law of Health and Safety at Work (1982), para. 3.2.
[8] 1974 Act, ss. 33(1) and 47(1).
[9] 1974 Act, s. 47(1).
[10] 1974 Act, s. 16(1) and (2).
[11] 1974 Act, s. 17.

operation of the unified health and safety regime.[12] In addition, there is also a Health and Safety Executive (HSE) which has operational responsibility for enforcing the relevant statutory provisions[13] on health and safety and also has the power to appoint inspectors.[14] Inspectors have important powers of entry, examination and investigation[15] and can issue both improvement notices[16] and prohibition notices.[17]

THE APPLICATION AND GENERAL PURPOSES OF THE ACT

5.9 As already noted, the 1974 Act applies generally to persons rather than to premises. However, there is an exclusion for persons who employ another, or are themselves employed, as domestic servants in a private household.[18] The Act and any regulations made under it apply to the Crown[19] subject to a number of important qualifications. Thus the provisions on improvement notices and prohibition notices do not apply to the Crown,[20] nor do the provisions as to offences.[21] Despite the fact that the provisions as to offences do not apply to the Crown they do apply to persons in the public service of the Crown as they apply to other persons.[22] Crown immunity no longer extends to a health authority or a health board[23]; nor does it apply to NHS Trusts.[24] The Act grants powers to Her

---

[12] 1974 Act, s. 11.
[13] This is defined as meaning the health, safety and welfare provisions of the 1974 Act, the health and safety regulations provided for by s. 15 and the existing statutory provisions like the Factories Act 1961 and the Offices, Shops and Railway Premises Act 1963.
[14] 1974 Act, ss. 18 and 19.
[15] 1974 Act, s. 20.
[16] 1974 Act, s. 21.
[17] 1974 Act, s. 22.
[18] 1974 Act, s. 51.
[19] 1974 Act, s. 48(1).
[20] 1974 Act, ss. 21–25.
[21] 1974 Act, ss. 33–42.
[22] 1974 Act, s. 48(2). It should be noted that the Crown employees are not prosecuted in lieu of the Crown. For a discussion of prosecution policy on this matter see "Employment," *Stair Memorial Encyclopaedia*, Vol. 9, para. 409.
[23] See National Health Service (Amendment) Act 1986, s. 2, repealed and replaced by the National Health Service and Community Care Act 1990. See, in particular, s. 60.
[24] 1990 Act, Pt. II.

Majesty by Order in Council to extend the operation of
the health, safety and welfare provisions of the Act
outside Great Britain.[25] This power has been exercised to
extend the 1974 Act within United Kingdom territorial
waters adjacent to Great Britain or a designated area[26] in
order to cover workers involved in the offshore oil and
gas industry and in mining and the loading, unloading
and fuelling of vessels and also divers.[27]

5.10 The health, safety and welfare provisions of the
1974 Act have effect with a view to

> (a)   securing the health, safety and welfare of
>   persons at work[28];
> (b)   protecting persons other than persons at work
>   against risks to health or safety arising out of
>   or in connection with persons at work;
> (c)   controlling the keeping and use of explosive
>   or highly flammable or otherwise dangerous
>   substances, and generally preventing the
>   unlawful acquisition, possession and use of
>   such substances; and
> (d)   controlling the emission into the atmosphere
>   of noxious or offensive substances from pre-
>   scribed premises.[29]

This provision sets the parameters for the operation of the
Act. However, it also influences the powers of HSC to
make regulations under section 15 and it also sets the
framework for the exercise of the general duty by HSC to
do such things and make such arrangements as it considers appropriate.[30] It is declared that risks arising out of
or in connection with the activities of persons at work are
to be treated as including risks attributable to the manner

---

[25] 1974 Act, s. 84(3).
[26] An area so designated by an Order made under the Continental Shelf
Act 1964.
[27] See Health and Safety at Work, Etc., Act 1974 (Application Outside
Great Britain) Order 1977 (S.I. 1977 No. 1232) as amended by S.I. 1989
No. 672.
[28] "Work" means work as an employee or as a self-employed person:
1974 Act, s. 52(1)(a).
[29] 1974 Act, s. 1(1), para. (d) is repealed by the Environmental Protection
Act 1990, s. 162, Sched. 16, Pt. I. However, at time of writing there has
been no appointed date of repeal.
[30] 1974 Act, s. 11(1).

of conducting an undertaking, the plant or substances used for the purposes of an undertaking and the condition of premises so used or any part of them.[31] The concept of "the relevant statutory provisions" is also central to the operation of the 1974 Act and many of the functions and powers which the 1974 Act creates apply in relation to these provisions. The relevant statutory provisions are the health, safety and welfare provisions of the 1974 Act, the health and safety regulations made under section 15 and the existing statutory provisions such as the Mines and Quarries Act 1954, the Factories Act 1961 and the Offices, Shops and Railway Premises Act 1963.[32]

The general duty

5.11 The 1974 Act, s. 2(1) lays down the basic general duty placed upon every employer which is to ensure, so far as reasonably practicable, the health, safety and welfare at work of all his employees. Like many of the other duties created by the 1974 Act the general duty under section 2(1) is not absolute but depends upon the notion of reasonable practicability. In considering the meaning of this phrase the courts have approved expressly the interpretation placed upon the same phrase in the earlier factories legislation.[33] It is clear that the mere fact that a precaution is physically possible does not mean that it is reasonably practicable.[34] Equally, the existence of a universal practice is not conclusive evidence that it is not reasonably practicable to use some other safer method: though it should be given as much weight as is appropriate depending on the surrounding circumstances of the case.[35] The correct approach is to make a computation in

---

[31] 1974 Act, s. 1(3).

[32] 1974 Act, s. 53(1).

[33] See, for example, the decision of McNeill J. in *West Bromwich Building Society v. Townsend* [1983] I.C.R. 257 applying the reasoning of the Court of Appeal in *Edwards v. NCB* [1949] 1 K.B. 704 and the House of Lords in *Marshall v. Gotham Co. Ltd* [1954] A.C. 360. See also the decision of the High Court of Justiciary in *Lockhart v. Kevin Oliphant Ltd*, 1993 S.L.T. 179 which also applies *Edwards* and *Marshall*.

[34] Dictum of Asquith L.J. in *Edwards* at p. 712 applied in both *Townsend* and *Lockhart*.

[35] *Martin v. Boulton & Paul (Steel Construction) Ltd* [1982] I.C.R. 367 (D.C.).

which the quantum of risk is balanced against the sacrifice in terms of cost, time or trouble involved in the measures necessary for averting that risk. Employers will only satisfy this test when they can show that there is a gross disproportion in the computation so that the risk is insignificant in relation to the sacrifice.[36] It should be noted that it is not the precautions in themselves which have to be reasonably practicable. It is the observance of the precautions that is required so far as may be reasonably practicable.[37] The 1974 Act, s. 40 makes it clear that in any criminal proceedings involving a failure to comply with a duty or requirement to do something so far as practicable or so far as reasonably practicable, the onus of proof is placed on the accused.

The particular duties

5.12 There is also a series of specific duties in section 2(2) which are without prejudice to the generality of an employer's duty under section 2(1). In *Bolton Metropolitan Borough Council v. Malrod Insulations Ltd*[38] Tudor Evans J. argued that the opening words of section 2(2) ensure that the general duty in section 2(1) is imported into section 2(2) and in *R. v. Swan Hunter Shipbuilders Ltd*[39] the Court of Appeal made it clear that the specific duties in section 2(2) were merely aspects of the wider general duty created by section 2(1). Nevertheless, where the prosecutor does rely on one of the specific duties in section 2(2) and the circumstances of the case do not establish this, it is not competent to fall back on the general duty in section 2(1) in order to obtain a conviction, since this does not give the accused fair notice of the charge against him.[40] It has also been argued in *West Bromwich Building Society v. Townsend*[41] that for a competent charge under section 2(1) to be laid particulars of the breach have to be given which indicate a breach independent of the specific duties listed in section 2(2). It was the view of McNeill J. in this case that section 2(1) was a safety net designed to catch any

---

[36] *per* Asquith L.J. in *Edwards* at p. 712.
[37] *per* Lord Keith of Avonholm in *Marshall* at p. 377.
[38] [1993] I.C.R. 358.
[39] [1981] I.C.R. 831.
[40] *Cardle v. David Carlaw Engineering (Glasgow) Ltd*, 1991 S.C.C.R. 807.
[41] [1983] I.C.R. 257.

breaches which could not be libelled under section 2(2). This latter view appears to underplay the importance of section 2(1) and does not necessarily accord with prosecution practice.[42]

5.13 Section 2(2) places specific duties on employers and fleshes out the broad general duty created by section 2(1). Thus the matters to which the general duty extends include in particular:

(a) the provision and maintenance of plant[43] and systems of work that are, so far as reasonably practicable, safe and without risks to health;

(b) arrangements for ensuring, so far as reasonably practicable, safety and absence of risks to health in connection with the use, handling, storage and transport of articles and substances[44];

(c) the provision of such information, instruction, training and supervision as is necessary to ensure, so far as reasonably practicable, the health and safety at work of employees;

(d) so far as reasonably practicable as regards any place of work under the employer's control, the maintenance of it in a condition that is safe and without risks to health and the provision and maintenance of means of access to and egress from it that are safe and without such risks;

(e) the provision and maintenance of a working environment for employees that is, so far as reasonably practicable, safe, without risks to health, and adequate as regards facilities and arrangements for their welfare at work.

These duties provide a statutory articulation of the common law obligations of employers towards their employees.[45]

---

[42] The matter is discussed in more detail in "Employment," *Stair Memorial Encyclopaedia,* Vol. 9, para. 427.

[43] "Plant" includes any machinery, equipment or appliance. See 1974 Act, s. 53(1).

[44] "Substance" means any natural or artificial substance (including micro-organisms), whether in solid or liquid form or in the form of a gas or vapour. See 1974 Act, s. 53(1).

[45] This matter is discussed by McNeill J. in *West Bromwich Building Society v. Townsend* [1983] I.C.R. 257 at p. 261.

5.14 The duty of employers under para. (a) to provide and maintain safe and risk-free plant and systems of work for their employees, applies to all employees "at work"[46] and is not confined to those engaged in the specific process for which the plant in question was made available.[47] The word "provide" has been given the same meaning as under factories legislation, namely "to supply or to make available."[48] This means that where there is a duty to provide safe plant, for example, and an employer makes available plant which is not safe there will be a breach of duty even though the unsafe plant in question has not been used or is not being used.[49]

5.15 The extent of the duty under para. (c) may be wider than first appears. In *R. v. Swan Hunter Shipbuilders Ltd,*[50] where the employers were not only charged with failing to provide a safe system of work under para. (a) but also with a failure to provide sufficient information and instruction under para. (c), the Court of Appeal held that this latter duty might entail providing information and instruction as to potential dangers to non-employees who are working in connection with an employer's business. In the present case, it was held that Swan Hunter did owe a duty under para. (c) to inform the employees of contractors of potential dangers, since the dangers arose in circumstances which affected the health and safety of the employers' own employees. The duty to inform is further extended by Regulations which require information relating to the health, safety and welfare of employees to be provided to them by means of posters or leaflets in the form approved by the Health and Safety Executive.[51]

5.16 The duty under para. (d) to provide a safe and risk-free place of work applies to any place which is under the

---

[46] Employees are at work throughout the time when they are in the course of their employment but not otherwise. See 1974 Act, s. 52(1)(b).

[47] *Bolton Metropolitan Borough Council v. Malrod Insulations Ltd* [1993] I.C.R. 358.

[48] See, for example, *Norris v. Syndic Manufacturing Co.* [1952] 2 Q.B. 135. Equally, there is no definition of the word "maintain" in the 1974 Act. If the courts' approach to the meaning of "provide" is followed, it is likely that they would apply the meaning of "maintained" to be found in the Factories Act 1961, s. 176(1), where it means maintained in an efficient state, in efficient working order, and in good repair.

[49] *Bolton Metropolitan Borough Council v. Malrod Insulations Ltd* [1993] I.C.R. 358.

[50] [1981] I.C.R. 831.

[51] See the Health and Safety Information for Employees Regulations 1989 (S.I. 1989 No. 682). Discussed at para. 6.3.

employer's control. The fact that the duty is not linked to ownership but to the employer's ability to control means that this duty could apply even where employees are working at the premises of another so long as the employer has control of those premises. HSC has suggested that "place of work" should have a broad meaning to include such things as open-air sites and temporary structures, and that the duty itself is wide-ranging.[52] Under para. (e) a safe working environment is likely to cover such things as heating, lighting, ventilation and noise and facilities for welfare at work should include the provision of washing facilities.[53]

Health and safety policy

5.17   The 1974 Act, s. 2(3) requires employers to prepare and as often as may be appropriate revise a written statement of their general policy with respect to the health and safety at work of their employees and the organisation and arrangements for the time being in force for carrying out that policy and to bring the statement and any revisions to the notice of all their employees. There is an exemption from this requirement for an employer who carries on an undertaking in which for the time being less than five employees are employed.[54] The basic duty placed upon the employer under section 2(3) is to prepare and thereafter revise a safety policy and to bring this policy and any revisions to the notice of all employees. This is the extent of the duty and there is no further statutory guidance on the structure or content of such policies nor any advice on how they should be brought to the attention of employees, though HSC has published guidance notes for such policies.[55] This provision has been criticised on the basis that it merely requires employers to prepare safety policies. It does not require them to be adequate.[56]

[52] See *A Guide to the Health and Safety at Work, etc., Act 1974.*
[53] See HSC Guide.
[54] See Employers' Health and Safety Policy Statements (Exception) Regulations 1975 (S.I. 1975 No. 1584) discussed in *Osborne v. Bill Taylor of Huyton Ltd* [1982] I.C.R. 168, where it was held that the phrase "for the time being" should be construed as meaning "at any one time."
[55] *Guidance Notes on Employers' Health and Safety Policy Statements for Health and Safety at Work* (1980).
[56] See Phil James, "Reforming British Health and Safety Law: A Framework for Discussion" (1992) 21 I.L.J. 83 at p. 87.

Employee involvement in health and safety

5.18 The 1974 Act, s. 2(4) empowers the Secretary of State to provide for the appointment by recognised trade unions of safety representatives from amongst the employees.[57] Such representatives must represent the employees in consultations with the employer. Moreover, employers have a duty to consult these representatives with a view to the making and maintenance of arrangements which will enable them and their employees to co-operate effectively in promoting and developing measures to ensure the employees' health and safety at work, and in checking the effectiveness of such measures.[58] There is a further duty on employers, if requested to do so by the safety representatives, to establish a safety committee which has the primary function of keeping under review the measures taken to ensure the health and safety at work of employees.[59]

5.19 The details of employee involvement in health and safety are provided by the Safety Representatives and Safety Committees Regulations 1977[60] and there is also an HSC Approved Code of Practice. Safety representatives can only be appointed by a recognised trade union[61] from amongst the employees where one or more employees are employed by an employer by whom it is recognised.[62] Employees appointed as safety representatives should so far as reasonably practicable have been employed by the employer throughout the preceding two years or have had at least two years' experience in similar employ-

---

[57] Under the 1974 Act, s. 2(5) it was possible for safety representatives to be appointed by workforce election. However, this provision was repealed by the Employment Protection Act 1975, ss. 116 and 125(3), Sched. 15, para. 2 and Sched. 18.

[58] 1974 Act, s. 2(6).

[59] 1974 Act, s. 2(7).

[60] S.I. 1977 No. 500 as amended by Management of Health and Safety at Work Regulations 1992 (S.I. 1992 No. 2051).

[61] "Recognised trade union" means an independent trade union as defined by the Trade Union and Labour Relations (Consolidation) Act 1992, s. 5 which the employer concerned recognises for the purpose of negotiations relating to or connected with one or more of the matters specified in s. 178 of that Act. See reg. 2(1).

[62] reg. 3(1). There is an exception for employees employed in a mine within the meaning of the Mines and Quarries Act 1954, s. 180. There are also special rules for members of the British Actors' Equity Association and the Musicians' Union. See reg. 8.

ment.[63] Employees cease to be safety representatives when the trade union which appointed them notifies the employer in writing that their appointment has been terminated or they cease to be employed at the workplace[64] or they resign.[65]

5.20 As well as having the general function under the 1974 Act, s. 2(4) to represent employees in consultation with the employer, safety representatives have the following functions:

(a)   to investigate potential hazards and dangerous occurrences at the workplace[66] (whether or not they are drawn to their attention by the employees they represent) and to examine the causes of accidents at the workplace;

(b)   to investigate complaints by any employee they represent relating to that employee's health, safety or welfare at work;

(c)   to make representations to the employer on matters arising from the above two paragraphs;

(d)   to make representations to the employer on general matters affecting the health, safety or welfare at work of employees at the workplace;

(e)   to carry out certain inspections;

(f)   to represent the employees they were appointed to represent in consultation at the workplace with inspectors of HSE and of any other enforcing authority;

(g)   to receive certain information from inspectors; and

---

[63] reg. 3(4).

[64] However, where safety representatives are appointed to represent employees at more than one workplace they need not cease to be safety representatives so long as they continue to be employed at any one of them. See reg. 3(3)(b).

[65] reg. 3(3)(a)–(c).

[66] "Workplace" means any place or places where the group or groups of employees a safety representative is appointed to represent are likely to work or are likely to frequent in the course of their employment or incidentally to it. See reg. 2(1).

(h)   to attend meetings of safety committees
where they attend in their capacity as safety
representatives in connection with any of the
above functions.[67]

5.21 Further guidance on the functions of safety representatives is provided by para. 5 of the Code of Practice.
It recommends that safety representatives should:

(a)   take all reasonably practical steps to keep
themselves informed of:
(i)   the legal requirements relating to the
health and safety of persons at work,
particularly those they represent:
(ii)   the particular hazards of the workplace
and the measures deemed necessary to
eliminate or minimise the risk deriving
from these hazards; and
(iii) the employer's health and safety policy
and the organisation and arrangements
for fulfilling that policy;
(b)   encourage co-operation between their
employer and the employees in promoting
and developing essential measures to ensure
the health and safety of employees and in
checking the effectiveness of these measures;
(c)   bring to the employer's notice normally in
writing[68] any unsafe or unhealthy conditions
or working practices or unsatisfactory
arrangements for welfare at work which come
to their attention whether on an inspection or
day-to-day observation. The report does not
imply that all other conditions and working
practices are safe and healthy or that the
welfare arrangements are satisfactory in all
other respects.

5.22 There are now additional duties of consultation
placed upon employers by the regulations.[69] Employers

---

[67] reg. 4(1)(a)–(h).
[68] The Code also recommends that making a written report does not
preclude a direct oral approach in the first instance, particularly in
situations where speedy remedial action is necessary. Oral discussion is
also most appropriate for minor matters.
[69] See reg. 4A inserted by the Management of Health and Safety at Work
Regulations 1992 (S.I. 1992 No. 2051), reg. 17, Sched.

must consult safety representatives in good time with regard to:

- (a) the introduction of any measure at the workplace which may substantially affect the health and safety of the employees the safety representatives concerned represent;
- (b) arrangements for nominating or appointing competent persons to assist them in undertaking the measures necesary to comply with the requirements and prohibitions imposed by the relevant statutory provisions[70];
- (c) any health and safety information they are required to provide to the employees by any relevant statutory provision;
- (d) the planning and organisation of any health and safety training they are required to provide to the employees by any relevant statutory provision; and
- (e) the health and safety consequences for the employees of the introduction and planning of new technologies into the workplace.[71]

Employers must also provide such facilities and assistance as safety representatives may reasonably require in order to carry out their functions.[72]

5.23 Safety representatives have the power to carry out inspections in three circumstances. First, they are entitled to inspect the workplace or a part of it if they have given the employer or his representative reasonable notice in writing of their intention to do so and they have not carried out an inspection in the previous three months.[73] However, further inspections can be carried out within the three-month period where there has been a substan-

---

[70] Under the Management of Health and Safety at Work Regulations 1992 (S.I. 1992 No. 2051), reg. 6, employers must appoint competent persons to assist in health and safety matters and under reg. 7(1)(b) they must appoint a sufficient number of competent persons to implement evacuation procedures from premises in the event of serious or imminent danger. Discussed at para. 6.21.

[71] reg. 4A(1)(a)–(e).

[72] reg. 4A(2).

[73] reg. 5(1). More frequent inspections can be carried out by agreement with the employer.

tial change in the conditions of work (whether because of
the introduction of new machinery or otherwise) or new
information has been published by HSC or HSE relevant
to the hazards of the workplace since the last inspection
and the employer has been consulted before the intended
inspection.[74] The employer is required to provide such
facilities and assistance as the safety representatives may
reasonably require (including facilities for independent
investigation by them and private discussion with the
employees) for the purposes of an inspection, but nothing
in this provision precludes the employer or his representative from being present in the workplace during an
inspection.[75]

5.24 Safety representatives also have specific inspection
functions where there has been a notifiable accident or
dangerous occurrence in a workplace or a notifiable
disease[76] has been contracted there. In such circumstances
they may inspect the part of the workplace concerned and
so far as is necessary for determining the cause they may
inspect any other part of the workplace and where it is
reasonably practicable to do so they must notify the
employer or his representative of their intention to carry
out the inspection. Such an inspection will only be
appropriate when it is safe for an inspection to be carried
out and the interests of employees in the group which
safety representatives are appointed to represent might be
involved.[77] As with the general inspection power,
employers are required to provide such facilities and
assistance as the safety representatives may reasonably
require, though the employer can be present on the
premises during the inspection.[78]

5.25 The third inspection power which safety representatives possess is to inspect relevant documents. If
safety representatives have given the employer reasonable notice, they are entitled to inspect and to take copies

---

[74] reg. 5(2).
[75] reg. 5(3).
[76] "Notifiable accident or dangerous occurrence" and "notifiable disease" mean any accident, dangerous occurrence or disease, as the case
may be, notice of which is required to be given by virtue of any of the
relevant statutory provisions. See reg. 6(3).
[77] See generally, reg. 6(1).
[78] reg. 6(2).

of any document relevant to the workplace or to the employees they represent which the employer is required to keep under any relevant statutory provision except the health records of identifiable individuals.[79] Employers must also make available to safety representatives the information, within their knowledge, necessary for safety representatives to fulfil their functions except:

(a) any information the disclosure of which would be against the interests of national security; or

(b) any information which they could not disclose without contravening a statutory prohibition; or

(c) any information relating specifically to individuals, unless they have consented to its disclosure; or

(d) any information the disclosure of which would, for reasons other than its effect on health, safety and welfare at work, cause substantial injury to the employer's undertaking or, where the information was supplied by some other person, to the undertaking of that other person; or

(e) any information obtained by the employer for the purpose of bringing, prosecuting or defending any legal proceedings.

5.26 The Code of Practice recommends that the sorts of information which should be provided by employers should include:

(a) information about the plans and performance of their undertaking and any changes proposed in so far as they affect the health, safety and welfare at work of their employees;

(b) information of a technical nature about hazards to health and safety and precautions deemed necessary to eliminate or minimise them, in respect of machinery, plant, equipment, processes, systems of work and substances in use at work, including any relevant information provided by consultants or

---

[79] reg. 7(1).

designers or by the manufacturer, importer or supplier of any article or substance used, or proposed to be used, at work by their employees;

(c)　information which the employer keeps relating to the occurrence of any accident, dangerous occurrence or notifiable industrial disease and any statistical records relating to such matters;

(d)　any other information specifically related to matters affecting the health and safety of employees, including the results of any measurements taken in the course of checking the effectiveness of health and safety arrangements; and

(e)　information on articles or substances which an employer issues to homeworkers.

Safety committees

5.27 A safety committee must be established by an employer where at least two safety representatives request in writing that the employer establish one.[80] Where such a request is made employers must comply with the following procedure:

(a)　they must consult with the safety representatives who made the request and with the representatives of recognised trade unions whose members work in any workplace where it is proposed that the safety committee will function;

(b)　they must post a notice stating the composition of the committee and the workplace(s) to be covered by it in a place where it may easily be read by the employees; and

(c)　the committee must be established not later than three months after the request for it.

As already noted, the general function of a safety committee is to keep under review the measures taken to ensure the health and safety at work of the employees. It

[80] reg. 9(1).

is obvious that the functions of safety representatives and those of safety committees are different. The functions of safety representatives are much more pro-active whereas the basic function of safety committees is to consider and appraise management's health and safety policies. It is vital, therefore, that there is effective co-ordination between the two groups.

The right to time off

5.28 An employer must permit a safety representative to take such time off with pay during the employee's working hours as is necessary for the purposes of his functions[81] and to undergo such training in aspects of those functions as may be reasonable in all the circumstances having regard to any relevant provisions of an HSC approved code of practice relating to time off for training.[82] The Code of Practice recommends that as soon as possible after their appointment safety representatives should be permitted time off with pay to attend basic training facilities approved by the TUC or by the union which appointed them. Further training, similarly approved, should be undertaken where the safety representative has special responsibilities or where such training is necessary to meet changes in circumstances or relevant legislation.

5.29 The length of such training cannot be rigidly prescribed. However, the Code recommends that basic training should take into account the functions of safety representatives, of safety committees and of trade union policies and practices in relation to:

(a) the legal requirements relating to health and safety at work, particularly of the group of persons they directly represent;

(b) the nature and extent of workplace hazards, and the measures necessary to eliminate or minimise them; and

---

[81] Namely, the general functions in the 1974 Act, s. 2(4) and the specific functions listed in reg. 4(1)(a)–(h).

[82] reg. 4(2). See the Code of Practice: Time Off for the Training of Safety Representatives (1978).

> (c) the health and safety policy of employers, and the organisation and arrangements for fulfilling those practices.

The Code also suggests that safety representatives will have to acquire new skills in order to carry out their functions, including safety inspections, and in using basic sources of legal and official information and information provided by the employer on health and safety matters.

5.30 The Code also explains the obligations of trade unions as far as the training of safety representatives is concerned. When a trade union wishes a safety representative to receive relevant training it should inform management of the course that it has approved and supply a copy of the syllabus, indicating its contents, if the employer asks for it. Unions should give the employer at least a few weeks' notice regarding the safety representatives who have been nominated for a particular course and the numbers attending should be those which are reasonable in the circumstances, bearing in mind such factors as the frequency of such courses and the operational requirements of the employer. As the Code makes clear, many of these issues are best resolved by agreement between management and unions. In considering whether time off for training is necessary, it has been held that the Code carries great weight but it is not decisive of the issue.[83] Further, although the Code recommends that training courses should be approved by the TUC or a union this is not a mandatory legal requirement.[84] Thus, although union approval for courses is a factor to be taken into account, it is not illegal for employers to organise their own courses. In such a case it will be a question for the industrial tribunal to decide whether an employer-provided course is adequate, particularly as regards the representational responsibilities of safety representatives.[85]

5.31 Where the employer has either failed to permit a safety representative to take time off or has failed to pay

---

[83] *White v. Pressed Steel Fisher* [1980] I.R.L.R. 176 (E.A.T.).
[84] *Cf.* the provisions on time-off for union duties in the Trade Union and Labour Relations (Consolidation) Act 1992, s. 168. It is provided by s. 168(2) that any training courses in aspects of industrial relations must be approved by the TUC or an independent trade union.
[85] *White v. Pressed Steel Fisher* [1980] I.R.L.R. 176 (E.A.T.).

him for any time off, there is a right of complaint to an industrial tribunal.[86] A safety representative must submit such a complaint within three months of the date when the failure occurred or within such further period as the tribunal considers reasonable where it is satisfied that it was not reasonably practicable for the complaint to be presented within the three months.[87] Where the tribunal finds the complaint to be well-founded it will make a declaration to that effect and can award compensation of such amount as it considers just and equitable in all the circumstances having regard to the employer's default and the employee's loss.[88] Where the tribunal finds that the employer has failed to pay the employee the whole or part of the required amount, the tribunal must order the employer to pay to the employee the amount which it finds due.[89]

Protection of safety representatives and safety committee members

5.32 There is now legislation which protects safety representatives and members of safety committees from being subjected to any detriment[90] and which makes it unfair[91] to dismiss them where they have performed, or propose to perform, any functions as a safety representative or a member of a safety committee.[91a] There are also protections for employees who have been designated by the employer to carry out activities in connection with preventing or reducing health and safety risks and for employees who bring to the employer's attention harmful circumstances where there is either no safety representative nor any safety committee or it was not reasonably

[86] The Safety Representatives and Safety Committees Regulations 1977, reg. 11(1).
[87] reg. 11(2).
[88] reg. 11(3).
[89] reg. 11(4).
[90] See the Employment Protection (Consolidation) Act 1978, s. 22A(1)(b) as inserted by the Trade Union Reform and Employment Rights Act 1993, s. 28, Sched. 5, para. 1; and see para. 7.24.
[91] See EPCA, s. 57A(1)(b) inserted by the Trade Union Reform and Employment Rights Act 1993, s. 28, Sched. 5, para. 3. There is no qualifying period nor upper age-limit applicable to health and safety dismissals. See EPCA, ss. 64(3) and (4) as amended by the 1993 Act.
[91a] And see Chap. 7, para. 7.29.

practicable for the employee to raise the matter through them.[92] Employees who leave or propose to leave or refuse to return to their place of work in circumstances of danger which they reasonably believe to be serious and imminent or who take or propose to take appropriate steps to protect themselves or other persons from danger in similar circumstances are also protected.[93]

Duties of employers and the self-employed to persons other than employees

5.33 Employers must conduct their undertakings in such a way as to ensure, so far as reasonably practicable, that persons not in their employment who may be affected thereby are not exposed to risks to their health and safety.[94] It is important to ascertain what is required of employers as regards the conduct of their undertakings. In *RMC Roadstone Products Ltd v. Jester*[94a] the Divisional Court held that an employer's mere capacity or opportunity to exercise control over the activity of an independent contractor was not enough to bring that activity with the ambit of section 3(1). It was necessary to show either the exercise of some actual control or a duty to exercise such control. This approach has now been disapproved by the Court of Appeal in *R. v. Associated Octel Co. Ltd*[94b] where it was stated that it was not necessary to show that the employer had some actual control over how the work is done. Instead the ingredients of an offence under section 3(1) are that the accused is (a) an employer (b) who so conducts his undertaking (c) as to expose to risk to health and safety (d) a person not employed by him (e) who may be affected by such conduct of the accused's undertakings. This means that if there is a risk of injury to the health and safety of the employees of an independent contractor or members of the public a prima facie case of liability will be established when there is actual injury as a result of the conduct of that operation. A similar duty also

---

[92] EPCA, ss. 22A(1)(a) and (c) (detriment) and ss. 57A(1)(a) and (c) (dismissal). See also paras. 5.40 and 7.24.
[93] EPCA, ss. 22A(1)(d) and (e) (detriment) and ss. 57A(1)(d) and (e) (dismissal).
[94] 1974 Act, s. 3(1).
[94a] [1994] I.C.R. 456; [1994] I.R.L.R. 330.
[94b] [1994] I.R.L.R. 540.

applies to the self-employed to conduct their undertakings in such a way as to ensure that they and other persons (not being their employees) are not exposed to health and safety risks.[95] The Secretary of State also has the power, by regulations, to prescribe the circumstances and the manner in which employers and the self-employed must give prescribed information to persons other than employees who may be affected by the way that the undertaking is conducted as might affect their health and safety.[96]

5.34 It is clear that the general duty provided for by section 3(1) can impose a duty to inform persons who are not the employer's own employees. In *R. v. Swan Hunter Shipbuilders Ltd*[97] the Court of Appeal held that the duty under section 3(1) to conduct the undertaking in such a way as to avoid risks to the health and safety of persons other than employees was wide enough to include an obligation to provide information and instruction to the employees of others. The fact that section 3(3) specifically requires an employer to give information to persons not in his employment does not limit any obligation under section 3(1), since the former provision refers only to limited information in limited circumstances to be prescribed by regulations which have not yet been made. This approach has been followed in Scotland where it has been confirmed that there is no mutual inconsistency between section 3(1) and section 3(3), since section 3(3) is limited in application and relates only to prescribed cases, prescribed circumstances, and prescribed information in a prescribed manner.[98] On the other hand, section 3(1) requires information and instruction on how to avoid risks to health and safety subject only to the requirement of reasonable practicability.

5.35 It is also the case that the conduct of the undertaking is not confined to the hours when the employer's own

---

[95] 1974 Act, s. 3(2). The scope of this duty has been amended by the Genetically Modified Organisms (Contained Use) Regulations 1992 (S.I. 1992 No. 3217) and the Health and Safety (Dangerous Pathogens) Regulations 1981 (S.I. 1981 No. 1011) so as to apply to any activity involving genetic modification or dangerous pathogens.

[96] 1974 Act, s. 3(3). At time of writing no regulations have been made under this provision.

[97] [1981] I.C.R. 831.

[98] See *Carmichael v. Rosehall Engineering Works Ltd*, 1984 S.L.T. 40; [1983] I.R.L.R. 480.

employees are actually in the premises doing their jobs.[99] Section 3(1) is more general in scope and does not depend upon the process of the undertaking being actively carried on so that it will also apply when the premises have been closed for maintenance. A prosecution under section 3(1) is competent so long as there is a risk of exposure to danger: it is not necessary to prove that the risk has actually materialised. Thus in a case involving the risk of legionella infection from an air-conditioning cooling tower it was sufficient for conviction merely to prove that legionella bacteria might emerge so as to expose members of the public to the possibility of danger: it was not necessary also to show that the bacteria did get into the atmosphere and were available to be inhaled.[1]

Duties of persons concerned with premises to persons other than employees

5.36 The 1974 Act also imposes general duties on owners, occupiers and others, such as maintenance contractors, as regards their control of non-domestic premises. A duty is owed by persons to those who are not their employees but who use non-domestic premises[2] made available to them as a place of work or as a place where they may use plant or substances provided for their use there and the duty applies to such premises and other non-domestic premises used in connection with them.[3] The duty applies to persons having control of any premises or matter in connection with the carrying on by them of a trade, business or other undertaking (whether for profit or not).[4] The application of this duty is wide enough to cover the common parts of a block of flats (the

[99] *R. v. Mara* [1987] I.C.R. 165.
[1] *R. v. Board of Trustees of the Science Musem* [1993] I.C.R. 876; [1994] I.R.L.R. 25.
[2] There is no specific definition of non-domestic premises in the 1974 Act. However, s. 53(1) defines "domestic premises" as meaning premises occupied as a private dwelling (including any garden, yard, garage, outhouse or other appurtenance which is not used in common by the occupants of more than one such dwelling), and directs that "non-domestic premises" should be construed accordingly. It is wide enough to cover a children's indoor play centre. See *Moualem v. Carlisle City Council, The Times,* July 8, 1994.
[3] 1974 Act, s. 4(1).
[4] 1974 Act, s. 4(4).

hall, landing and staircases and lifts) since the common
parts are not domestic premises and, therefore, in accordance with section 53(1) if they are premises at all they
must be non-domestic premises.[5] Such common parts will
be made available as a place of work or as a place where
plant and substances might be used as required by section
4(1) when lift engineers or electricians attend at the block
to maintain or repair the lifts or electrical installations or
when the common parts are redecorated by contractors.[6]

5.37 Any person who has, to any extent, control of
premises[7] or of the means of access to or egress from
them or of any plant or substance in such premises has a
duty to take such measures as it is reasonable for a person
in his position to take to ensure, so far as is reasonably
practicable, that the premises, all means of access or
egress and any plant or substance are safe and without
risks to health.[8] This provision requires a prosecutor to
establish three things. The prosecutor must prove, first,
that the premises are unsafe and constitute a risk to
health, second, what persons have at that time any
degree of control of those premises and, third, that it is
reasonable for one or more of the persons having a degree
of control to take measures which would ensure safety.
Once a prosecutor has fulfilled these requirements the
onus shifts to the accused to prove that it was not
reasonably practicable to take the measures in question.[9]
The reasonableness of the measures is to be judged in the
light of the person's knowledge of the anticipated use for
which the premises have been made available and of the
extent of his control and knowledge, if any, of the actual
use thereafter. But the person need not take further
measures against unknown and unexpected events.[10] A
person is to be treated as a person who has control of

[5] *Westminster City Council v. Select Management Ltd* [1985] I.C.R. 353.
[6] *Select Management, ibid.* See, in particular, the judgment of Parker L.J.
at p. 357.
[7] The fact that the control can be to any extent means that this provision
has been widely construed. In *T. Kilroe & Sons Ltd v. Gower* [1983]
Crim.L.R. 548 contractors who were hired to demolish a factory were
held to have sufficient control of the premises even though most of the
work had been delegated to sub-contractors.
[8] 1974 Act, s. 4(2).
[9] *H.M. Inspector of Factories v. Austin Rover Group Ltd* [1989] I.R.L.R. 404
(H.L.).
[10] See the speech of Lord Jauncey, *ibid.*, at pp. 410–411.

premises when he has, by virtue of any contract or tenancy, an obligation of any extent in relation to the maintenance or repair of any non-domestic premises or of any means of access to or egress from them or as regards the safety or health risks arising from plant or substances in those premises.[11]

MANAGEMENT OF HEALTH AND SAFETY AT WORK REGULATIONS

5.38 The above provisions constitute the core duties created by the Act since they apply to employers as regards their own employees (s. 2), employers and the self-employed as regards persons who are not their employees (s. 3) and the controllers of premises (s. 4). Persons who may owe duties under any of these provisions should also take into account the provisions of the Management of Health and Safety at Work Regulations 1992.[12] These regulations provide more specific direction as to how to carry out the general duties of sections 2–4 and, most importantly, introduce the principle of risk assessment. Regulation 3(1) requires every employer to make a suitable and sufficient assessment of the risks to the health and safety of his employees to which they are exposed while they are at work and the risks to the health and safety of others who are not in his employment arising out of the conduct of his undertaking. Where the persons working in the undertaking include women of child-bearing age and the work is of a kind which could involve risk to the health and safety of a new or expectant mother[12a] or to that of her baby, the risk assessment must include an assessment of risk as regards any processes or working conditions, or physical, biological or chemical agents which might affect the health and safety of that mother or baby.[12b] Where the risk cannot be avoided by

---

[11] 1974 Act, s. 43.

[12] S.I. 1992 No. 2051, as amended by S.I. 1994 No. 2865. These Regulations are also discussed at para. 6.21.

[12a] "New or expectant mother" means an employee who is pregnant; who has given birth within the previous six months; or who is breastfeeding. See reg. 1(2).

[12b] reg. 13A(1) as inserted by S.I. 1994 No. 2865, reg. 2(3). References to risk, in relation to risk from any infectious or contagious disease, are references to a level of risk at work which is in addition to the level to which a new or expectant mother may be expected to be exposed outside the workplace—reg. 13A(4).

taking action which is required to be taken under the relevant statutory provisions the employer must, if it is reasonable to do so, and would avoid such risks, alter the new or expectant mother's working conditions or hours of work.[12c] If it is not reasonable to alter the working conditions or hours of work, or if it would not avoid such risk, the employer must suspend the employee from work for so long as is necessary to avoid that risk.[12d] The duties to alter working conditions or hours of work and the duty to suspend from work do not apply unless the new or expectant mother has notified the employer in writing that she is pregnant, has given birth within the previous six months, or is breastfeeding.[12e] It should be noted that unlike the rest of the Management Regulations the risk assessment duties owed by an employer to new or expectant mothers do give rise to civil liability.[12f] Generally the assessment is to be done for the purpose of identifying the measures the employer needs to take to comply with the requirements and prohibitions imposed by the relevant statutory provisions. A similar assessment should be conducted by self-employed persons as regards risks to their own health and safety and the health and safety of persons not in their employment arising out of the conduct of their undertaking.[13] Employers and the self-employed are also required to keep their risk assessments under review and to make any necessary changes.[14] Employers who employ five or more employees must record the significant findings of the assessment and any group of employees who are especially at risk.[15]

5.39 The purpose of risk assessment is best described by the Approved Code of Practice which has been produced by HSC. It declares:

"The purpose of the risk assessment is to help the employer or self-employed person to determine

---

[12c] reg. 13A(2).

[12d] reg. 13A(3).

[12e] reg. 13C(1). The employer is also entitled to request the employee to produce a certificate from a registered medical practitioner or a registered midwife showing that she is pregnant—reg. 13C(2)(a).

[12f] regs. 15(1) and (2) as amended by S.I. 1994 No. 2865, reg. 2(5); *i.e.* those created by reg. 13A(1).

[13] reg. 3(2).

[14] reg. 3(3).

[15] reg. 3(4).

what measures should be taken to comply with the employer's or self-employed person's duties under the 'relevant statutory duties.' This phrase covers the general duties in the [1974 Act] and the more specific duties in the various Acts and Regulations (including these Regulations) associated with [it]. Regulation 3 does not itself stipulate the measures to be taken as a result of the risk assessment. The measures in each workplace will derive from compliance with other health and safety duties . . . taking carefully into account the risk assessment. In essence, the risk assessment guides the judgment of the employer or the self-employed person, as to the measures they ought to take to fulfil their statutory obligations."[16]

5.40 The Regulations also place a number of additional duties on employers which complement and enhance the basic requirement of risk assessment. Employers must make and give effect to appropriate health and safety arrangements, having regard to the nature of the activities and size of undertaking, for the effective planning, organisation, control, monitoring, and review of preventive and protective measures[17] and provide such health surveillance as is appropriate to the health and safety risks identified by the assessment.[18] Competent persons can be appointed by employers to assist them in undertaking the measures necessary to comply with the requirements and prohibitions of the relevant statutory provisions.[19] Employers must also establish procedures to be followed in the event of serious and imminent danger to persons at work in the undertaking.[20] They must nominate a sufficient number of people to implement these procedures as far as evacuation from the premises is concerned, and no employee should have access to a restricted area unless he has received adequate health and safety instructions.[21]

---

[16] See paras. 7 and 8.
[17] reg. 4(1). Employers with five or more employees must record their arrangements — reg. 4(2). "Preventive and protective measures" are the measures which have been identified in the assessment as the measures required to be taken so as to comply with the requirements and prohibitions imposed by the relevant statutory provisions — reg. 1(2).
[18] reg. 5.
[19] reg. 6(1).
[20] reg. 7(1)(a).
[21] regs. 7(1)(b) and (c).

The regulations also ensure that employees become aware of these arrangements by requiring the employer to provide them with comprehensible and relevant information on:

(a) the risks to their health and safety identified by the assessment;

(b) the preventive and protective measures;

(c) procedures for serious and imminent danger;

(d) the identity of persons nominated to implement evacuation procedures; and

(e) the risks associated with any shared workplace.[22]

5.41 Further, the Regulations also contain provisions which are relevant to the duties owed by controllers of premises under the 1974 Act, s. 4. Employers who share a workplace must co-operate with one another so as to ensure compliance with the requirements and prohibitions of the relevant statutory provisions, take all reasonable steps to co-ordinate those measures and inform the other employers concerned of the health and safety risks to their employees.[23] Employers and self-employed persons must ensure that the employer of any employees from an outside undertaking who are working in their undertaking are provided with comprehensible information on the risks to those employees' health and safety and the measures which have been taken to comply with the requirements and prohibitions of the relevant statutory provisions.[24]

OTHER DUTIES IN 1974 ACT

Duties of persons in control of premises

5.42 The 1974 Act, s. 5, places duties on persons having control of a prescribed class[25] of premises to use the best

---

[22] reg. 8.

[23] reg. 9(1). These duties also extend to the self-employed — reg. 9(2).

[24] reg. 10(1).

[25] See the Health and Safety (Emissions into the Atmosphere) Regulations 1983 (S.I. 1983 No. 943) which prescribe the class of premises covered by this provision and the substances which are to be treated as noxious or offensive.

practicable means for preventing the emission into the atmosphere from the premises of noxious or offensive substances and for rendering harmless and inoffensive such substances as may be emitted. The provision has been the subject of considerable amendment by the Environmental Protection Act 1990, s. 162(1), Sched. 15, para. 14, and is prospectively repealed by section 162(2) and Sched. 16, Part I of that Act from a date to be appointed.

Duties of manufacturers as to articles for use at work

5.43 The 1974 Act, s. 6, imposes a series of duties in respect of articles and substances for use at work. This provision has been the subject of considerable amendment, most importantly by the Consumer Protection Act 1987. The basic thrust of the provision is to place duties on any person who designs, manufactures, imports or supplies[26] any article for use at work[27] or any article of fairground equipment. The duties only operate in relation to things done in the course of a trade, business or other undertaking and to matters within their control.[28] The key duties are:

(a) to ensure, so far as reasonably practicable, that the article is so designed and constructed that it will be safe and without risks to health at all times when it is being set, used, cleaned or maintained by a person at work;

(b) to carry out or arrange for the carrying out of such testing and examination as may be necessary for performing the above duty;

(c) to take such steps as are necessary to secure that persons supplied with an article are provided with adequate information about the use for which the article has been designed or

---

[26] "Supply" means supplying articles by way of sale, lease, hire or hire-purchase, whether as principal or agent for another — 1974 Act, s. 53(1).
[27] It is necessary that the article be designed, etc., for use at work. This requirement is criticial and it will mean, for example, that there is unlikely to be any protection under s. 6(1) when the article is being tested to discover whether it is suitable for use at work. See *McKay v. Unwin Pyrotechnics Ltd* [1991] Crim.L.R. 547.
[28] 1974 Act, s. 6(7).

has been tested and about any conditions necessary to ensure that it is safe and without risks to health; and

(d)   to take such steps as are necessary to secure, so far as is reasonably practicable, that revisions of the information are provided as are necessary by reason of its becoming known that anything gives rise to a serious risk to health and safety.[29]

5.44   The 1974 Act, s. 6(2) requires designers and manufacturers of articles for use at work to carry out any necessary research with a view to the discovery, and so far as is reasonably practicable, the elimination or minimisation of health and safety risks. There are also duties placed upon those responsible for the erection or installation of any article for use at work to ensure, so far as is reasonably practicable, that nothing about the way in which the article is erected or installed makes it unsafe or a risk to health.[30] Manufacturers, importers and suppliers of any substance must:

(a)   ensure, so far as is reasonably practicable, that the substance will be safe and without risk to health at all times when it is being used, handled, processed, stored or transported by a person at work or in non-domestic premises;

(b)   carry out or arrange for the carrying out of any necessary testing and examination;

(c)   take such steps as are necessary to secure that persons supplied with the substance are provided with adequate information about any risks to health and safety to which the inherent properties of the substance may give rise, about the results of any relevant tests and about any necessary conditions as regards the use, etc. or disposal of the substance; and

(d)   take such steps as are necessary to secure, so far as is reasonably practicable, that all necessary revisions of information are provided.[31]

[29]   1974 Act, s. 6(1)(a)–(d).
[30]   1974 Act, s. 6(3).
[31]   1974 Act, s. 6(4)(a)–(d).

Duties of employees at work

5.45 It is the duty of employees to take reasonable care for the health and safety of themselves and of other persons who may be affected by their acts or omissions at work.[32] Employees also owe a duty of co-operation as regards any duty or requirement imposed on the employer or any other person by any of the relevant statutory provisions so far as is necessary to enable that duty or requirement to be performed or complied with.[33] Both the duty of care and the duty of co-operation only apply while the employee is at work. Employees are at work throughout the time that they are in the course of their employment, but not otherwise.[34] This issue was discussed in *Coult v. Szuba*,[35] where the court observed that, although there was extensive authority on the meaning of course of employment in a civil law context, this was the first time that the phrase had had to be interpreted in the context of penal legislation. In the context of the civil cases it is necessary for the phrase to be liberally construed, but that approach should not be applied when interpreting criminal legislation. At the end of the day the issue is primarily one of fact. However, the mere fact that an employee has clocked in for work does not necessarily mean that he is automatically within the course of his employment.

5.46 The duties of employees have been extended by the Management of Health and Safety at Work Regulations 1992. Under regulation 12(1) employees have duties to use any machinery, equipment, dangerous substance, transport equipment, means of production or safety device provided by the employer in accordance with any training and instruction in the use of that equipment which is provided by the employer in compliance with the requirements and prohibitions of any relevant statutory provision. Moreover, employees must also inform

---

[32] 1974 Act, s. 7(a). This duty can undoubtedly extend to members of the public and may be judged by reference to the employee's seniority. See *Skinner v. H.M. Advocate*, 1994 S.C.C.R. 316.

[33] 1974 Act, s. 7(b).

[34] 1974 Act, s. 52(1)(b).

[35] [1982] I.C.R. 380. See also *Thomson v. Barbour*, 1994 S.C.C.R. 485 where the fact that the employee could not be proved to have been at work at the critical time was considered to be fatal to the prosecutor's case.

their employer or any other employee with specific responsibility for health and safety of any work situation which could reasonably be considered a serious and immediate danger to health and safety, and of any matter which could reasonably be considered to represent a shortcoming in the employer's protection arrangements for health and safety. These later duties only arise where the situation or matter either affects the health and safety of the employee or arises out of or in connection with his own activities at work, and has not previously been reported to the employer or to any other employee.[36]

Other duties

5.47 No person shall intentionally or recklessly interfere with or misuse anything provided in the interests of health, safety and welfare in pursuance of any of the relevant statutory provisions.[37] HSC has made it clear that the things which are covered by this provision include fire escapes and fire extinguishers, perimeter fencing, warning notices for particular hazards, protective clothing, guards for machinery and special containers for dangerous substances.[38] It must be shown that the thing was provided in the interests of health, safety or welfare. Thus it is not a breach of this provision to interfere with or misuse a thing which has been provided for another purpose.[39]

5.48 No employer is to levy or permit to be levied on any employee any charge in respect of anything done or provided in pursuance of any specific requirement of the relevant statutory provisions.[40] This prohibition against charging only operates where there is a specific statutory requirement to do or provide a thing. It will not apply in relation to the general duties of sections 2–6 of the 1974 Act which, in any case, are usually hedged around by requirements of reasonable practicability.[41]

---

[36] See generally, reg. 12(2).
[37] 1974 Act, s. 8.
[38] Discussed in *Stair Memorial Encyclopaedia*, Vol. 9, para. 467.
[39] *Tearle v. Cheverton & Laidler Ltd* (1969) 7 K.I.R. 364 (a case under the Factories Act 1961, s. 143(1) (repealed)).
[40] 1974 Act, s. 9.
[41] See, for example, *Associated Dairies Ltd v. Hartley* [1979] I.R.L.R. 171.

ADMINISTRATION

5.49 The 1974 Act creates two bodies corporate to be called the Health and Safety Commission (HSC) and the Health and Safety Executive (HSE).[42] HSC consists of a chairman appointed by the Secretary of State and between six and nine other members who are also appointed by the Secretary of State.[43] Before appointing the members of HSC, the Secretary of State is required to consult with organisations representing employers (for three members), organisations representing employees (for three other members) and as to any other members, organisations representing local authorities and such other organisations, including professional bodies, the activities of whose members are concerned with the general purposes of the Act.[44] HSE consists of three persons of whom one is appointed by HSC with the approval of the Secretary of State to be director and the other two are appointed by HSC with the approval of the Secretary of State and after consulting the director.[45] The functions of HSC and HSE, and of their officers and servants, are performed on behalf of the Crown.[46]

5.50 HSC has the general duty to do such things and make such arrangements as it considers appropriate for the general purposes of the Act.[47] This general function is subject to the duty (a) to submit to the Secretary of State from time to time particulars of what it proposes to do in order to perform its functions; (b) to ensure that its activities are in accordance with proposals approved by the Secretary of State, and (c) to give effect to any directions given by the Secretary of State.[48] HSC also has the following specific duties:

(a) to assist and encourage persons concerned with matters relevant to the general purposes to further those purposes;

(b) to make such arrangements as it considers appropriate for the carrying out of research, the publication of the results of research and

[42] 1974 Act, s. 10(1).
[43] 1974 Act, s. 10(2).
[44] 1974 Act, s. 10(3)(a)–(c).
[45] 1974 Act, s. 10(5).
[46] 1974 Act, s. 10(7).
[47] 1974 Act, s. 11(1).
[48] 1974 Act, s. 11(3).

the provision of training and information in connection with those purposes, and to encourage research and the provision of training and information;

(c)   to make such arrangements as it considers appropriate for securing that government departments, employers, employees, organisations representing employers and employees respectively, and other persons concerned with matters relevant to any of those purposes are provided with an information and advisory service and are kept informed of, and adequately advised on, such matters; and

(d)   to submit from time to time to the authority having power to make regulations under any of the relevant statutory provisions such proposals as it considers appropriate for the making of regulations.[49]

5.51 HSC also possesses a number of other powers. It can enter into agency agreements with government departments or other persons to perform functions on behalf of either HSC or HSE, and can by agreement undertake functions of a Minister of the Crown, government department or other public authority[50] (with or without payment), being functions which in the opinion of the Secretary of State can appropriately be performed by the Commission in connection with any of its functions.[51] HSC also has the power to provide (with or without payment) services or facilities to government departments and public authorities,[52] to appoint persons or committees to advise it[53] and to carry out or arrange for or make payments for research and to disseminate information derived from that research.[54]

5.52 HSC also has powers to direct investigations and inquiries.[55] This power can be exercised as regards any

[49] 1974 Act, s. 11(2).
[50] No regulation-making power can be delegated under this power. See 1974 Act, s. 13(2).
[51] 1974 Act, s. 13(1)(a) and (b).
[52] 1974 Act, s. 13(1)(c).
[53] 1974 Act, s. 13(d). HSC can remunerate such persons and has the power to pay travelling and subsistence allowances — s. 13(1)(e).
[54] 1974 Act, s. 13(1)(f).
[55] See generally 1974 Act, s. 14.

accident, occurrence or other matter whatsoever which HSC thinks it necessary or expedient to investigate for any of the general purposes of the Act or with a view to making regulations for those purposes.[56] In such circumstances it is immaterial whether or not HSE has responsibility for enforcing any of the relevant statutory provisions which relate to the matter in question.[57] Accordingly, HSC may at any time direct HSE or authorise any other person to investigate and make a special report on any matter, or with the consent of the Secretary of State direct that an inquiry be held into any such matter.[58] HSC has the power to make public any special report which it has commissioned.[59] Where the inquiry is concerned with a matter which has caused the death of any person, unless the Lord Advocate otherwise directs, no inquiry with regard to that death can be held under the Fatal Accidents and Sudden Deaths Inquiries (Scotland) Act 1976.[60]

5.53 HSE has the specific duties to exercise on behalf of HSC such of its functions as HSC directs it to exercise and to give effect to any directions given to it by HSC: although HSC cannot give directions as to the enforcement of the relevant statutory provisions in any particular case.[61] HSE must also, if so requested by a Minister of the Crown, provide him with information about HSE's activities in connection with any matter with which he is concerned and provide him with relevant expert advice from any of its officers or servants.[62] HSE also has the power to do anything (except borrow money) which is calculated to facilitate, or is conducive or incidental to, the performance of any of its functions.[63]

ENFORCEMENT

5.54 It is the duty of HSE to make adequate arrangements for the enforcement of the relevant statutory pro-

---

[56] 1974 Act, s. 14(1).
[57] 1974 Act, s. 14(1).
[58] 1974 Act, s. 14(2). See also the Health and Safety Inquiries (Procedure) Regulations 1975 (S.I. 1975 No. 335) as amended by S.I. 1976 No. 1246. Inquiries should be held in public except where the Regulations provide otherwise — 1974 Act, s. 14(3).
[59] 1974 Act, s. 14(5).
[60] 1974 Act, s. 14(7).
[61] 1974 Act, s. 11(4).
[62] 1974 Act, s. 11(5).
[63] 1974 Act, s. 11(6).

visions except to the extent that some other authority or class of authorities is made responsible for their enforcement.[64] The Secretary of State has the power by Regulations to make local authorities responsible for the enforcement of the relevant statutory provisions.[65] The Regulations may also make provision for the division of responsibilities between the Executive and local authorities and for securing that notice of any such division is brought to the notice of persons affected by it.[66] The Secretary of State has made Regulations which assign enforcement responsibilities to both HSE and local authorities.[67] The Regulations authorise islands and district councils in Scotland to enforce the relevant statutory provisions for certain types of activities in non-domestic premises.[68] A local authority will be the enforcing authority where the main activity relates to such matters as the sale of goods for retail or wholesale distribution, office activities, catering activities, consumer services or the arts, sports, games, entertainments or other cultural or recreational activities.[69] On the other hand, HSE has the power of enforcement in such areas as mines and quarries, fairgrounds, construction work and agricultural activities.[70] HSC has the power to resolve any uncertainties as regards the division of responsibilities.[71]

5.55 Where a local authority has been designated the enforcing authority it is the duty of that authority to make adequate arrangements for the enforcement within its area of the relevant statutory provisions and to perform the enforcement duty and any other functions conferred on it in accordance with any guidance given by HSC.[72] HSC has powers to investigate and report to the Secretary of State in the case of a local authority which is defaulting as regards its enforcement responsibilities.[73] The Secretary of State has the power to make a default order which may

---

[64] 1974 Act, s. 18(1).
[65] 1974 Act, s. 18(2)(a).
[66] 1974 Act, s. 18(2)(b).
[67] See the Health and Safety (Enforcing Authority) Regulations 1989 (S.I. 1989 No. 1903).
[68] reg. 2(1).
[69] reg. 3(1) and Sched. 1.
[70] reg. 3(1) and Sched. 2.
[71] reg. 6(2).
[72] 1974 Act, s. 18(4).
[73] 1974 Act, s. 45(1).

require the authority to perform specified enforcement functions within a specified time.[74] A failure to comply with the order may result in the authority's responsibilities being transferred to HSE.[75]

5.56 Day-to-day enforcement lies with the inspectors who are appointed by enforcing authorities.[76] Under section 19(1) every enforcing authority may appoint as inspectors such persons having suitable qualifications as it thinks necessary for carrying into effect the relevant statutory provisions within its field of responsibility and may terminate such appointments. Every appointment of a person as an inspector must be made by an instrument in writing specifying which of the powers conferred on inspectors by the relevant statutory provisions are to be exercisable by the person so appointed and an inspector can only exercise the powers as are so specified.[77] Inspectors when seeking to exercise their powers may be required to produce their instruments of appointment or duly authenticated copies.[78]

POWERS OF INSPECTORS

5.57 Inspectors can exercise the following powers so as to carry into effect any of the relevant statutory provisions within the field of responsibility of their enforcing authority:

(a) at any reasonable time (or in dangerous situations, at any time) to enter any premises;

(b) to take with them a constable if they have reasonable cause to apprehend any serious obstruction in the execution of their duty;

(c) on entering premises, to take with them any other person duly authorised by their enforcing authority and any necessary equipment or materials;

---

[74] 1974 Act, s. 45(3) and (4).
[75] 1974 Act, s. 45(5).
[76] For further information on how HSE organises its six inspectorates, see *Stair Memorial Encyclopaedia*, Vol. 9, paras. 486 and 487.
[77] 1974 Act, s. 19(2).
[78] 1974 Act, s. 19(4).

(d) to make such examination and investigation as may be necessary in the circumstances;

(e) to direct that premises where there is a power of entry must be left undisturbed (whether generally or in particular respects) for so long as is reasonably necessary to enable examination and inspection;

(f) to take such measurements and photographs and make such recordings as are necessary for any examination or investigation;

(g) to take samples of any articles or substances found in any premises where there is power of entry, and of the atmosphere in or in the vicinity of those premises;

(h) in the case of articles or substances likely to cause danger to health or safety, to cause them to be dismantled or subjected to any process or test[79];

(i) to take possession of such articles or substances for so long as is necessary in order to examine them, prevent any tampering with them, and to ensure that they are available in any proceedings for an offence[80];

(j) to require any person whom there is reasonable cause for believing may have information relevant to any examination or inspection to answer questions and sign a declaration of the truth of the answers[81];

[79] This power must be exercised in the presence of persons who have responsibilities in relation to those premises where that person so requests unless the inspector considers that such an arrangement would be prejudicial to the safety of the State — 1974 Act, s. 20(4). The inspector also has duties to consult appropriate persons in order to ascertain the dangers of dismantling the article or substance or subjecting it to any process or test — 1974 Act, s. 20(5).

[80] An inspector who exercises this power must leave a notice with a responsible person or fixed to a conspicuous position giving particulars of the article or substance and stating that he has taken possession of it; where it is practicable a portion of any sample that is taken away must be given to the responsible person — 1974 Act, s. 20(6). It is interesting that although an inspector exercising powers under para. (i) must fulfil notice requirements no such requirement operates under para. (g) which grants the inspector a specific power to take samples. See *Laws v. Keane* [1982] I.R.L.R. 500 (H.J.C.) doubting *Skinner v. John G. McGregor (Contractors) Ltd*, 1977 S.L.T. (Sh. Ct.) 83.

[81] Such questioning should take place *in camera* except for any persons nominated by the individual and persons who are allowed to be present by the inspector — s. 20(2)(j).

(k) to require the production of, inspect, and take copies of any books or documents required by the relevant statutory provisions and any other books or documents which must be seen for the purpose of any examination or investigation;

(l) to require any person to afford such facilities and assistance as are necessary to enable inspectors to exercise their powers; and

(m) to exercise any other power which is necessary for carrying into effect the relevant statutory provisions within the field of responsibility of the enforcing authority.

The powers of an inspector do not extend to compelling the production by any person of any document which could be withheld on grounds of legal professional privilege from production in an action in the Court of Session on an order for the production of documents.[82]

Improvement notices and prohibition notices

5.58 As was noted at the beginning of this chapter, the Robens Committee preferred administrative enforcement over criminal sanctions which they thought should only be applied where punishment would be generally expected and supported by the public. The most important recommendation as regards administrative sanctions was the grant of powers to inspectors to serve inspection notices and prohibition notices with a right of appeal to industrial tribunals. The 1974 Act, ss. 21–24 fulfils these recommendations and creates the framework for the operation of these specific administrative powers and the arrangements for appeals.

5.59 If an inspector is of the opinion that a person is contravened one or more of the relevant statutory provisions or has contravened one or more of those provisions in circumstances that make it likely that the contravention will continue or be repeated he can serve an improvement notice. The notice will:

[82] 1974 Act, s. 20(8).

(a) state that he is of the opinion that a relevant statutory provision is being contravened;

(b) specify the provision which is being contravened;

(c) give particulars of the reasons for the inspector's opinion; and

(d) require the person to remedy the contravention within such period as may be specified in the notice.[83]

It is insufficient for the inspector to assert in an improvement notice that he is of the opinion that the employer is contravening the general duties of section 2(1) without stating which of the particular provisions are being contravened. Such a defect will not be cured by the inspector giving reasons for his opinion. A proper notice should either identify the contravention by reference to the specific duties or, if some contravention not so identifiable is alleged, give particulars of it.[84]

5.60 The more draconian administrative remedy, a prohibition notice, applies to any activities which are being or are likely to be carried on by or under the control of any person, being activities to which the relevant statutory provisions apply.[85] A prohibition notice can be served by an inspector where he is of the opinion that the above activities involve a risk of serious personal injury and will be served on the person who is carrying on or is likely to carry on those activities or who has control of them.[86] The prohibition notice must:

(a) state that the inspector has the required opinion;

(b) specify the matters which in his opinion give rise to the risk;

(c) where in his opinion any of those matters involves a contravention of any of the relevant statutory provisions, he must state that

---

[83] 1974 Act, s. 21. The notice may (but need not) include directions as to the measures to be taken to remedy the contravention specified in the notice, and any such directions may be framed by reference to approved codes of practice and so as to afford the employer the choice of different ways of remedying the contravention — s. 23(2).

[84] *Per* McNeill J. in *West Bromwich Building Society Ltd v. Townsend* [1983] I.C.R. 257 at p. 269.

[85] 1974 Act, s. 22(1).

[86] 1974 Act, s. 22(2).

he is of that opinion, specify the provision(s)
as to which he is of that opinion, and give
particulars as to why he is of that opinion;
and

(d)   direct that the activities to which the notice
relates shall not be carried on by or under the
control of the person on whom the notice is
served unless the matters specified in the
notice as giving rise to the risk and any
associated contraventions of specified provisions have been remedied.[87]

Such a direction can take effect either at the end of the
period specified in the notice or, if the notice so declares,
immediately.[88]

5.61 There is a right of appeal to an industrial tribunal
against the service of either of the above notices.[89] Such an
appeal is instigated by sending a notice of appeal to the
Secretary within 21 days from the date of service of the
notice.[90] The tribunal has the power either to cancel or
affirm the notice and, if it affirms it, can do so either in its
original form or with such modifications as the tribunal
may in the circumstances think fit.[91] In the case of an
appeal against an improvement notice the bringing of that
appeal has the effect of suspending the operation of the
notice until the final disposal of the appeal.[92] The bringing
of an appeal against a prohibition notice has the same
effect if, but only if, on the application of the appellant
the tribunal so directs (and then only from the giving of
the direction).[93]

Grounds for appeal

5.62 It would seem that the employer's financial position
is not a relevant ground on which to base an appeal

---

[87] 1974 Act, s. 22(3). See also s. 23(2) as regards references to approved
codes of practice in directions and affording employees the choice
between different ways of remedying the contravention.
[88] 1974 Act, s. 22(4).
[89] 1974 Act, s. 24. For the procedure applicable to such appeals, see
generally the Industrial Tribunals (Constitution and Rules of Procedure)
(Scotland) Regulations 1993 (S.I. 1993 No. 2688) Sched. 4.
[90] Sched. 4, reg. 2(1). Although this period can be extended where the
tribunal is satisfied that it was not reasonably practicable for the appeal
to be brought within the time — reg. 2(2).
[91] 1974 Act, s. 24(2).
[92] 1974 Act, s. 24(3)(a).
[93] 1974 Act, s. 24(3)(b).

against a notice. In *Harrison (Newcastle-under-Lyme) Ltd v. Ramsey*,[94] where the company argued that it could not comply with the notice because it was in financial difficulties, the tribunal rejected such a defence because otherwise the company would be able to make economic gains and undercut competitors at the expense of the safety of its employees. However, there may be circumstances where the tribunal will be prepared to extend the time for compliance with the notice for financial reasons.[95]

5.63 Much may turn on the relevant statutory provisions which form the basis of the notice and the standard of care which those provisions create. If the provisions create absolute requirements then there will be no scope for assessing the risk as against the cost of the necessary remedial action.[96] On the other hand, in many cases tribunals may have to conduct such an assessment because the relevant statutory provisions require employers to do all that is reasonably practicable. In *Associated Dairies Ltd v. Hartley*,[97] where the company appealed against a notice requiring suitable safety footwear to be provided free of charge, the tribunal considered that there was no statutory requirement that such footwear should be provided and that the general duty under the 1974 Act, s. 2, for securing safety at work was based on the standard of reasonable practicability. In such circumstances, the tribunal concluded that since the cost of providing the necessary footwear free of charge was disproportionate to the risk of employees being injured it was not reasonably practicable for such footwear to be supplied without charge. Nonetheless, in other cases tribunals have been prepared to accept the terms of the notice unmodified because the sacrifice in terms of cost is not disproportionate to the risks involved.[98] Equally, it is

---

[94] [1976] I.R.L.R. 135.

[95] *Otterburn Mill v. Bullman* [1975] I.R.L.R. 223 (time limit extended because of the impact on the business of fencing all the machines at once). Extensions of time may also be given for other reasons. See, for example, *D. J. M. Campion and A. J. Campion v. Hughes* [1975] I.R.L.R. 291 (extension of time to enable consent for work from the local authority).

[96] See, for example, *Sutton & Co. Ltd v. Davies* [1978] IDS Brief 149 (although no accident in 27 years notice affirmed because duty to fence was absolute).

[97] [1979] I.R.L.R. 17.

[98] See, for example, *Belhaven Brewery Co. Ltd v. McLean* [1975] I.R.L.R. 370 (risk justified expensive requirement of improvement notice).

no defence to argue that the breach is a trivial one which
is also being committed by many other employers who
have not been served with notices.[99]

5.64 As we have already seen, the 1974 Act, s. 24(2),
empowers tribunals to modify notices. This power
enables tribunals not only to reduce the scope of the
notice but also to add to or increase its requirements.[1]
However, this power does not permit a tribunal to amend
a notice so as to include allegations that the employer was
breaching other provisions of the Act which are not
specified in the notice.[2] But tribunals may have the power
to amend a notice in order to correct technical matters
where there is evidence of a plain and continuing breach
of the Act.[3] Moreover, where it is alleged that the notice is
invalid as being imprecise or vague, a tribunal should not
deal with that matter as a preliminary point. Instead, the
tribunal should hear the whole case and, if it concludes
that the notice is imprecise or vague, it should modify the
notice so as to remedy this defect.[4]

Other powers

5.65 Inspectors also have powers to deal with causes of
imminent danger. Where an inspector finds an article or
substance in premises which he has power to enter and
which he believes is a cause of imminent danger of
serious personal injury, he may seize it and cause it to be
rendered harmless (whether by destruction or otherwise).[5] Before it is rendered harmless the inspector must
take a sample of the article or substance, if it is one of a
batch, and if practicable give it to a responsible person at
the premises where it was found.[6] There are also requirements obliging the inspector, after the article or substance
has been rendered harmless, to give a written report of
his action to the responsible person and the owner of the

[99] *South Surbiton Co-operative Society v. Wilcox* [1975] I.R.L.R. 292.
[1] *Tesco Stores Ltd v. Edwards* [1977] I.R.L.R. 120.
[2] *British Airways Board v. Henderson* [1979] I.C.R. 77. But note also *West
Bromwich Building Society v. Townsend* [1983] I.C.R. 257, discussed at
para. 5.59 above.
[3] *Harrison (Newcastle-under-Lyme) v. Ramsey* [1976] I.R.L.R. 135.
[4] *Chrysler (U.K.) Ltd v. McCarthy* [1978] I.C.R. 939 (D.C.).
[5] 1974 Act, s. 25(1).
[6] 1974 Act, s. 25(2).

article or substance where the owner is not the responsible person.[7] There are also provisions in the 1974 Act concerning the power of customs officers to detain articles and substances,[8] indemnification of inspectors,[9] the power of HSC, HSE and the enforcing authorities to obtain information which HSC needs for the discharge of its functions[10] and as regards restrictions on the disclosure of any such information.[11]

OFFENCES

5.66 It is an offence under the 1974 Act for a person:

(a) to fail to discharge a duty created by sections 2—7;

(b) to contravene section 8 or section 9;

(c) to contravene any health or safety regulations or any requirement or prohibition imposed under any of these regulations (including any requirement or prohibition to which he is subject by virtue of the terms of, or any condition or restriction attached to any licence, approval, exemption, or other authority issued, given or granted under the regulations);

(d) to contravene any requirement imposed by or under any regulations made under section 14 for the purpose of directing investigations and inquiries or intentionally obstructing any person exercising powers in connection with investigations or inquiries;

(e) to contravene any requirement imposed by an inspector under section 20 (general powers) or section 25 (power to deal with cause of imminent danger);

(f) to prevent or attempt to prevent any other person from appearing before an inspector or from answering any questions that the person is required to answer under section 20 (2);

---

[7] 1974 Act, s. 25(3).
[8] 1974 Act, s. 25A.
[9] 1974 Act, s. 26.
[10] 1974 Act, s. 27.
[11] 1974 Act, s. 28.

(g)   to contravene any requirement or prohibition imposed by an improvement notice or a prohibition notice[12];

(h)   intentionally to obstruct an inspector or to obstruct a customs officer in the exercise or performance of their powers or duties;

(i)   to contravene any requirement imposed by a notice requiring the disclosure of information under section 27 (1);

(j)   to use or disclose any information for another purpose in contravention of section 27 (4) or section 28;

(k)   to make a statement which he knows to be false or recklessly to make a statement which is false where the statement is made in purported compliance with a statutory requirement to furnish any information or for the purpose of obtaining the issue of a document to himself or another person;

(l)   intentionally to make a false entry in any register, book, notice or other document required by the relevant statutory provisions to be kept, served or given or, with intent to deceive, to make use of any such entry which he knows to be false;

(m)   with intent to deceive, to use a document issued or authorised to be issued under any of the relevant statutory provisions or required for any purpose or to make or have in his possession a document so closely resembling any such document as to be calculated to deceive;

(n)   falsely to pretend to be an inspector; or

(o)   to fail to comply with an order made by a court under section 42.[13]

5.67 The Act also creates a series of penalties applicable to the above offences. A person guilty of an offence which consists of a failure to discharge a duty imposed by sections 2—6 is liable on summary conviction to a fine not

---

[12] It is no defence to such a charge that the accused has complied with the notice so far as reasonably practicable since this is irrelevant to an offence under s. 33(1)(g). See *Deary v. Mansion Hide Upholstery Ltd* [1983] I.C.R. 610.

[13] 1974 Act, s. 33(1)(a)–(o).

exceeding £20,000,[14] and on conviction on indictment to an unlimited fine.[15] A person guilty of an offence under paragraph (d), (f), (h) or (n) or an offence under paragraph (e) where it consists of a requirement imposed by an inspector under section 20 is liable on summary conviction to a fine not exceeding level 5 on the standard scale.[16] A person guilty of an offence under paragraph (g) or (o) is liable on summary conviction to imprisonment for a term not exceeding six months, or a fine not exceeding £20,000, or both; and on conviction on indictment to imprisonment for a term not exceeding two years, or an unlimited fine, or both.[17] A person guilty of any other offence created by section 33(1) or of an offence under any of the existing statutory provisions, being an offence for which no other penalty is specified, is liable on summary conviction to a fine not exceeding £5,000, and on conviction on indictment, if the offence is covered by section 33(4), to imprisonment for a term not exceeding two years, or an unlimited fine, or both; and in any other case to a fine.[18] The offences covered by section 33(4), where a higher penalty can be imposed on indictment, are:

(a)   an offence consisting of a contravention of any of the relevant statutory provisions by doing otherwise than under the authority of a licence issued by HSE where such a licence is necessary under the relevant statutory provisions;

(b)   an offence consisting of a contravention of a term, condition or restriction attached to any such licence;

(c)   an offence consisting of acquiring or attempting to acquire, possessing or using an explosive article or substance in contravention of the relevant statutory provisions;

---

[14] It is clear that there is no yardstick by which one can test whether a fine of £20,000 is excessive except by considering whether all the relevant circumstances have been taken into account. See *Kvaerner Govan Ltd v. H.M. Advocate,* 1992 S.C.C.R. 10. One relevant circumstance will be the serious consequences of the risk for employees. See *R. v. Sanyo Electrical Manufacturing (U.K.) Ltd* (1992) 156 J.P. 863 (C.A.).

[15] 1974 Act, s. 33(1A) as inserted by the Offshore Safety Act 1992, s. 4(2), (6).

[16] 1974 Act, s. 33(2).

[17] 1974 Act, s. 33(2A) as inserted by the Offshore Safety Act 1992, s. 4(3), (6).

[18] 1974 Act, s. 33(3).

(d)   an offence under paragraph (j).

There are special provisions in section 34 concerning time limits for bringing criminal proceedings under section 33.[19]

SPECIAL PROVISIONS ON OFFENCES

5.68   Where the commission by any person of an offence under any of the relevant statutory provisions is due to the act or default of some other person, that other person is guilty of an offence, and the person may be charged with and convicted of the offence, whether or not proceedings are taken against the first-mentioned person.[20] "Act or default " requires the wrongful act or default of the other person.[21] Accordingly, no prosecution will be competent when the act or default of the other person only became unlawful as a result of legislation enacted subsequently.[22] There is no need to prove *mens rea* or negligence under this provision if the original offence is constituted without the need for *mens rea* or negligence.[23] It is competent to prosecute persons for wrongful acts or defaults where the original offence would have been committed by the Crown but for the fact that section 33 does not bind the Crown.[24] It should also be noted that the above provisions are subject to what may be specified in health and safety regulations.[25]

5.69   It is clear law that when a a statute declares that the act or default of any person is an offence such an offence applies equally to bodies corporate.[26] However, the 1974 Act creates additional rules which ensure that not only the body corporate but also its directors, managers, secretary and other similar officers can be prosecuted. It is

[19] For a discussion on s. 34, see *Stair Memorial Encyclopaedia*, Vol. 9, para. 513.
[20] 1974 Act, s. 36(1).
[21] *Noss Farm Products Ltd v. Lilico* [1945] 2 All E.R. 609 (D.C.).
[22] *Noss Farm Products Ltd*, above.
[23] *Lamb v. Sunderland and District Creamery Ltd* [1951] 1 All E.R. 923 (D.C.).
[24] 1974 Act, s. 36(2).
[25] 1974 Act, s. 36(3).
[26] Interpretation Act 1978, s. 5 and Sched. 1.

provided by section 37(1) that where an offence under any of the relevant statutory provisions committed by a body corporate is proved to have been committed with the consent or connivance of, or to have been attributable to any neglect on the part of, any director, manager, secretary or other similar officer of the body corporate or a person who was purporting to act in such a capacity, he as well as the body corporate is guilty of an offence and can be proceeded against and punished accordingly.[27]

5.70 There appears to be no direct authority on the meaning of the word "connivance" although it has been submitted that the state of mind is one of "wilful blindness" — *i.e.* an intentional shutting of the eyes to something of which the percipient would, in his own interests, prefer to remain unaware.[28] "Neglect" presupposes the existence of some obligation or duty on the part of the person charged with neglect[29] and applies to any neglect in duty to which the contravention of the safety provisions was attributable.[30] The need for the offence to be attributable to the neglect is also broadly construed. In *Wotherspoon v. H.M. Advocate*[31] the court considered that:

> "any degree of attributability will suffice and in that sense it is evident that the commission of a relevant offence by a body corporate may well be found to be attributable to failure on the part of each of a number of directors, managers or officers to take certain steps which he could and should have taken in the discharge of the particular functions of his particular office."

The director of roads of a regional council has been held to fall within the class of person who can be prosecuted under this provision.[32] However, it would seem that only managers who have the power and responsibility for

---

[27] Where the affairs of a body corporate are managed by its members, the provision applies in relation to the acts and defaults of a member in connection with his functions of management as if he were a director of the body corporate — 1974 Act, s. 37(2).

[28] See J. Hendy and M. Ford, *Health and Safety* (2nd ed., 1993), Introductory Note 6.

[29] *Wotherspoon v. H.M. Advocate*, 1978 J.C. 74.

[30] *Armour v. Skeen*, 1977 J.C. 15.

[31] 1978 J.C. 74.

[32] *Armour v. Skeen*, 1977 J.C. 15.

deciding corporate policy and strategy are capable of being prosecuted.[33]

THE USE OF REGULATIONS AND CODES OF PRACTICE

5.71 It is clear that one of the principal objectives of the 1974 Act is for the older laws on health and safety to be progressively replaced by a system of regulations and approved codes of practice operating with other provisions of the 1974 Act so as to improve standards of health, safety and welfare.[34] The 1974 Act, ss. 15 and 16 play a crucial role in achieving this objective by granting powers to make regulations and by authorising HSC to approve and issue codes of practice.

5.72 The Secretary of State for Employment, the Minister of Agriculture, Fisheries and Food, or the Secretary of State and the Minister acting jointly have the power to make Regulations for any of the general purposes of the Act.[35] Regulations can also be made for any of the purposes specified in Schedule 3 to the Act.[36] Health and safety regulations:

    (a)   may repeal or modify any of the existing statutory provisions;

    (b)   may exclude or modify for specified classes of case any of the general duties in sections 2—9 or any of the existing statutory provisions;

    (c)   may make a specified authority or class of authorities responsible, to such extent as may be specified, for the enforcement of any of the relevant statutory provisions;

---

[33] *R. v. Boal* [1992] Q.B. 591.
[34] 1974 Act, s. 1(2).
[35] 1974 Act, s. 15(1).
[36] These include the manufacture, supply, design, construction, guarding, repair, maintenance, marking, testing, import and transport of articles and substances; the licensing of activities; the regulation of persons allowed to perform certain functions; health; conditions of work; welfare; protective clothing; fire risks; emission of substances; training; notification and recording of accidents; animals; dangers to premises or persons; powers of search in connection with fire risks; action after accidents; power to employers and others to make rules and give directions; and powers to local and public authorities to make bye-laws.

(d)   may impose requirements by reference to the approval of HSC or any other specified body or person;

(e)   may provide for references, in the regulations to any specified document to operate as references to that document as revised or reissued from time to time;

(f)   may provide (either unconditionally or subject to conditions, and with or without limit of time) for exemptions from any requirement or prohibition imposed by or under any of the relevant statutory provisions;

(g)   may enable exemptions from any requirement or prohibition imposed by or under any of the relevant statutory provisions to be granted (either unconditionally or subject to conditions, and with or without limit of time) by any specified person or by any person authorised in that behalf by a specified authority;

(h)   may specify the person or classes of person who, in the event of a contravention of a requirement or prohibition imposed by or under the regulations, are to be guilty of an offence, whether in addition to or to the exclusion of other persons or classes of person;

(i)   may provide for any specified defence to be available in proceedings for any offence under the relevant statutory provisions either generally or in specified circumstances;

(j)   may exclude proceedings on indictment in relation to offences consisting of a contravention of a requirement or prohibition imposed by or under any of the existing statutory provisions, the general duties of sections 2—9 or health and safety regulations;

(k)   may restrict the punishments which can be imposed in respect of any of the offences mentioned in para. (j) other than the maximum fine on conviction on indictment; and

(l)   in the case of regulations made for any purpose mentioned in the Offshore Safety Act 1992, s. 1(1), may provide that any offence consisting of a contravention of the regulations, or of any requirement or condition imposed by or under them, shall be punish-

able on conviction on indictment by imprisonment for a term not exceeding two years, or a
fine, or both.[37]

It is legitimate for health and safety regulations to take the
form of regulations applying to particular circumstances
only or to a particular case only (for example, regulations
applying to particular premises only).[38]

5.73 HSC has the power for the purposes of providing
practical guidance with respect to the general duties of
sections 2—7 or of health and safety regulations or of any
of the existing statutory provisions to approve and issue
such codes of practice (whether prepared by it or not) as
in its opinion are suitable for that purpose.[39] HSC may
also approve such codes of practice issued or proposed to
be issued by other bodies.[40] HSC cannot approve a code of
practice without the consent of the Secretary of State, and
must, before seeking his consent, consult any government department or other body that appears to HSC to be
appropiate and may have to consult such government
departments and other bodies by virtue of the directions
of the Secretary of State.[41] HSC also has the power from
time to time to revise the whole or any part of a code of
practice or withdraw its approval from any code subject to
the consent of the Secretary of State and after appropriate
consultation.[42] There are also notifictation requirements as
regards the approval, revision, or withdrawal of approval
for any code.[43]

5.74 A failure to observe a provision of a code of practice
does not of itself render a person liable to any civil or
criminal proceedings; but there are special provisions
where in any criminal proceedings a party is alleged to
have committed an offence by reason of a contravention
of any health and safety provision for which there is an

---

[37] 1974 Act, s. 15(2)–(6).
[38] 1974 Act, s. 15(8).
[39] 1974 Act, s. 16(1)(a).
[40] 1974 Act, s. 16(1)(b).
[41] 1974 Act, s. 16(2).
[42] 1974 Act, s. 16(4) and (5).
[43] 1974 Act, s. 16(3) and (6). In the case of the approval of a code, HSC is
required to issue a notice in writing identifying the code, stating the date
on which it takes effect and specifying the provisions for which it is
approved.

approved code of practice.[44] In such a case any provision of the code which appears to the court to be relevant to the requirement or prohibition alleged to have been contravened is admissible in evidence in the proceedings. If it is proved that there was at any material time a failure to observe any provision of the code, commission of an offence must be taken as proved unless the court is satisfied that the requirement or prohibition could be complied with other than by way of observance of the code.[45]

[44] 1974 Act, s. 17(1).
[45] 1974 Act, s. 17(2).

CHAPTER 6

SELECTED AREAS OF STATUTORY REGULATION

INTRODUCTION

6.1 It is the purpose of this chapter to consider some of the delegated legislation made under the Health and Safety at Work Act 1974, s. 15, in more detail. First, we shall consider some basic statutory regulations of general effect such as the Health and Safety (First-Aid) Regulations 1981.[1] Thereafter we will discuss certain specific and specialised statutory provisions which regulate health and safety in particular industries or in relation to particular types of activity. In this part of the chapter we shall consider certain regulations such as the Control of Lead at Work Regulations 1980[2] and the Control of Substances Hazardous to Health Regulations 1988[3] which comply largely with earlier European Directives. Next we shall examine the remaining regulations made in 1992 which were intended to comply with the more recent European Directives made under Article 118A of the Treaty of Rome and which have not yet been discussed in this book.[4] Finally, the chapter will conclude with a brief examination of the regulatory regime applicable in offshore installations. This regime has been revolutionised as a result of

[1] S.I. 1981 No. 917.
[2] S.I. 1980 No. 1248. See also the Lead and Ionic Compounds Directive 82/605.
[3] S.I. 1988 No. 1657. These regulations originally gave effect to earlier European Directives such as the Chemical, Physical and Biological Agents at Work Directive 80/1107. They were substantially amended in 1992 in order to comply with the Carcinogens Directive 90/394.
[4] The Personal Protective Equipment at Work Regulations 1992 (S.I. 1992 No. 2966); the Manual Handling Operations Regulations 1992 (S.I. 1992 No. 2793) and the Health and Safety (Display Screen Equipment) Regulations 1992 (S.I. 1992 No. 2792). We shall also consider some aspects of the Management of Health and Safety at Work Regulations 1992 (S.I. 1992 No. 2051).

the recommendations of the Cullen Report[5] which led to the enactment of the Offshore Safety Act 1992 and the making of the Offshore Installations (Safety Case) Regulations 1992.[6]

SELECTED GENERAL REGULATIONS

(a) Health and Safety (First-Aid) Regulations 1981

6.2 These Regulations[7] require employers[8] to provide equipment and facilities and such number of suitable persons as is adequate and appropriate in the circumstances so that first-aid[9] can be rendered to employees who are injured or become ill at work.[10] Persons will not be suitable to provide first aid unless they have undergone such training and have such qualifications as HSE may approve for the time being and have such additional training, if any, as may be appropriate in the circumstances of the case.[11] Where a suitable person is absent in temporary and exceptional circumstances it is sufficient compliance if the employer appoints a person to take charge of the situation throughout the period of the absence both in relation to an injured or ill employee who will need help from a medical practitioner or nurse and the adequate and appropriate equipment and facilities which must be provided.[12] Employers would usually be expected to provide suitable persons qualified in first-aid.[13] However, it is possible for them to appoint a person

[5] Cm. 1310 (1990).
[6] S.I. 1992 No. 2885.
[7] S.I. 1981 No. 917. There is also an Approved Code of Practice and a Guidance Note published by HSE.
[8] For exemptions from the regulations, see reg. 7. For the special position of mines see reg. 7(e) and reg. 8, and for the application of the Regulations offshore see reg. 9.
[9] "First-aid" means (a) in cases where a person will need help from a medical practitioner or nurse, treatment for the purposes of preserving life and minimising the consequences of injury and illness until such help is obtained, and (b) treatment of minor injuries which would otherwise receive no treatment or which do not need treatment by a medical practitioner or nurse. See reg. 2(1).
[10] regs. 3(1) and (2).
[11] reg. 3(2)(a) and (b).
[12] reg. 3(3).
[13] See Code of Practice, para. 32.

to take charge instead of providing a person qualified in first-aid where having regard to the nature of the undertaking, the number of employees at work and the location of the establishment it would be adequate and appropriate to do so.[14] Employers also have an obligation to inform their employees about arrangements for first-aid, including the location of equipment, facilities and personnel[15] and self-employed persons are required to take care of their own health and safety by the provision of adequate and appropriate first-aid equipment.[16]

(b) Health and Safety Information for Employees Regulations 1989

6.3 These Regulations[17] require employers to furnish information relating to health, safety and welfare to their employees either by means of a poster in a form approved and published by HSE or by means of a similarly approved leaflet which is given to each employee.[18] It is the duty of the employer to ensure that any approved poster is kept displayed in a readable condition and at a reasonably accessible place and in such a position in that place so that it can be easily seen and read.[19] The Regulations also require that the name and address of the enforcing authority and the address of the employment medical advisory service be written clearly and indelibly on the poster in the appropriate space.[20] Where employers distribute the leaflet to their employees the same information should be provided in a written notice which accompanies it.[21]

---

[14] reg. 3(4).
[15] reg. 4.
[16] reg. 5.
[17] S.I. 1989 No. 682.
[18] regs. 3 and 4.
[19] reg. 4(1)(a). HSE has the power to approve revisions to the posters and leaflets and employers must incorporate such changes into their literature. See reg. 3(2) and reg. 4(3).
[20] reg. 5(1).
[21] reg. 5(3).

(c) Control of Industrial Major Accident Hazards Regulations 1984

6.4 The purpose of these Regulations[22] is to prevent and limit the effects of accidents arising from any industrial activity[23] involving dangerous substances. The Regulations apply to any operation in an industrial installation[24] which involves one or more dangerous substances,[25] unless that operation is incapable of producing a major accident hazard, and to the storage of specified quantities of certain substances listed in the Regulations.[26]

6.5 A manufacturer[27] who has control of an industrial activity must at any time provide evidence including documents to show that he has identified the major accident[28] hazards and has taken adequate steps to prevent such major accidents and to limit their consequences to persons and the environment, and provide persons working on the site with the information, training and equipment necessary to ensure their safety.[29] Where a major accident occurs on a site, the manufacturer must forthwith notify HSE of that accident. HSE must obtain the following information from the manufacturer as soon as it becomes available—

[22] S.I. 1984 No. 1902 as amended by S.I. 1985 No. 2023, S.I. 1986 No. 294, S.I. 1988 No. 1462, S.I. 1990 No. 2325 and S.I. 1994 No. 118 which removes the exemption for industrial activities carried out at sites operated by disposal authorities. The Regulations are intended to implement Council Directive 82/501 on the major accident hazards of certain industrial activities.
[23] The Regulations have wide effect. However, they do not apply to nuclear installations, defence installations, factories, magazines or stores licensed under the Explosives Act 1875 or mines or quarries. See reg. 3.
[24] See reg. 2(1). Sched. 4 lists the industrial installations which are covered by the Regulations.
[25] For the definition of "dangerous substance" see reg. 2(1) and Scheds. 1–3.
[26] See Sched. 2.
[27] "Manufacturer" means a person having control of an industrial activity. See reg. 2(1).
[28] "Major accident" means an occurrence (including, in particular, a major emission, fire or explosion) resulting from uncontrolled developments in the course of an industrial activity, leading to a serious danger to persons, whether immediate or delayed, inside or outside the installation, or to the environment, and involving one or more dangerous substances. See reg. 2(1).
[29] reg. 4(2).

(a)   the circumstances of the accident;
(b)   the dangerous substances involved;
(c)   the data available for assessing the effects of the accident on persons and the environment; and
(d)   the emergency measures taken.[30]

The manufacturer must also provide a statement of the steps envisaged to alleviate the medium or long-term effects of the accident, if any, and to prevent its recurrence.[31] HSE is required to collect, where possible, the information necessary for a full analysis of the accident and to send to the European Commission certain specified information.[32]

6.6   There are special rules which apply when a manufacturer has control of an industrial activity involving specified dangerous substances.[33] In such cases a manufacturer cannot undertake any industrial activity unless a written report has been prepared containing certain specified information and that report has been sent to HSE at least three months before the commencement of the activity.[34] Such reports must be kept up-to-date[35] and the manufacturer can be required to give further information relating to the activity to HSE if HSE so requires it.[36] Manufacturers are also required to prepare and keep up-to-date adequate on-site emergency plans detailing how major accidents will be dealt with on the site where the industrial activity is carried on.[37] The local authority[38] in whose area the industrial activity is being carried on has a

---

[30] reg. 5(1)(a). See also reg. 5(3) which makes it clear that a manufacturer who has already notified a major accident to HSE under the Reporting of Injuries, Diseases and Dangerous Occurrences Regulations 1985 is to be deemed to have complied with the notification requirements of these Regulations. The 1985 Regulations are discussed at para. 6.7.

[31] reg. 5(1)(b).

[32] reg. 5(2). The information to be provided to the European Commission is listed in Sched. 5.

[33] The industrial activities to which these special rules apply are defined by reg. 6. For information on the types of substances and quantities required see Scheds. 2 and 3.

[34] reg. 7(1). HSE can agree to a shorter period.

[35] reg. 8.

[36] reg. 9.

[37] reg. 10.

[38] The appropriate local authority is a regional or islands council. See reg. 2(1).

corresponding obligation to prepare and keep up-to-date an adequate off-site emergency plan.[39] The manufacturer also has a responsibility to prepare and supply information to persons likely to be in the area of the activity and to make that information publicly available.[40] The local authority can assist the manufacturer in the dissemination of such information.[41]

(d) Reporting of Injuries, Diseases and Dangerous Occurrences Regulations 1985

6.7 These Regulations[42] place reporting requirements on the responsible person in relation to accidents at work, certain prescribed diseases and dangerous occurrences. The responsible person will usually be the employer.[43] Where any person as a result of an accident arising out of or in connection with work, dies or suffers certain specified injuries or conditions[44] or where there is a dangerous occurrence[45] the responsible person must forthwith notify the enforcing authority[46] by the quickest practicable means and must within seven days send a report to that authority on an approved form.[47] In addition, the responsible person must, as soon he knows, inform the enforcing authority in writing of the death of an employee as a result of an accident at work which is the cause of his death within one year of the accident whether or not the accident has already been reported.[48] Responsible persons

---

[39] reg. 11. This plan should be prepared after consulting the manufacturer, HSE and any other appropriate person.

[40] reg. 12(1). The manufacturer can consult the local authority and appropriate persons, but remains responsible for the accuracy, completeness and form of the information. See reg. 12(2).

[41] reg. 12(3).

[42] S.I. 1985 No. 2023 as amended by S.I. 1988 No. 1729, S.I. 1989 No. 1457 and S.I. 1992 No. 743.

[43] See reg. 2(1).

[44] These are listed in reg. 3(2) and include certain fractures and amputations, eyesight loss and any other injury which requires the person to be admitted immediately into hospital for more than 24 hours.

[45] See reg. 2(1) and Sched. 1.

[46] See the 1974 Act, s. 18 and the Health and Safety (Enforcing Authority) Regulations 1989 (S.I. 1989 No. 1903) discussed in Chap. 5, para. 5.54.

[47] reg. 3(1). The duty to notify applies not only in the case of accidents to employees etc., but will also apply to accidents to visitors and customers. See *Woking Borough Council v. BHS plc, The Times,* November 4, 1994.

[48] reg. 4.

are also required to report forthwith to the enforcing authority where a person at work suffers from one of a number of specified diseases and his work involves a specified activity.[49] There are also reporting requirements as regards gas incidents.[50] Finally, the responsible person must also keep records of any injury or condition, dangerous occurrence or disease which has to be reported.[51]

SPECIAL REGULATIONS

(a) Control of Lead at Work Regulations 1980

6.8 These Regulations[52] place duties on employers to protect their employees and other persons who are exposed to lead at work.[53] They are accompanied by an Approved Code of Practice which provides detailed guidance for each regulation. The exposure to lead must come through the use of lead in such a form that it is likely to be inhaled, ingested or otherwise absorbed by persons: the regulations do not apply to lead given off from the exhaust systems of motor vehicles on public roads.[54] It would seem that any such exposure should be significant and that there will be no breach of duty when the work involves merely intermittent exposures of short duration.[55] The basic duty is for employers and the self-employed, where any work may expose persons to lead, to assess that work to determine the nature and degree of that exposure.[56] Employers also have obligations to ensure that adequate[57] information, instruction and training is given to their employees who are liable to be exposed to lead so that they are aware of the risks from lead and the precautions which should be observed.[58]

---

[49] reg. 5(1). For specified diseases and specified activities see Sched. 2.
[50] reg. 6.
[51] reg. 7(1).
[52] S.I. 1980 No. 1248 as amended by S.I. 1990 No. 305 and S.I. 1992 No. 2966. These Regulations comply substantially with the Lead and Ionic Compounds Directive 1982 (82/605).
[53] reg. 3.
[54] See generally the definition of lead in reg. 2(1).
[55] *Hewett v. Alf Brown's Transport Ltd* [1992] I.C.R. 530 (C.A.).
[56] reg. 4(1).
[57] "Adequate" means adequate having regard only to the nature and degree of exposure to lead.
[58] reg. 5(a).

6.9 There are also a series of regulations which are intended to control the exposure to and spread of contamination by lead at the workplace. Thus every employer must, so far as is reasonably practicable, provide such control measures for materials, plant and processes as will adequately control the exposure of employees to lead otherwise than through the use of respiratory protective equipment or protective clothing.[59] However, there are also special provisions requiring the provision of appropriate respiratory equipment to employees who are liable to be exposed to airborne lead.[60] The Regulations also place obligations on employers to provide adequate washing and changing facilities,[61] to ensure that suitable arrangements are made for employees to eat, drink and smoke in a place which is not liable to be contaminated with lead[62] and to secure the cleanliness of workplaces, premises, plant, respiratory protective equipment and protective clothing.[63] Most importantly, every employer, his employees and every self-employed person must, so far as reasonably practicable, prevent the spread of contamination by lead from the place where work is being carried out. The regulations also place obligations on employers as regards the proper use or application of control measures and protective equipment[64] and their maintenance in an efficient state, in efficient working order and good repair.[65] Finally, employers are required to have adequate air monitoring procedures[66] and there are detailed rules about the medical surveillance of employees who are employed on work which involves exposure to lead.[67]

(b) Control of Asbestos at Work Regulations 1987

6.10 A similar safety regime to that applicable for lead was created for asbestos by the 1987 Regulations.[68] The

[59] reg. 6.
[60] reg. 7.
[61] reg. 9.
[62] reg. 10.
[63] reg. 11.
[64] reg. 13.
[65] reg. 14.
[66] reg. 15.
[67] See generally reg. 16.
[68] S.I. 1987 No. 2115 as amended by S.I. 1988 No. 712, S.I. 1992 No. 2966 and S.I. 1992 No. 3068. They fulfil the requirements of the Asbestos Directive 1983 (83/477) as amended by E.C. Directive 91/382.

Regulations impose duties on employers for the protection of employees who may be exposed to asbestos at work and of other persons who are liable to be affected by such work.[69] Employers are not permitted to carry out any work involving exposure to asbestos unless they have identified the type of asbestos involved in the work and have treated it accordingly.[70] Moreover, there must be an adequate assessment of the nature and degree of exposure to asbestos and an indication of the steps to be taken to prevent or reduce to the lowest level reasonably practicable that exposure.[71] Employers must also notify the enforcing authority when work with asbestos is to be undertaken[72] and must ensure that adequate information, instruction and training is given to employees about the risks from asbestos and the precautions to be observed.[73] The basic obligation placed upon employers is to prevent the exposure of their employees to asbestos, but where this is not reasonably practicable to reduce exposure to asbestos to the lowest level reasonably practicable by measures other than by the use of respiratory protective equipment.[74] Thereafter, the Regulations impose control mechanisms, maintenance requirements and medical surveillance along similar lines to those already discussed for the Control of Lead at Work Regulations.[75]

(c) Control of Substances Hazardous to Health Regulations 1988

6.11 These Regulations[76] constitute some of the most important and far-reaching provisions on health and safety promulgated since the 1974 Act. They are intended to provide a comprehensive and systematic approach to the control of exposure to most substances hazardous to

---

[69] reg. 3.
[70] reg. 4.
[71] regs. 5(1) and (2).
[72] reg. 6.
[73] reg. 7.
[74] reg. 8.
[75] See regs. 9–17.
[76] S.I. 1988 No. 1657 as amended by S.I. 1990 No. 2026, S.I. 1991 No. 2431, S.I. 1992 No. 2382, S.I. 1992 No. 2966, S.I. 1993 No. 745 and S.I. 1994 No. 3246. This last amendment implements the Biological Agents Directive (90/679) and extends the regulations to cover offshore oil and gas installations.

health in all types of work and workplace. The original regulations which implement some of the earlier Directives of the European union[77] were the subjects of considerable amendment in 1992 in order to comply with the Carcinogens at Work Directive.[78] The effect has been to create an extensive but flexible code of conduct as regards the health risks associated with virtually all work activities[79] where substances which are hazardous to health are used or produced. The regulations are also accompanied by a general Approved Code of Practice and by a number of other Codes of Practice which focus attention on the health risks associated with specific substances and specific activities.

6.12 The cornerstone of these Regulations is reg. 3 which places a duty on all employers[80] as regards the health risks of their employees and other persons, whether at work or not, who may be affected by the work carried on by employers as regards substances hazardous to health. A substance means any natural or artificial substance whether in solid or liquid form or in the form of a gas or vapour (including micro-organisms).[81] Such a substance becomes hazardous to health if it satisfies any of the following—

> (a) it is a substance which is listed as being dangerous for supply within the meaning of the Chemicals (Hazard Information and Packaging) Regulations 1993[82] and for which an indication of danger specified for that substance by the 1993 Regulations is very toxic, toxic, harmful, corrosive or irritant;

[77] See, for example, the Chemical, Physical and Biological Agents at Work Directive 80/1107.

[78] 90/394.

[79] There are some limited exceptions where the COSHH Regulations do not apply. See reg. 5. For our purposes the most important exclusions are where the activities are already covered by the Control of Lead at Work Regulations 1980 or the Control of Asbestos at Work Regulations 1987.

[80] For the purposes of these Regulations a self-employed person is to be treated as both an employer and employee except for monitoring and health surveillance purposes. See reg. 3(2).

[81] reg. 2(1).

[82] S.I. 1993 No. 1746.

(b)   it is a substance for which the COSHH Regulations specify a maximum exposure limit[83] or for which HSC has approved an occupational standard;

(c)   it is a micro-organism which creates a hazard to the health of any person;

(d)   it involves dust of any kind, when present at a substantial concentration in air;

(e)   it is a substance which is not already covered but which creates comparable hazards to the health of any person.[84]

6.13 Key to the application of the Regulations is reg. 6 which places obligations on employers not to carry on any work which is liable to expose any employees to any substances hazardous to health unless they have made a suitable and sufficient assessment of the health risks created by that work and of the steps that need to be taken in order to comply with the Regulations. Any such assessment must be reviewed regularly and forthwith if there is reason to suspect that the assessment is no longer valid or there has been a significant change in the work to which it relates.[85] It is clear that the focus for the health risk assessment is the employer's own work activities and that the preventive and precautionary measures which an employer will be required to introduce as a result of that assessment will be consistent with the risks which it has identified. Nevertheless, the Regulations provide guidance as to the sorts of precautions which employers should introduce.

6.14 These are as follows –

(1)   preventing exposure to substances hazardous to health or, where this is not reasonably practicable, securing adequate control of exposure[86];

---

[83] See Sched. 1.
[84] reg. 2(1).
[85] reg. 6(2).
[86] reg. 7(1). So far as reasonably practicable, such prevention is to be secured by measures other than the provision of personal protective equipment – reg. 7(2). It should be noted, however, that there are special rules for carcinogens. See reg. 7(2A).

(2) taking all reasonable steps to ensure that any control measure, personal protective equipment, or other thing or facility so provided is properly used and applied[87];

(3) ensuring that any control measure is maintained in an efficient state, in efficient working order and in good repair[88];

(4) monitoring the exposure of employees to substances hazardous to health in accordance with a suitable procedure[89];

(5) ensuring that employees who are or are liable to be exposed to a substance hazardous to health are subject to suitable health surveillance arrangements[90];

(6) providing employees who may be exposed to substances hazardous to health with such information, instruction and training as is suitable and sufficient for them to know the risks to health created by such exposure and the precautions which should be taken.[91]

(d) Electricity at Work Regulations 1989

6.15 These Regulations[92] are intended to provide a comprehensive framework of control as regards the use of electricity at work and they place duties of compliance on employers, the self-employed, managers of mines or quarries and employees.[93] Regulation 3(1) lays down a general requirement that all electrical systems[94] must at all times be of such construction as to prevent danger. There are also similar requirements as regards the maintenance

---

[87] reg. 8(1).
[88] reg. 9(1).
[89] reg. 10(1).
[90] reg. 11(1).
[91] reg. 12(1).
[92] S.I. 1989 No. 635.
[93] See generally reg. 3. The Regulations do not apply to the master or crew of a sea-going vessel or their employer, nor do they apply to any person in relation to an aircraft or hovercraft moving under its own power – reg. 32.
[94] "System" means an electrical system in which all the electrical equipment is, or may be, electrically connected to a common source of electrical energy, and includes such source and such equipment – reg. 2(1).

of electrical systems.[95] In addition, every work activity, including operation, use, and maintenance of a system and work near a system must be carried out in such a manner as not to give rise to danger.[96] All of these duties are based upon the standard of reasonable practicability indicating that a balance should be struck between the steps necessary to prevent the dangers and the dangers themselves. However, as the HSE's Guidance Notes make clear, given that the most obvious danger associated with electricity is electrocution the Regulations may in practice impose a fairly high standard of care.

6.16 There are also other duties created by the Regulations where the standard is one of reasonable practicability. Thus under regulation 6 electrical equipment[97] which may reasonably foreseeably be exposed to mechanical damage; the effects of the weather, natural hazards, temperature or pressure; the effect of wet, dirty, dusty or corrosive conditions; or any flammable or explosive substance must be of such construction or as necessary protected so as to prevent, so far as reasonably practicable, danger arising from such exposure. Equally, under regulation 7 there are duties, so far as reasonably practicable, to ensure that all conductors in a system which may give rise to danger are either suitably covered with insulating material or have such precautions taken in respect of them as will prevent danger. It has been held under the equivalent provision of earlier regulations that the purpose of this regulation is to protect employees against the consequences of doing things by reason of inadvertence or inattention which they would not normally do.[98]

6.17 Other duties impose a standard which is strict so that they do not involve issues of reasonable practicability. Any protective equipment provided to persons working on or near electrical equipment must be suitable

---

[95] reg. 4(2).
[96] reg. 4(3).
[97] "Electrical equipment" includes anything used, intended to be used or installed for use, to generate, provide, transmit, transform, rectify, convert, conduct, distribute, control, store, measure or use electrical energy.
[98] See *R. v. Sanyo Electrical Manufacturing (U.K.) Ltd* [1992] 156 J.P. Reports 863 (C.A.) — decided under the Electricity (Factories Act) Special Regulations 1944 (S.R. & O. 1944 No. 739).

for the use for which it is provided, be maintained in a condition suitable for that use, and be properly used.[99] No electrical equipment should be put into use where its strength and capability may be exceeded in such a way as may give rise to danger.[1] The Regulations also impose requirements through earthing or by other suitable means to prevent dangers arising from conductors becoming charged[2] and as regards the need for suitable precautions to prevent dangers from breaks in the electrical continuity when a circuit conductor is connected to earth.[3] Every joint and connection in a system must be mechanically and electrically suitable for use[4] and efficient means, suitably located, must be provided for protecting every part of the system from excess of current.[5]

6.18 There must be suitable means for cutting off the supply of electricity to any electrical equipment and for isolating that equipment[6] and adequate precautions must be taken to prevent electrical equipment which has been made dead becoming electrically charged when work is being carried out on or near it.[7] There are regulations about the need for adequate precautions for electrical equipment made dead,[8] as regards work on or near live conductors,[9] and in relation to the provision of adequate space, access and lighting for work on or near all electrical equipment.[10] Finally, it is unlawful for a person to work on any activity where technical knowledge or experience is necessary to prevent danger or injury, unless he possesses such knowledge or experience or is properly supervised.[11]

6.19 As already noted, the Regulations place obligations of compliance as far as matters which are within their control on employers, the self-employed and managers of

[99] reg. 4(4).
[1] reg. 5.
[2] reg. 8.
[3] reg. 9.
[4] reg. 10.
[5] reg. 11.
[6] reg. 12(1).
[7] reg. 13.
[8] reg. 13.
[9] reg. 14.
[10] reg. 15.
[11] reg. 16.

mines and quarries.[12] As far as employees are concerned
they have duties while at work to co-operate with their
employer so far as is necessary to enable any duty placed
upon that employer to be complied with and to comply
with the regulations in relation to matters which are
within their control.[13] This ensures that both the employer
and employee can be guilty of an offence under the
regulations and that actions for breach of statutory duty
are also competent against both. This state of affairs may
cause problems for employees suing on the basis of the
employer's alleged breach of duty where it is claimed that
they were also in default under the regulations.[14]

OTHER "EUROPEAN" REGULATIONS

6.20 The acceptance of the Single European Act by the
Member States of the European Community in 1987 has
had a major impact on the development and implementa-
tion of health and safety laws throughout the European
Union. The amendments to the Treaty of Rome which
SEA brought about not only ensured that for the first time
there was a specific article, *viz.* Article 118A, dealing with
health and safety issues but they also enabled approval
for such measures to be given by means of a system of
Qualified Majority Voting in the Council of Ministers.
There can be no doubt that the directives of the European
Union which have been made since the Framework Directive[15] was approved in 1989 constitute a major source of
law on health and safety matters. As has already been
noted, the United Kingdom Government has accepted
these European initiatives and has enacted the necessary
compliance measures by means of regulations made
under section 15 of the Health and Safety at Work Act
1974. Some of these regulations have already been discussed in earlier chapters. For example, the Workplace

---

[12] reg. 3(1). For the special provisions for mines and quarries see Pt. III.
[13] reg. 3(2).
[14] See, for example, *Ginty v. Belmont Building Supplies Ltd* [1959] 1 All
E.R. 414.
[15] See the EC Council Directive on the introduction of measures to
encourage improvements in the safety and health of workers at work:
89/391/EEC. For further information on the European dimension see
para. 2.7–2.11.

(Health, Safety and Welfare) Regulations 1992[16] and the
Provision and Use of Work Equipment Regulations 1992[17]
were discussed in Chapter 4 and the risk assessment
requirements of the Management of Health and Safety at
Work Regulations 1992[18] were discussed in Chapter 5. It is
now time to consider some of these regulations in a
different context and to examine the other "European"
regulations which have not yet been discussed in this
book.

(a) Management of Health and Safety at Work Regulations 1992

6.21 As well as implementing the framework directive,[19]
these regulations are also intended to comply with the
temporary workers directive.[20] As already noted, their
most significant contribution to UK health and safety laws
has been the introduction of detailed requirements for
risk assessment.[21] Employers now have an obligation to
conduct a risk assessment exercise both for their
employees and for others so as to identify the measures
that should be taken in order to comply with health and
safety laws.[22] There are similar obligations placed on the
self-employed as regards risks to their own health and
safety and those of others.[23] However, there can be no
doubt that the Management Regulations also strengthen
the UK health and safety regime by creating a number of
additional obligations on both employers and employees.
Much of what follows arises as a logical extension of the
risk assessment exercise and the conclusions which it
reaches. It is central to such an exercise that information
about the risks and the preventive and protective measures is distributed widely. Accordingly, the Management
Regulations also contain provisions intended to ensure
that employees and other persons are aware of the
hazards and their own responsibilities in relation to them.

[16] S.I. 1992 No. 3004.
[17] S.I. 1992 No. 2932.
[18] S.I. 1992 No. 2051, as amended by S.I. 1994 No. 2865.
[19] EC directive on the introduction of measures to encourage improvements in the safety and health of workers at work 89/391/EEC.
[20] 91/383/EEC. HSC has published an Approved Code of Practice to
accompany the Regulations.
[21] See paras. 5.38–5.41.
[22] reg. 3(1).
[23] reg. 3(2).

6.22 Key aspects of the rest of the Regulations are as follows:

(1) Health and safety arrangements and health surveillance: Employers must make and give effect to appropriate arrangements having regard to the nature of their activities and the size of their undertakings for the effective planning, organisation, control, monitoring and review of any preventive and protective measures.[24] Employers must also provide such health surveillance as is appropriate to the risks identified by the assessment.[25]

(2) Health and safety assistance: Employers are required to appoint one or more competent persons to assist them in undertaking the necessary measures to comply with the requirements and prohibitions imposed by any of the relevant statutory provisions.[26] A person can be regarded as competent where he has sufficient training and experience or knowledge and other qualities to enable him properly to assist in undertaking the necessary measures.[27] Such a person need not necessarily be an employee and special information responsibilities are placed upon the employer when the competent person is not in his employment.[28] Employers may also have to inform the competent person(s) about persons working in the undertaking who are on fixed-term contracts or are employed in a employment business.[29]

(3) Procedures for serious and imminent danger: Every employer must establish and give effect to appropriate procedures which should be followed in the event of serious and imminent danger to workers in the undertaking. Competent persons must be nominated to implement these procedures as far as evacuation from premises is concerned, and the employer must ensure that no employee should have access to an area which is

[24] reg. 4(1). Employers employing five or more employees must record their arrangements — reg. 4(2).
[25] reg. 5.
[26] reg. 6(1). The number of persons appointed, the time available to fulfil their functions and the means at their disposal must be adequate having regard to the size of the undertaking, the risks and the distribution of those risks through the undertaking — reg. 6(3).
[27] reg. 6(5).
[28] See reg. 6(4)(a).
[29] reg. 6(4)(b).

restricted on health and safety grounds unless adequate health and safety instruction has been provided to the employee concerned.[30] In particular, the appropriate procedures must, so far is practicable, ensure that persons at work who are exposed to serious and imminent danger are informed of the nature of the hazard and the steps which have been taken to protect them from it, enable those persons to stop work and immediately proceed to a place of safety when they are exposed to serious, imminent and unavoidable danger and prevent those persons from resuming work where there is still a serious and imminent danger.[31]

(4) Information to Employees: Employers are required to provide their employees with comprehensible[32] and relevant information on the risks to their health and safety identified by the assessment, the preventive and protective measures, the procedures for serious and imminent danger, the persons responsible for evacuation procedures, and the risks associated with shared workplaces.[33]

(5) Shared workplaces and visiting workers: Employers who share a workplace must co-operate with one another in order to comply with the requirements and prohibitions of the relevant statutory provisions and take all reasonable steps to co-ordinate their preventive and protective measures and inform the other employers of the risks to their employees' health and safety from the conduct of their undertakings.[34] Every employer and self-employed person must provide comprehensible information to the employer of employees from an outside undertaking who are working in his undertaking as regards the health and safety risks associated with that undertaking and the requirements and prohibitions of any of the relevant statutory provisions.[35]

(6) Capabilities and training: Employers must take into account an employee's health and safety capabilities

---

[30] reg. 7(1).
[31] reg. 7(2).
[32] The Code of Practice advises that for information to be comprehensible it must be capable of being understood by the employees to whom it is addressed.
[33] reg. 8.
[34] reg. 9(1).
[35] reg. 10(1).

when entrusting tasks and must provide adequate health and safety training to new employees and those exposed to new or increased risks either because of a transfer or change of responsibilities or through the introduction of new work equipment, new technology or a new or changed system of work.[36] Training must be repeated periodically where appropriate, be adapted to take account of any new or changed health and safety risks and take place during working hours.[37]

(8) Duties of employees: Employees have duties to use any machinery, equipment, dangerous substance, transport equipment, means of production or safety device in accordance with the training that they have received and the instructions regarding use which have been provided to them in compliance with the requirements and prohibitions of any relevant statutory provisions.[38] Employees must also inform their employer or any other employee with specific health and safety responsibilities as regards any work situation which represents a serious and immediate danger to health and safety and any shortcoming in the employer's protection arrangements for health and safety.[39]

(9) Temporary workers: Regulation 13 is intended to comply with the Temporary Workers Directive by placing information responsibilities on employers and the self-employed for employees on fixed-term contracts, those employed to perform a specific task, and those provided by employment agencies. Such people must be provided with information about any special occupational qualifications or skills to be held by such employees if they are to carry out their work safely and any health surveillance required to be provided to them. This information should be provided before the employees commence their duties.

(10) Worker participation: As already noted,[40] the regulations amend the Safety Representatives and Safety Committees Regulations 1977[41] by placing additional

---

[36] regs. 11(1) and (2).
[37] reg. 11(3).
[38] reg. 12(1).
[39] reg. 12(2). These duties are discussed in more detail at para. 5.45.
[40] See para. 5.22.
[41] S.I. 1977 No. 500.

responsibilities on employers to consult in good time safety representatives as regards (a) the introduction of protective and preventive measures; (b) the arrangements for the appointment of safety assistants and those responsible for implementing evacuation arrangements; (c) the health and safety information provided to employees; (d) the planning and organisation of health and safety training and (e) the health and safety consequences of new technology.[42]

(11) Duties to new or expectant mothers: As already noted, a risk assessment must take account of the health and safety risks to new and expectant mothers.[42a] Moreover, employers must suspend from work a new and expectant mother[42b] who works at night where a certificate from a registered medical practitioner or a registered midwife shows that it is necessary for her health or safety that she should not be at work for any period specified in the certificate.[42c]

Finally, it should be noted that a breach of any duty imposed by the Regulations does not confer a right of action in any civil proceedings, except as regards the risk assessment obligations in regulation 13A(1) owed to new or expectant mothers.[43]

(b) Workplace (Health, Safety and Welfare) Regulations 1992

6.23 These Regulations[44] are intended to implement the Workplace Directive[45] of the European Union and are accompanied by an HSC Approved Code of Practice. They took effect for new workplaces on January 1, 1993 and will apply to workplaces in existence before that date on January 1, 1996. They are discussed in detail in

---

[42] reg. 17 and Sched.
[42a] See para. 5.38.
[42b] "New or expectant mother" means an employee who is pregnant; who has given birth within the previous six months; or who is breastfeeding – reg. 1(2).
[42c] reg. 13B as inserted by S.I. 1994 No. 2865, reg. 2(3).
[43] reg. 15(1) and (2) as amended by S.I. 1994 No. 2865, reg. 2(5).
[44] S.I. 1992 No. 3004.
[45] See EC Directive on minimum safety and health requirements for the workplace 89/654/EEC.

Chapter 4.[46] As already noted, the regulations provide very detailed rules about the health and safety requirements for the working environment and provide for both criminal and civil liability. They exclude from their compass workplaces which are in the nature of ships; building operations and engineering construction works; involving the extraction of mineral resources; or workplaces which are situated in the immediate vicinity of another workplace involving the extraction of mineral resources. The Regulations also repeal a whole host of earlier regulations[47] and some key provisions of the Factories Act 1961[48] and the Offices, Shops and Railway Premises Act 1963.[49]

(c) Provision and Use of Work Equipment Regulations 1992

6.24 These Regulations[50] are intended to implement the Work Equipment Directive[51] and are accompanied by HSE Guidance Notes. As was noted in Chapter 4,[52] one of the key aspects of these Regulations is the repeal of the fencing provisions of the Factories Act 1961.[53] Instead, the Regulations provide new provisions requiring measures to be taken to prevent access to dangerous parts of machinery or to any rotating stock bar or to stop the movement of any dangerous part of machinery or rotating stock bar when any person enters a danger zone. The Regulations apply to new machinery from January 1, 1993 and in the case of existing machinery the obligations under these Regulations operate from January 1, 1997. They can be enforced through both criminal penalty and civil liability.

---

[46] See paras. 4.66–4.76.
[47] See Sched. 2, Pt. II.
[48] In particular, Factories Act 1961, ss. 1–7, 18, 28, 29, 57–60 and 69. See Sched. 2, Pt. I.
[49] Offices, Shops and Railway Premises Act 1963, ss.4-16. See Sched. 2, Pt. I.
[50] S.I. 1992 No. 2932.
[51] EC Directive on minimum safety and health requirements for the use of work equipment by workers at work 89/655/EEC.
[52] See paras. 4.44–4.57.
[53] Factories Act 1961, ss. 12–16. The regulations also repeal s. 17 and s. 19 and the Offices, Shops and Railway Premises Act 1963, s. 17. See Sched. 2, Pt. I. They also repeal a number of older regulations. See Sched. 2, Pt. II.

(d) Personal Protective Equipment at Work Regulations 1992

6.25 These Regulations[54] are intended to implement the Personal Protective Equipment Directive[55] and are accompanied by HSE Guidance Notes. The basic obligation placed upon employers[56] is to ensure that suitable personal protective equipment is provided to their employees[57] who may be exposed to a risk to their health or safety while at work unless it can be shown that the risk has been adequately controlled by other means which are equally or more effective.[58] "Personal protective equipment" means all equipment (including clothing affording protection against the weather) which is intended to be worn or held by a person at work and which protects him against one or more risks to his health and safety, and any addition or accessory designed to meet that objective.[59] However, there are exclusions for personal protective equipment which involves any of the following—

    (a)   ordinary working clothes and uniforms which do not specifically protect the health and safety of the wearer;

    (b)   offensive weapons used as self-defence or as deterrent equipment;

---

[54] S.I. 1992 No. 2966.

[55] EC Directive on minimum safety and health requirements for the use by workers of personal protective equipment at the workplace 89/656/EEC.

[56] There are exemptions for seagoing ships. See reg. 3(1).

[57] The Health and Safety at Work Act 1974, s. 9 ensures that an employer cannot charge the employee for the provision of such equipment.

[58] reg. 4(1). Self-employed persons must ensure that they are provided with suitable personal protective equipment for their own health and safety – reg. 4(2). Reg. 4 does not apply where other regulations require personal protective equipment to be provided in respect of health and safety risks. For our purposes the most important of these other regulations are the Control of Lead at Work Regulations 1980 (S.I. 1980 No. 1248), the Control of Asbestos at Work Regulations 1987 (S.I. 1987 No. 2115) and the Control of Substances Hazardous to Health Regulations 1988 (S.I. 1988 No. 1657).

[59] reg. 2(1). For examples of relevant protective equipment see para. 7 of the Guidance Notes. The Guidance Notes make clear that some types of personal protective equipment such as ear protectors and most types of respiratory protective equipment are unlikely to be covered by the PPE Regulations since they are covered by other regulations such as the COSHH Regulations.

(c)   portable devices for detecting and signalling risks and nuisances;

(d)   personal protective equipment used for protection while travelling on roads; and

(e)   equipment used during the playing of competitive sports.[60]

6.26 As noted above, the key requirement is for the personal protective equipment to be suitable. Equipment will not be suitable unless:

(a)   it is appropriate for the risks involved and the conditions at the place where the exposure to the risks may occur;

(b)   it takes account of ergonomic requirements and the state of health of the wearer;

(c)   it is capable of fitting the wearer correctly, if necessary after adjustments;

(d)   so far as practicable, it is effective to prevent or adequately control the risks involved without increasing overall risk;

(e)   it complies with any British enactment implementing any relevant Community directive[61] on design and manufacture of personal protective equipment.[62]

6.27 Although the need to provide suitable personal protective equipment is the key provision, the Regulations also place obligations on employers as regards the selection and compatibility and use and maintenance of personal protective equipment. Thus before choosing any personal protective equipment employers must ensure that an assessment is made to determine whether that equipment is suitable.[63] This assessment must include (a) an assessment of the health and safety risks which have not been avoided by other means, (b) the definition of the characteristics the equipment must have to be effective against those risks and (c) a comparison of those charac-

---

[60] reg. 3(2).
[61] The relevant directives are EC Directive 89/686/EEC and EC Directive 93/95/EEC implemented in the UK by the Personal Protective Equipment (EC Directive) Regulations 1992 (S.I. 1992 No. 3139 as amended by S.I. 1993 No. 3074).
[62] reg. 4(3).
[63] reg. 6(1).

teristics against the characteristics which the proposed equipment possesses.[64] Such an assessment must be reviewed if there is any reason to suspect that it is no longer valid or there has been a significant change in the matters to which it relates.[65] In addition, employers must ensure that where employees are required to wear two or more items of personal protective equipment each item is compatible and continues to be effective against the risks in question.[66]

6.28 The Regulations also require employers to take all reasonable steps to ensure that any personal protective equipment provided to employees is properly used.[67] Central to this requirement are the provisions of reg. 9(1) which place obligations on employers to ensure that employees are provided with the necessary information, instruction and training. Any such information, etc. should be adequate and appropriate[68] to enable employees to know (a) the risks which the personal protective equipment will avoid or limit, (b) the purpose for which and the manner in which that equipment is to be used, and (c) any action the employee needs to take to ensure that the equipment remains in an efficient state, in efficient working order and in good repair. There are corresponding obligations on employees to use personal protective equipment in accordance with any training and instructions as to its use[69] and to report to their employer any loss of or obvious defect in that equipment.[70]

6.29 As regards the upkeep of such equipment, regulation 7(1) requires every employer to ensure that any personal protective equipment provided to employees is maintained (including replaced or cleaned as appropriate) in an efficient state, in efficient working order and in good repair. The Guidance Notes make it clear that it is essential for employers to introduce an examination and maintenance schedule for all personal protective equip-

---

[64] reg. 6(2).
[65] reg. 6(3).
[66] reg. 5(1).
[67] reg. 10(1).
[68] Information and instruction will not be adequate and appropriate unless it is comprehensible to the employees concerned – reg. 9(2).
[69] reg. 10(2).
[70] reg. 11.

ment and to provide a sufficient stock of spare parts.[71] Employers are also required to provide appropriate accommodation for personal protective equipment when it is not being used[72] and employees must take all reasonable steps to ensure that it is returned to that accommodation after use.[73] The Regulations can be enforced by the application of both the criminal and civil law, and it is clear that both employers and employees can be responsible for breaches of statutory duty.

(e) Manual Handling Operations Regulations 1992

6.30 These Regulations[74] are intended to implement the Manual Handling Directive[75] and are accompanied by HSE Guidance Notes. They repeal earlier provisions in both the Factories Act 1961, s.72 and the Offices, Shops and Railway Premises Act 1963, s. 23 which concentrated solely on the weight of the load to be lifted. Instead the new Regulations take a wider and more ergonomic approach to the problem of employees moving loads. The basic aim of the Manual Handling Regulations is to prevent employees having to undertake any lifting operations which involve a risk of back injury: though the Regulations apply to the risk of any type of injury. Thus the primary obligation placed upon employers[76] is, so far as is reasonably practicable, to avoid the need for employees to undertake any manual handling operations at work which involve the risk of their being injured.[77] "Manual handling operations" means any transporting or supporting of a load (including the lifting, putting down, pushing, pulling, carrying or moving of it) by hand or by

---

[71] See paras. 45–47.

[72] reg. 8.

[73] reg. 10(4).

[74] S.I. 1992 No. 2793.

[75] EC Directive on the minimum safety and health requirements for the manual handling of loads where there is a risk particularly of back injury to workers 90/269/EEC.

[76] Similar duties are placed upon self-employed persons as regards themselves – reg. 2(2). There are also exemptions for sea-going ships – reg. 3.

[77] reg. 4(1)(a). "Injury" does not involve injury caused by any toxic or corrosive substance which (a) has leaked or spilled from a load, (b) is present on the surface of a load but has not leaked or spilled from it, or (c) is a constituent part of the load and "injured" is to be construed accordingly – reg. 2(1).

bodily force.[78] A load is defined to include any person and any animal,[79] so that the Regulations apply equally to nurses lifting patients and to farm workers lifting animals.

6.31 Although the principal and first obligation on employers is to avoid employees lifting loads, the Regulations recognise that there may be situations where this cannot be achieved. Thus where it is not reasonably practicable to avoid the need for employees to undertake any manual handling operations at work which involve the risk of injury, employers must

(a)   make a suitable and sufficient assessment of all such operations,[80]

(b)   take appropriate steps to reduce the risk of injury to those employees involved in manual handling operations to the lowest level reasonably practicable, and

(c)   take appropriate steps to provide such employees with general indications and, where it is reasonably practicable to do so, precise information on the weight of each load and the heaviest side of any load whose centre of gravity is not positioned centrally.[81]

The assessment must be reviewed by the employer if there is reason to suspect that it is no longer valid, or there has been a significant change in the operations to which it relates.[82] Employees have a duty to make full and proper use of any system of work which the employer has instituted so as to bring the risk of injury to the lowest level reasonably practicable.[83] The Regulations permit

[78] reg. 2(1).
[79] reg. 2(1).
[80] In this context employers must have regard to a list of factors and consider the corresponding questions all of which are specified in Sched. 1. The factors include the tasks, the loads, the working environment and individual capacity. The questions include the posture of employee's bodies, the unwieldiness of loads, the conditions of the working environment and whether the operations require unusual strength or height or could endanger pregnant women.
[81] reg. 4(1)(b). There is a very useful flow chart on p. 5 of the Guidance Notes which indicates the hierarchy of responsibilities placed upon employers by reg. 4(1).
[82] reg. 4(2).
[83] reg. 5.

both criminal prosecutions and civil actions for breach of statutory duty.

(f) Health and Safety (Display Screen Equipment) Regulations 1992

6.32   These Regulations[84] are intended to implement the Display Screen Equipment Directive[85] and are accompanied by HSE Guidance Notes. The effect of the Regulations is to ensure that for the first time in Britain there is a legal framework regulating the health and safety of persons using visual display units. The Regulations only apply where there is display screen equipment and the duties that they create only apply when there are users and operators. "Display screen equipment" means any alphanumeric or graphic display screen, regardless of the display process involved.[86] However, exempted from the Regulations are the following—

(a)   drivers' cabs or control cabs for vehicles or machinery;

(b)   display screen equipment on board a means of transport;

(c)   display screen equipment mainly intended for public operation;

(d)   portable systems not in prolonged use;

(e)   calculators, cash registers or any equipment having a small data or measurement display required for direct use of the equipment; and

(f)   window typewriters.[87]

6.33   "User" means an employee who habitually uses display screen equipment as a significant part of his normal work.[88] The critical question here is whether employees use a display screen as a *significant* part of their normal work and the Guidance Notes are particularly helpful in indicating examples of users and non-users and the criteria that should be adopted when resolving this

---

[84] S.I. 1992 No. 2792.
[85] EC Directive on minimum safety and health requirements for work with display screen equipment 90/270/EEC.
[86] reg. 1(2).
[87] reg. 1(4).
[88] reg. 1(2)(d).

issue.[89] "Operators" are self-employed persons who also habitually use display screen equipment as a significant part of their normal work.[90] The obligations under the Regulations fall largely on employers. As far as users are concerned, employers owe duties to their employees regardless of who it is that provided the workstation[91]; whereas in the case of operators, employers only owe duties to the self-employed when it is the employer who has provided the workstation and the operator uses that workstation for the employer's purposes.[92]

6.34 It is clear that critical to the application of the regulations is the concept of the "workstation." A workstation is an assembly comprising—

> (a) display screen equipment (whether provided with software determining the interface between the equipment and the user, a keyboard or any other input device),
> (b) any optional accessories to the equipment,
> (c) any disk drive, telephone, modem, printer, document holder, work chair, work desk, work surface or other item peripheral to the equipment, and
> (d) the immediate work environment around the equipment.[93]

Workstations first put into service on or after January 1, 1993 must comply with certain standards listed in the Schedule to the Regulations; whereas existing workstations (those in service on or before December 31, 1992) have to comply with these standards by December 31, 1996.[94]

---

[89] See the Guidance Notes at pp. 6–10. Some examples given of definite users are secretaries, journalists, air traffic controllers and graphic designers, some examples of possible users are scientists and airline check-in clerks whereas the Guidance Notes make clear that senior managers are definitely not users. These are merely examples and a better guide are the criteria listed in para. 12 and the chart provided on p. 10.

[90] reg. 1(2)(b).

[91] Thus employees working at home or at another employer's workstation are nonetheless covered.

[92] See generally reg. 3.

[93] reg. 1(2(e).

[94] See reg. 3 and Sched. The Schedule contains detailed rules on the equipment, environment and interface between computer and user/operator required for workstations.

6.35 Consistent with many of the other "European" Regulations the Display Screen Regulations require employers to carry out an assessment of the risks associated with display screen equipment. Thus regulation 2(1) requires employers to perform a suitable and sufficient analysis of workstations so as to assess the health and safety risks to which users and operators are exposed. Once this has been completed employers must then reduce the risks identified by the assessment to the lowest extent reasonably practicable.[95] Any such assessment must be reviewed if there is reason to suspect that it is no longer valid or there has been a significant change in the matters to which it relates.[96] Employers must also plan the activities of users so that their daily work on display screen equipment is periodically interrupted by such breaks or changes of activity as reduce their workload at that equipment.[97]

6.36 A central provision of the Regulations concerns eye and eyesight tests for employees. Employers owe obligations both to users and to employees who are to become users to ensure that they are provided with an appropriate eye and eyesight test[98] which must be carried out by a competent person.[99] Such tests should be carried out whenever an employee who is a user at the date of coming into force of the Regulations or who is an employee who is to become a user so requests it, at regular intervals thereafter, and on request where a user experiences visual difficulties which may reasonably be considered to be caused by work on display screen equipment.[1] No employee can be required to undergo an eye and eyesight test against his or her will.[2] Employers may also be required to provide users with special corrective appliances appropriate for their work where normal

---

[95] reg. 2(3).

[96] reg. 2(2).

[97] reg. 4. For general guidance on this issue see the Guidance Notes at paras. 44 and 45.

[98] This will be a "sight test" as defined by the Opticians Act 1989, s. 36(2). See Guidance Notes, para. 50.

[99] reg. 5(1).

[1] reg. 5(1) and regs 5(3) and (4). An original test should, in the case of users, be carried out as soon as practicable after the request and, in the case of employees who will become users, be carried out before that employee becomes a user – reg. 5(2).

[2] reg. 5(6).

corrective appliances cannot be used and the result of any eye and eyesight test shows such provision to be necessary.[3]

6.37 Finally, the Regulations also place training and information responsibilities on employers. As regards training, users and employees who are to become users must be provided with adequate health and safety training in the use of any workstation upon which they may be required to work and that training must be updated when a workstation is substantially modified.[4] As regards information, users and operators must be provided with adequate information about all aspects of health and safety relating to their workstations and the measures taken in accordance with the risk assessment and the requirements for workstations specified in the Schedule to the Regulations.[5] Employers must also provide users with adequate information concerning their daily work routine and any substantial modification in their workstations and also as regards eye and eyesight tests and training requirements.[6] The Regulations give rise to both criminal and civil liability.

THE OFFSHORE HEALTH AND SAFETY REGIME

6.38 Until recently the major statute dealing with health and safety on offshore installations was the Mineral Workings (Offshore Installations) Act 1971. This Act enabled regulations to be made for the safety of offshore installations and for the safety, health and welfare of persons aboard such installations. It placed obligations on the concession owner and owner of the installation and required the appointment of an installation manager who was given general responsibility for safety, health and welfare on the installation and who was also required to maintain order and discipline on the rig. Many of its provisions have now been repealed: though much remains, particularly as far as the responsibilities of the oil

---

[3] reg. 5(5). Under the Health and Safety at Work Act 1974, s.9, an employer cannot charge the employee for such appliances.
[4] reg. 6.
[5] reg. 7(1).
[6] regs. 7(2) and (3).

installation manager are concerned. Moreover, under the original provisions of the 1971 Act responsibility for the enforcement of the Act was placed upon the Department of Energy – this responsibility has now been transferred to HSE.[7]

6.39 The legal catalyst for much of this change was the Offshore Safety Act 1992 which was enacted so as to implement the recommendations of the Cullen Report[8] into the *Piper Alpha* disaster which had claimed the lives of 165 men. This report was highly critical of the safety regime applicable on offshore installations and made a number of significant and important recommendations. For our purpose, three of Lord Cullen's 106 recommendations are worthy of particular comment. The first was his recommendation that there should be regulations requiring the operator of every offshore installation to submit a "safety case" for acceptance by HSE. The safety case would have to demonstrate that the risks of a major accident had been assessed adequately and that suitable measures had been applied to control risks and ensure the safety of everybody on board. The second major recommendation was that existing offshore health and safety legislation should be progressively repealed by new regulations. These new regulations were to be "goal-setting" rather than specific as to the measures which had to be taken. Third, responsibility for offshore health and safety should be transferred to HSE.

6.40 The Offshore Safety Act 1992 fulfils three major purposes. First, it extends the coverage of the general purposes of the Health and Safety at Work Act 1974, s. 1(1)(a)–(d). The 1992 Act makes it clear that the general purposes will apply to—

(a) the safety, health and welfare of persons on offshore installations or engaged on pipe-line works;

(b) the safety of such installations and the prevention of accidents on or near them;

---

[7] See generally the Offshore Safety (Repeals and Modifications) Regulations 1993 (S.I. 1993 No. 1823).
[8] See *Report of the Public Inquiry into the Piper Alpha Disaster* (Cm. 1310) published on Nov. 12, 1990.

(c)   the proper construction and safe operation of
       pipe-lines and the prevention of damage to
       them; and
(d)   the safe dismantling, removal and disposal of
       offshore installations and pipe-lines.[9]

Second, it declares that current offshore safety legislation
should be added to the list of relevant statutory provisions which are specified in the 1974 Act, Sched. 1.[10] As
relevant statutory provisions, offshore safety legislation is
now subject to the 1974 Act, s. 1(2) and can be progressively replaced by a system of regulations and approved
codes of practice. Moreover, it also ensures that offshore
safety legislation can be enforced by HSE. Third, section 1
ensures that the existing statutory provisions can be
repealed or modified by health and safety regulations
made under the 1974 Act, s. 15, and allows for such
regulations to be made about any of the matters which are
specified in the general purposes of the 1974 Act as
modified for offshore installations by the 1992 Act.[11] The
1992 Act clearly enables earlier offshore safety legislation
to be repealed and replaced by the goal-setting regulations which Lord Cullen has recommended. Just as
important, it has enabled the Secretary of State to introduce regulations for safety cases.

(a) Offshore Installations (Safety Case) Regulations 1992

6.41   These Regulations[12] were made under powers
granted to the Secretary of State by the 1974 Act, s. 15 and
the 1992 Act, s. 1(2), and fulfil the recommendations of
Lord Cullen on this issue. They are entirely consistent
with the thrust of the "European" Regulations since they
require a full assessment of installations so as to identify
the risks and introduce the necessary protective and
preventive measures. There are also requirements for the
carrying out of safety audits by independent persons. The
key requirement is for operators to prepare a safety case
for their installation and to send it to HSE.[13] No offshore

---

[9] 1992 Act, s.1(1).
[10] 1992 Act, ss. 1(1) and (3).
[11] 1992 Act, s. 1(2).
[12] S.I. 1992 No. 2885.
[13] reg. 4(1).

installation can be operated until such a case has been prepared and sent to HSE and it has been accepted by the Executive.[14]

6.42 The Regulations specify the requirements for a safety case[15] and make it clear that any such case must include sufficient particulars to demonstrate that:

(a)   the management system[16] is adequate to ensure that the relevant statutory provisions will be complied with in relation to the installation and any activity on or connected with it;

(b)   adequate arrangements have been established for audits[17] and reports;

(c)   all hazards with the potential to cause a major accident have been identified; and

(d)   risks have been evaluated and measures taken to reduce the risks to persons affected by those hazards to the lowest level that is reasonably practicable.[18]

A safety case should be revised by the operator as often as is appropriate[19] and there are obligations on the operator to ensure that the procedures and arrangements laid out in the safety case are followed.[20]

(b) Offshore Installations (Safety Representatives and Safety Committees) Regulations 1989

6.43 The importance of the oil installation manager in offshore health and safety matters has already been noted. Such persons have particular responsibility under

---

[14] reg. 4(2).
[15] See Sched. 1 for the safety case requirements for the design of a fixed installation, and Sched. 2 for the operation of a fixed installation. Sched. 3 lists the requirements for a mobile installation.
[16] "Management system" means the organisation and arrangements established by the operator for managing the undertaking – reg. 8(4)(b).
[17] "Audit" is a systematic assessment of the adequacy of the management system carried out by persons who are sufficiently independent of the system to ensure that the assessment is objective.
[18] reg. 8(1).
[19] reg. 9.
[20] reg. 10(1).

the 1989 Regulations[21] as regards safety representatives and safety committees on offshore installations. These Regulations were made by the Secretary of State for Energy under powers granted to him by the Mineral Workings (Offshore Installations) Act 1971 and are different from the Safety Representatives and Safety Committees Regulations 1977.[22] The major difference is that the 1989 Regulations do not depend upon the existence of an independent trade union recognised for collective bargaining purposes. Instead, the 1989 Regulations permit a workforce to nominate and elect safety representatives on the basis of constituencies established and maintained by the installation manager.

6.44 There must be at least two constituencies on each installation with a maximum of 40 members and every member of the workforce must be assigned to a constituency.[23] It is the duty of the installation manager to establish these constituencies and he can take into account such factors as the areas of the installation, its activities, the employers of members of the workforce and such other objective criteria as may be applied.[24] There must be a safety representative for each constituency and any member of the constituency can stand for election so long as he is nominated and seconded by two other members of the constituency.[25] If there is more than one candidate nominated for election as a safety representative in a constituency it is the duty of the installation manager to conduct a secret ballot where every member has the right to vote for one candidate.[26] Once elected, a safety representative has the right to conduct investigations and to make representations to the installation manager on behalf of the constituency members.[27] Safety representatives also have the right to paid time off in order to exercise their functions and to undertake training.[28]

6.45 The owner of an offshore installation where one or more safety representatives have been elected also has a

---

[21] S.I. 1989 No. 971.
[22] S.I. 1977 No. 500 discussed in Chap. 5 at paras. 5.20–5.26.
[23] reg. 5(2).
[24] reg. 5(1).
[25] reg. 9(1).
[26] reg. 11(1).
[27] See generally reg. 16.
[28] reg. 26.

duty to establish a safety committee. This committee is chaired by the installation manager and is made up of all the safety representatives together with one other person appointed by the manager and other persons co-opted unanimously by the committee.[29] The committee exercises important functions such as the power to keep under review the measures taken to ensure the occupational health and safety of the workforce and the arrangements for training of safety representatives, and the right to consider the causes of accidents, dangerous occurrences and causes of occupational ill-health and to make representations to the installation manager about them.[30]

(c) Offshore Safety (Protection against Victimisation) Act 1992 (Repealed)

6.46 Another one of Lord Cullen's key recommendations was that offshore safety representatives should be protected against victimisation by making it automatically unfair to dismiss them for exercising their safety functions. The 1992 Act sought to implement this recommendation but went further than Lord Cullen by ensuring that protection was also granted to members of safety committees and that the extent of the protection applied to both dismissal and action short of dismissal. The statute was repealed by the Trade Union Reform and Employment Rights Act 1993 and replaced by provisions added by the 1993 Act to the Employment Protection (Consolidation) Act 1978.[31] The effect is to ensure that safety representatives and members of safety committees on offshore installations enjoy the same level of protection from being subjected to a detriment or dismissal as their counterparts onshore.[32]

---

[29] reg. 20.
[30] See generally reg. 22(1).
[31] See EPCA, s. 22A (detriment) and EPCA, s. 57A (dismissal).
[32] This issue is discussed in Chap. 5 at para. 5.32 and Chap. 7 at para. 7.24.

CHAPTER 7

REMEDIES AND INSURANCE

INTRODUCTION

7.1 As has been made clear in earlier chapters, enforcement of performance of duties in the field of health and safety at work is the province of both criminal and civil procedure. Broadly[1] it can be asserted that those duties which are common law in their origin are the subject of civil procedures and remedies while duties which are statutory are either enforced only through criminal sanctions or through both criminal sanctions and a civil law action for breach of statutory duty at the instance of a party injured or killed. This chapter seeks to outline those civil law remedies and also insurance, both private and State.

The range of remedies

7.2 By far the most common civil law remedy for death or personal injury sustained at work is an action for damages for breach of the employer's duty of care. However an action for damages may also lie for breach of statutory duty[2] and for breach of contract[3]; similarly, because of the ambit of the implied contractual term, a breach of duty may also justify use of self-help remedies like retention and lien as well as the rescission of the contract and ground a claim of constructive dismissal[4]

---

[1] Of course there are many situations in which the common law triggers a criminal procedure as a result of a crime committed in the course of employment (*e.g.* assault on a fellow employee or employer or committing the crime of malicious mischief by deliberately damaging the property of the employer), but these sanctions would be the normal result of the criminal conduct and are not specific to work situations.

[2] See Chap. 4, paras. 4.10 *et seq.*

[3] See Chap. 3, para. 3.4.

[4] *Ibid.*

221

and, although unlikely, there is no reason why persistently breaching the duty of care owed to an employee could not lead to an employer being the subject of an interdict.[5] Far more likely the matter would be drawn to the attention of the Health and Safety Inspector (or other enforcing authority) who is empowered to issue an Improvement or Prohibition Notice.[6] The range of remedies open to an employee would also include (1) the special rights against action short of dismissal and dismissal itself and (2) the maternity suspension provisions on health and safety grounds both introduced by the Trade Union Reform and Employment Rights Act 1993.[7]

Damages — contract or delict?

7.3 The purpose of an award of damages is — "so far as possible, to effect *restitutio in integrum* and to restore the pursuer to the position he would have been in if the contract had been performed, or the legal duty to him duly implemented."[8] However, if the initial injury is made worse by the conduct of the pursuer he cannot recover damages for loss attributable to his own lack of care.[9] Although the employer's duty to his employee may be expressed as contractual or delictual it is important to note that the basis of the claim can produce different results and while one claim may be viable the other may not.[10] Thus it may be that an action in contract cannot proceed because of an exemption clause[11] or because the contract may have been retrospectively reduced. Also, and probably more importantly, the heads of loss recoverable in delict are different from those recoverable in contract. Thus the rules of remoteness of damage are not

---

[5] See S. Robinson, *The Law of Interdict*, pp. 126 *et seq.*
[6] See Chap. 5, paras. 5.56 *et seq.*
[7] Trade Union Reform and Employment Rights Act 1993, ss. 25 and 28; see *post*, paras. 7.25.
[8] Walker *Principles of Scottish Private Law*, Bk. IV, p. 292.
[9] *McKew v. Holland & Hannen & Cubitts*, 1970 S.L.T. 68 (H.L.); and see Chap. 3, para. 3.16.
[10] In this respect see the interesting article by Prof. J.M. Thompson "Delictual Liability between Parties to a Contract," 1994 S.L.T. (News) 29.
[11] *Golden Sea Produce Ltd v. Scottish Nuclear plc*, 1992 S.L.T. 942. Note however that s. 16(1) of the Unfair Contract Terms Act 1977 prevents the exclusion of liability in respect of death or personal injury.

the same in contract and delict. In the former, liability extends only for the consequences of the breach which should have been contemplated at the time the contract was entered into so that loss not reasonably foreseeable by the defender at the time of contracting, having regard to his state of knowledge — imputed and actual — is too remote to be recoverable.[12] On the other hand, in a delictual action there is liability for the harm which immediately results from the breach of duty and for all the other direct consequences thereof provided these were reasonably foreseeable, and as has been pointed out,[13] although Lord Kinloch's statement that "[t]he grand rule on the subject of damages is, that none can be claimed except such as naturally and directly arise out of the wrong done and such as may reasonably be supposed to have been in the view of the wrongdoer"[14] was made *obiter* it is an accurate statement of Scots law governing liability for both the immediate and subsequent consequences of negligence when properly construed. Although there may be different views as to the correct test to be applied for determining questions relating to the remoteness of damage[15] it is not disputed that the law of delict is generally more favourable to the pursuer in a personal injuries claim than the law of contract. While damages for breach of contract have included a sum in respect of *solatium*[16] the dichotomy between contractual and delictual claims is amply illustrated by *Black v. Gibson*[17] in which both breach of a building contract and negligence were pleaded: the Lord Ordinary allowed a proof before answer of the averments relating to damages for anxiety, worry and the onset or exacerbation of illness since the claim alleged fault as well as breach of contract.[18]

---

[12] Bell, *Comm.* I, 478–479; *Prin.* s. 33; *Hadley v. Baxendale* (1854) 9 Ex. 341; *Victoria Laundry v. Newman* [1949] 2 K.B. 528; and see the more recent review of the position in *Haberstich v. McCormick & Nicholson*, 1975 S.C. 1.

[13] Gloag and Henderson, *Introduction to the Law of Scotland* (9th ed. 1987), para. 34.14.

[14] *Allan v. Barclay* (1864) 2 M. 873 at p. 874.

[15] For an interesting discussion of the test for remoteness of damage see W. A. Wilson, *Introductory Essays on Scots Law* (2nd ed., 1984), p. 126 *et seq.*

[16] See the cases referred to by W. W. McBryde, *The Law of Contract in Scotland* (1987), p. 481.

[17] 1992 S.L.T. 1076.

[18] See also *Palmer v. Beck*, 1993 S.L.T. 485, in which an award of damages for *solatium* was refused in an action for breach of warrandice.

Similarly in an action for wrongful dismissal a pursuer is generally not entitled to a sum in respect of loss of reputation and injury to feelings — at least not until the House of Lords reconsiders its decision in *Addis v. Gramophone Co. Ltd.*[19]

7.4 On the other hand in a personal injuries claim based on delict or breach of statutory duty the pursuer is entitled to sums in respect of (a) *solatium*[20] for the pain and suffering caused by the injuries and for loss of faculties, mental or physical, including loss of or impairment of senses and, if the injured person's expectation of life has been reduced by the injuries and the injured person was or is likely to become aware of that, the court in assessing the amount of damages due by way of *solatium* will have regard to the extent the injured person will suffer in consequence of being aware of the reduction in the expectation of life[21]; (b) patrimonial loss including loss of earnings past and prospective[22] and, where the injuries cause diminished expectation of life, it is to be assumed that the pursuer will survive until the date when he would have been expected to die if he had not sustained the injuries with account being taken of living expenses the pursuer would have reasonably incurred until the notional date of death[23]; and (c) expenses necessarily and reasonably incurred in, for example, medical treatment.

Calculating the award of damages

7.5 Detailed examination of the calculation of an award of damages is beyond the scope of this work,[24] but this

---

[19] [1909] A.C. 488; *per* Browne-Wilkinson V.-C. in *O'Laoire v. Jackel International Ltd* [1991] I.R.L.R. 170 (C.A.). And see *Re B.C.C.I.* [1994] I.R.L.R. 282 in which the English High Court reviewed the law in *Addis* and *O'Laoire*.

[20] Solatium may include an element for loss of congenial employment: *Stark v. Lothian and Borders Fire Board*, 1993 S.L.T. 652.

[21] Damages (Scotland) Act 1976, s. 9A inserted by Damages (Scotland) Act 1993, s. 5: the effect of s. 9A is to supersede decisions like *Dalgleish v. Glasgow Corporation*, 1976 S.C. 32 which supported the award of *solatium* for reduced life expectancy even if the injured person was unaware of it.

[22] A multiplier is used depending on the number of years for which the loss may be expected to continue.

[23] Damages (Scotland) Act 1976, s. 9.

[24] For such a detailed coverage, reference may be made to McEwan and Paton *Damages in Scotland* (2nd ed., 1989).

section attempts to set out some general rules which may be of particular relevance to personal injuries claims and to offer some examples from case law of the rules in operation.

Provisional and interim damages

7.6 Until the enactment of the Administration of Justice Act 1982[25] damages for personal injuries were assessed once and for all at the end of the proof.[26] However, that Act introduced a major innovation, namely an award of provisional damages, by providing that where (a) in an action for damages for personal injuries it is proved or admitted to be a risk that at some definite or indefinite time in the future the injured person will, as a result of the act or omission which gave rise to the cause of action, develop or suffer some serious deterioration in his physical or mental condition and (b) the responsible person was a public authority or public corporation or insured or otherwise indemnified in respect of the claim the court may order damages to be awarded to the injured person and that the injured person may apply for a further award of damages.[27] It is not enough merely to aver a possible future deterioration in condition: the pursuer has to aver and prove a causal link between that deterioration and the act or omission in question.[28] Provisional damages have been awarded where there was a serious risk of the injured person developing epilepsy[29] or mesothelioma but have been refused where the original injury was a damaged lumbar disc which gave rise to some risk of prolapse with ensuing complications.[30]

7.7 Provisional damages are to be distinguished from interim damages which are to mitigate the suffering of the injured person or to assist relatives pending the outcome of the action for damages. The procedure whereby an application for interim damages may be made was introduced in 1974[31] and is competent at the instance of the

---

[25] s. 12.
[26] Walker, *Delict* (2nd ed.) p. 462.
[27] Administration of Justice Act 1982, s. 12.
[28] *Paterson v. Costain Mining Ltd*, 1988 S.L.T. 413.
[29] *Lappin v. Britannia Airways*, 1989 S.L.T. 181.
[30] *Meek v. Burton Gold Medal Biscuits Ltd*, 1989 S.L.T. 338; and see *McMenemy v. Argyll Stores Ltd*, 1992 S.L.T. 971.
[31] Rules of Court, r. 89A introduced by Act of Sederunt, May 14, 1974; a similar procedure is available in the sheriff court.

pursuer after defences have been lodged. If the court is satisfied that the defender has admitted liability or if the pursuer would succeed without a substantial finding of contributory negligence it may order the defender to make a payment of interim damages.

Loss of earnings

7.8 Where personal injury has resulted in loss of earnings the loss is calculated having regard to earnings after deduction of Income Tax,[32] National Insurance contributions[33] and pension contributions.[34] When the National Insurance scheme was introduced in 1948 it was provided[35] that in an action for damages for personal injuries (whether based on contract or delict) there shall, in assessing those damages, be taken into account against any loss of earnings which has accrued or probably will accrue to the injured person from the injuries one-half of the value of any rights which have accrued or which will accrue in respect of certain state benefits. However in order to permit the government to recover moneys paid out there has now been introduced a new scheme which results in the deduction of the total amount of specified benefits.[36] Under the scheme the Secretary of State is granted the right to recover from those making payments of damages for personal injuries a sum representing certain state benefits paid during the period of five years, or until the making of the payment in final discharge of any claim, if sooner. The defender must not make any payment under a decree or settlement until he has obtained from the Department of Social Security Compensation Recovery Unit a certificate of the total benefits paid to the pursuer and must deduct the amount of such benefits from the damages payable and account for it to the Department of Social Security. The benefits to which

---

[32] *British Transport Commission v. Gourlay* [1956] A.C. 185.
[33] *Gibney v. Eric Johnson Stubbs (Scotland) Ltd,* 1987 S.L.T. 132.
[34] *Dews v. NCB* [1987] 3 W.L.R. 38 (H.L.).
[35] Law Reform (Personal Injuries) Act 1948, s. 2.
[36] Social Security Act 1989, s. 22, Sched. 4 now included in Pt. IV of the Social Security Administration Act 1992.

the scheme applies are (a) sickness benefit,[37] (b) invalidity pension and allowance, (c) unemployment benefit, (d) attendance and mobility allowances, (e) retirement and severe disablement allowances, (f) family credit and (g) income support.

7.9 However, certain payments are not to be taken into account to reduce the amount of damages.[38] Where a payment is not the subject of an express statutory provision its treatment must depend on its intrinsic nature and not its source,[39] and it has been held that a government retraining allowance should be deducted in full,[40] but not Family Income Supplement on the view that it is indistinguishable from wages.[41] Nor, in the absence of a contractual term to the effect, should there be deducted from an award of damages in respect of loss of earnings against an employer a sum representing monies paid under an incapacity insurance to which the employer and the employee have contributed.[42] In some recent cases an award has been made for loss of employability to reflect the modern economic conditions of inflation and unemployment which may result in a reluctance on the part of employers to engage people with disabilities. The purpose of an award to reflect loss of employability is to recognise the disadvantage of such people in the employment market.[43] However, while the Scottish courts have

[37] Note that the House of Lords has held that payments to an incapacitated employee made under an employer's health insurance scheme have to be taken into account when assessing damages for loss — *Hussain v. New Taplow Paper Mills Ltd* [1988] 2 W.L.R. 266 (H.L.). *Cf. Smoker v. London Fire Authority* [1991] I.C.R. 449 (H.L.) in which *Hussain* was narrowly distinguished on the grounds that what the injured employee received was wages as opposed to an insurance benefit. *Sed quaere?* Sickness and Invalidity Benefits will be replaced by Incapacity Benefit in April 1995, see para. 7.37a.
[38] Administrative Justice Act 1982, s. 10 excludes from the scheme (a) contractual payments, (b) pensions payable out of public funds, (c) payments from public funds for period after date of award of damages designed to secure minimum subsistence level, (d) redundancy payments, (e) payments by an employer which employee is bound to repay and (f) any payment of a benevolent nature, *e.g.* from British Coal under the N.C.B. Pneumoconiosis Compensation Scheme.
[39] *per* Lord Reid in *Parry v. Cleaver* [1920] A.C. 1, at p. 15.
[40] *Ward v. Tarmac*, 1972 S.L.T. (Notes) 52.
[41] *Webb v. Macauley*, 1988 S.L.T. 138. *Cf. Gaskill v. Preston* [1981] 3 All E.R. 427.
[42] *Wood v. British Coal Corporation* [1991] I.C.R. 449 (H.L.).
[43] This type of award seems to have originated in *Smith v. Manchester* [1974] K.I.R. 1.

made awards specifically to reflect loss of employability,[44] in other situations the award is difficult to distinguish from an award representing loss of future earnings.[45]

Other losses

7.10 Loss of future pension rights is recoverable,[46] as are the costs of nursing care[47] and reasonable medical expenses.[48] Where necessary services like nursing care and attendance have been or are likely to be rendered to the injured person by a relative, then in the absence of an express agreement that no payment shall be made for those services, the person who has incurred liability shall pay to the injured person a sum which represents reasonable remuneration for those services and the injured person has a duty to account to such a relative for any damages recovered[49]; and for that reason the House of Lords has held in an English appeal that where the provider of the services was the tortfeasor there could be no ground for requiring him to pay to the injured plaintiff a sum representing the value of the services which he had rendered since the plaintiff would then have to repay that sum to him (the provider of the services).[50] Similarly the person responsible for the personal injuries is made liable to pay to the injured person a reasonable sum in respect of the inability of the injured person to render certain

[44] *Kirkpatrick v. Scott Lithgow Ltd*, 1987 S.L.T. 654.
[45] See *Douglas v. NCB*, 1977 S.L.T. 14; *Marshall v. Bertrams Ltd*, 1985 S.L.T. 80.
[46] *Barratt v. Strathclyde Fire Brigade*, 1984 S.L.T. 325.
[47] *MacIntosh v. NCB*, 1988 S.L.T. 348; *Tuttle v. Edinburgh University*, 1984 S.L.T. 172.
[48] As to whether these may include private medical treatment the Law Reform (Personal Injuries) Act 1948, s. 2(4), provides that there shall be disregarded in determining the reasonableness of such expenses the possibility of avoiding or reducing them by taking advantage of facilities available under the National Health Service.
[49] Administration of Justice Act 1982, s. 8 as amended by Law Reform (Miscellaneous Provisions) (Scotland) Act 1990, s. 69. Note that s. 8(4) provides that a relative shall have no right of action in delict against the person responsible for the personal injuries. See, for example, *Prentice v. William Thyne Ltd*, 1989 S.L.T. 336 (£400 awarded for necessary services rendered by wife).
[50] *Hunt v. Severs, The Times*, May 2, 1994.

personal services.[51] It is sufficient if the injured person or the deceased would personally have provided the services and they were provided for benefit of the person claiming.[52]

Multipliers and multiplicands

7.11 Resort is made to multipliers and multiplicands when assessing damages for future loss of, for example, wages, support and services, for damages for nursing care[53] and for damages for the expenses involved in a curatory.[54] The multiplicand reflects the pursuer's loss of net earnings at the date of proof, no allowance being made for possible increase in his earnings had he not been injured. The appropriate multiplier is to be determined by having regard to various factors including the age of the pursuer, his likely retirement age, the nature of his injuries and whether the incapacity is temporary or permanent, with discounts to reflect the investment opportunities arising on receipt of a large capital sum, the regularity of work record, supervening illness and the risk of redundancy.[54a]

Claims by relatives

7.11a Where a relative is injured, but not fatally, his family have no right to recover damages in respect of ruined family life, *solatium*, expenses or loss of support,[55]

[51] Administration of Justice Act 1982, s. 9. The services are such as (i) might have been expected to have been rendered by the injured person, (ii) would ordinarily be obtainable on payment and (iii) would have been given gratuitously to a relative. See *Worf v. Western SMT Co. Ltd*, 1987 S.L.T. 317 (injured father had tutored children before injuries), *Fox v. NCR (Nederland) BV*, 1987 S.L.T. 401 (son lost services (board and lodging and use of car) after parents' death).
[52] *Ingham v. John Russell (Transport) Ltd*, 1991 S.L.T. 739 (I.H.) (carrying out services in form of extensive DIY, maintenance and garden work held to fall within s. 9).
[53] *MacIntosh v. NCB*, 1988 S.L.T. 348.
[54] *Forsyth's Curator v. Govan Shipbuilders Ltd*, 1989 S.L.T. 91.
[54a] *O'Neil v. British Coal Corporation*, 1991 S.L.T. 467. Reference may also be made to the Ogden actuarial tables: see C.N, McEachran *O'Brien's C.B. v. British Steel*, 1992 S.L.T. (News) 139.
[55] *Robertson v. Turnbull*, 1980 S.C. 108; 1982 S.L.T. 96 (H.L.). Note the provisions of the Damages (Scotland) Act 1976, s. 1(5) which prevent account being taken of "any insurance money, benefit, pension or gratuity paid as a result of the deceased's death"; applied in *Bews v. Scottish Hydro Electric plc*, 1992 S.L.T. 749 (O.H.).

and where a spouse has had to give up work to look after an injured spouse the former has no right to damages for loss of earnings[56] although the injured person himself may be able to claim for the loss of the spouse's earnings.[57] However, where the injuries are fatal surviving relatives have a right to recover damages where there was an existing close relationship[58] between the relative and the deceased. According to the Damages (Scotland) Act 1976[59] a loss of society award was to be made for the loss of such non-patrimonial benefit as the relative might have expected to derive from the deceased's society and guidance if he had not died replacing the award of *solatium* for grief and suffering on the death of a relative.[60] However, more recently, following the recommendation of the Scottish Law Commission[61] the basis of the award has been clarified to include compensation for all or any of the following — (a) distress and anxiety endured by the relative in contemplation of the suffering of the deceased person before his death, (b) grief and sorrow caused by the deceased's death or (c) the loss of such non-patrimonial benefit as the relative might have been expected to derive from the deceased's society and guidance if he had not died[62] and is no longer to be referred to as a loss of society award.[63] Also relatives are entitled to the net loss of financial support since the date of death together with any reasonable expenses incurred in connection with the deceased's funeral.[64] To make a calculation of future loss of support a multiplier is used and an award of provisional damages to an injured person does not, in the event of the injured person dying, bar a claim by relatives, but when quantifying loss of support account must be taken of such part of the provisional award relating to future patrimonial loss as was intended to compensate the deceased for a period beyond the date on

---

[56] *Collins v. SSEB*, 1977 S.L.T. 93.

[57] *Jack v. Alexander McDougall & Co. (Engineers) Ltd*, 1973 S.C. 13, and see *Gordon v. Muir*, 1980 S.L.T. (Notes) 51.

[58] See Damages (Scotland) Act 1976, Sched. 1.

[59] s. 1(4).

[60] *Dingwall v. Walter Alexander & Sons (Midland) Ltd*, 1981 S.L.T. 313.

[61] *Report on Effect of Death on Damages* (1992).

[62] Damages (Scotland) Act 1976, s. 1(4) as inserted by Damages (Scotland) Act 1993, s. 1(1).

[63] Damages (Scotland) Act 1993, s. 7(1).

[64] Damages (Scotland) Act 1976, s. 1(3). It is not necessary to establish a legal duty of support in order to prove dependency (*ibid.*, s. 1(6)).

which he died.[65] Provision is now made to transmit the rights of a deceased relative to his executor.[66] Thus for deaths on or after April 19, 1993 a claim for damages for both *solatium* and patrimonial loss is transmitted to the executor of a deceased person but only in respect of the period prior to the death,[67] and any right to damages which is vested in the relative concerned immediately before his death is transmitted to the relative's executor but only insofar as the period immediately before the relative's death.[68]

Interest

7.11b Under the Interest on Damages (Scotland) Acts 1958 and 1971 a court, having made an award of damages, is required to consider the matter of interest on that award. Interest on patrimonial loss runs from the date of the injury or accident although the court has a discretion to alter this[68a] and the award has to be apportioned between past loss (up to the date of proof) and future loss. Interest may be awarded only on the former at one half of the average court rate from the date of the injury to the proof. Where the award includes a sum in respect of *solatium*, interest (at the average court rate for the period) is awarded on past *solatium* in respect of the period from the date of the injury to whenever the pain and suffering ended which may, of course, have been before the proof; in respect of *solatium* for the period after the proof interest is awarded at one half of the average court rate until the time the court estimates the pain and suffering will reduce.[68b] These rules regarding interest in personal injuries cases are in addition to the normal rules by which interest is awarded at the court rate from the date of decree until payment by the defender.

---

[65] Damages (Scotland) Act 1976, s. 5A inserted by Damages (Scotland) Act 1993, s. 1(3).
[66] Damages (Scotland) Act 1976, ss. 1A, 3 as inserted by Damages (Scotland) Act 1993, ss. 2, 3.
[67] *Ibid.*
[68] Damages (Scotland) Act 1976, s. 1A as inserted by Damages (Scotland) Act 1993, s. 2.
[68a] *McRae v. Reid and Mallick Ltd,* 1961 S.L.T. 96.
[68b] See *Keicher v. NCB,* 1988 S.L.T. 318; *Preston v. Grampian Health Board,* 1988 S.L.T. 435.

Prescription and limitation

7.11c Liability in respect of personal injuries or death prescribes after 20 years [68c] however a claim for reparation must be brought within 3 years.[68d] In the case of a claim for personal injuries that period begins to run from (a) the date on which the injuries were sustained, or where the act or omission was a continuing one, the date the act or omission ceased, whichever is the later or (b) if later than the above date, the date on which the pursuer became aware of the following: (i) that the injuries were sufficiently serious to justify his bringing an action, (ii) that the injuries were in part at least attributable to an act or omission and (iii) the defender was a person to whose act the injuries were attributable, or the employer of such a person.[68e] A similar period of limitation operates where death has resulted from personal injuries.[68f] However in each case the court has a discretion to allow a later claim where it would be equitable to do so.[69g]

Some examples of the principles in application

7.12 Detailed examination of the calculation of an award of damages for personal injury is beyond the scope of this work, but the following recent cases demonstrate by way of examples, how the matter is approached by the courts.

Stark v. Lothian and Borders Fire Board[69]

7.13 S was a 26-year-old firefighter who suffered burns to about 24 per cent of his body while fighting a fire. He developed post-traumatic stress disorder and had returned to employment which was less congenial. He sued his employers for damages to include a sum in respect of assistance (in the form of changing his bedding, dressing and undressing, cooking meals, changing ban-

---

[68c] Prescription and Limitation (Scotland) Act 1973, s. 7.
[68d] *Ibid.*, ss. 17, 18.
[68e] Periods of nonage and legal disability of the pursuer are disregarded (*ibid.*, s. 17(3)). And see *McLaren v. Harland & Wolff Ltd*, 1991 S.L.T. 85 (O.H.).
[68f] Prescription and Limitation (Scotland) Act 1973, s. 18.
[68g] *Ibid.*, s. 19A; and see, for example, *Anderson v. John Cotton (Colne) Ltd*, 1991 S.L.T. 696 (O.H.).
[69] 1993 S.L.T. 652 (O.H.).

dages, applying medication and driving him about). The Lord Ordinary held that he would never be fit enough to return to firefighting and that in his new work in the Board's community education department there were no promotion prospects and his employment was less secure. Had he remained a firefighter he would have had reasonable prospects of promotion to leading fireman by 1991. However S would probably not have achieved any higher work.

Assistance and services. Counsel were agreed that £3,000 would be appropriate for services.

Future loss. A multiplier of 12 (years) was applied to a multiplicand of £750 the difference between a leading fireman's salary and the salary in S's new job producing £9,000 and for future disadvantage in the labour market £3,000.

Solatium. An overall award of £26,000 for pain and suffering, post-traumatic stress disorder and loss of job satisfaction.

McVey v. Central Regional Council[70]

7.14 M, a 33-year-old labourer, was injured when a pneumatic drill fell on his foot causing permanent ligament damage and rendering him unfit for any work involving prolonged walking or standing. He was probably fit for sedentary work but none was likely to be available. He sued his employers for damages.

Solatium. Agreed at £6,500.

Future loss. The difference between likely earnings and earnings had he not been disabled — £12,638 (the multiplicand) to which a multiplier of 5 was applied producing £63,190.

Haining v. Babcock Energy Ltd[71]

7.15 H was a 59-year-old, right-handed, semi-skilled labourer whose left hand was trapped in a machine causing a crushing and degloving injury. Most of his index finger was affected by infection. He returned to work after six months but he suffered continuing pain and was unable to follow his pre-accident hobby of competitive rowing, and his injury interfered with his

---

[70] 1994 S.L.T. 190.
[71] 1994 S.L.T. 107.

other hobby of breeding and keeping pigeons; also, while he could still carry out home decorating after his accident he found this work was much more difficult and he could do it only very slowly, although he had not been required to employ professional decorators since the accident.

Solatium. Having heard evidence and submissions on *solatium* the Lord Ordinary stated:

"Turning to the question of solatium counsel for the defenders submitted that the sum of £4,000 would be appropriate. In this connection reference was made to *Boyes v. Carnation Foods Ltd*, 1986 S.L.T. 145, which involved the loss of the terminal phalanx of the right forefinger. The pursuer had been off work for 15 weeks and was awarded solatium of £2,250 which represented £3,352 in current monetary values. It was accepted that this case stood at the lower end of the scale. Reference was also made to *Jackson v. Tayside Health Board*, 1980 S.L.T. (Notes) 57 . . . in which solatium had been assessed at £2,000 . . . now £4,300. In *Lind v. Lord Advocate*, 1982 S.L.T. 277 the pursuer had suffered injuries which resulted in partial amputation of the ring finger of the dominant right hand. The award of solatium was £2,250 . . . now £4,900. In *Anderson v. Thomas Case Ltd*, 1987 S.L.T. 564 there had been the loss by the pursuer of the top of the thumb of his dominant hand. This had resulted in an award of £4,000 . . . now £5,640. It was contended that that was a more serious injury than that of the pursuer. Finally reference was made to *Renwicks v. Bison Concrete Ltd*, 1988 S.L.T. 343, a case in which the pursuer's dominant right hand was crushed . . . leaving him with deformed fingers, a weakened grip and substantial reduction in manual dexterity. In that case solatium had been £4,250 . . . now £5,560. It was contended that this case was more serious than that of the pursuer.

"It is quite apparent that the pursuer's ability to use his left hand has been materially reduced by them. He continues to find difficulty in performing certain tasks with that hand and continues to experience pain in it from time to time, especially in his employment . . . the injuries have brought about a very serious deterioration in the quality of the pursuer's non-working life . . . (for example) his ability to carry on his hobby of rowing, which plainly occupied a very large place in his life prior to the accident . . . and enjoy his hobby of breeding and racing pigeons. . . . While the injury involved in *Hodge v. British Coal Corporation (No. 2),* 1992 S.L.T. 913[72] was plainly less severe than that of the pursuer the treatment carried out was by no means success-ful. . . . in all the circumstances an award of £9,000 would be appropriate."

Home decorating costs. As the evidence demonstrated that the pursuer was still able to do home decorating, albeit with greater difficulty and more slowly, the Lord Ordinary opined "having regard to the pursuer's con-tinued ability to do home decorating work . . . it would not be appropriate for me to make an award to represent that state of affairs."

Williamson v. G. B. Papers plc[73]

7.16 W, a 59-year-old office cleaner, injured herself in a fall on an oily substance on a factory floor. In her fall she twisted her ankle and also strained her neck. She was off work for about 12 weeks. She sued her employers for damages for, *inter alia,* out-of-pocket expenses and for services to be rendered by her husband and son.

Regarding the provision of services Lord Ordinary Cullen stated:

"[f]inally the pursuer made a claim in respect of services which her husband and her son required to perform for her in dealing with activities such as washing, ironing and shopping. The pursuer sug-gested under reference to the case of *Smith v. Chief Constable, Central Scotland Police,* 1991 S.L.T. 634 that a figure between £800 and £1,000 was justified with respect of the past, with £250–£300 in respect of the future. I do not consider that the evidence led was sufficiently detailed to enable figures of this magni-tude to be awarded . . . it would be appropriate to

---

[72] In *Hodge* the original injury was of a very minor nature although following a complicated series of treatments including amputations the ultimate result was loss of the right middle finger and an award of £7,000 for *solatium* was made.
[73] 1994 S.L.T. 173.

assess the past services in the sum of £400 . . . and the future in the sum of £100."

McLaren v. Harland & Wolff Ltd[73a]

7.16a M was employed as a plumber by H between 1953 and 1960 and thereafter worked as a driver. In 1983 he was diagnosed to be suffering from asbestosis and while he claimed benefit from the Department of Health and Social Security he made no claim against his former employers. After his death in 1988 his widow and children brought actions against H alleging that he died as a result of asbestosis while in employment with them.

On limitation Lord Migdale stated:[73b]

"I conclude that this is an action in which it seems to me to be equitable to allow this case to proceed in terms of s.19A of the 1973 Act. In coming to this conclusion I accept as relevant the various factors founded on by Counsel for the defenders" (no reasonable excuse for M failing to appreciate the possibility raising an action against H, in 1985 M told a doctor who advised making a claim to DHSS that the suggestion had already been made in 1983 when M was still working, by not following up the suggestion about a claim to the DHSS M indicated that he was merely inactive on the question of compensation from H) "in addition to the weighty point of loss of benefit to the defenders by the termination of these proceedings. I do not however consider that any of these other factors are factors of great additional weight in the . . . present case. It is true that had M raised an action timeously H might have had him medically examined . . . prior to his death. There might possibly have been a *post mortem* examination. However it is clear that M's condition was thoroughly monitored by medical experts independent of any question of litigation during the period of seven years prior to his death. No material prejudice is expressly averred by H in relation to the question of medical causation and no medical evidence was led for H at the preliminary proof. . . I regard it as at best for the defenders speculative

[73a] 1991 S.L.T. 85 (O.H.).
[73b] *Ibid.*, p. 89.

whether they are prejudiced on the medical aspects and I am not satisfied that this factor has been shown to be weighty factor in favour of the defenders. So far as the loss of the evidence of M himself is concerned a partial but only partial answer to this point is that the loss of such evidence may well be more of a disadvantage in proving the case to M than to H rebutting it. . . . I regard it important that this action involves averments to regular exposure of M to asbestos over a lengthy period and not for example to an allegation of a single transient event on which a witness no longer available could prospectively have provided evidence. There was evidence that in a case such as the present where employment in conditions involving exposure to asbestos dust is proved, where asbestosis is proved to be contracted many years later and where there is no other apparent significant exposure to asbestos dust, liability is not in practice a live issue.

On the other hand I consider that there are factors which as a matter of equity weigh heavily in favour of the pursuers. . . . I am satisfied that M was quite unaware at any time that he had a prospective right of action against the H. Nor do I consider that any such unawareness was unreasonable. When he died M had been away from employment in the shipyards for 28 years. For the last 24 he was working as a driver. . . . As such he was a member of the TGWU and as a member of the transport section would not receive information about hazards and compensation regarding such matters as asbestosis. It appears that M did not happen to have contact . . . with anyone who might have suggested to him that he had a right to compensation from H namely a suggestion which would have caused M to go to a lawyer for advice . . . what is important for present purposes is that I am satisfied that it was no fault of the late M that no action was raised during his lifetime and there was not material delay in raising the action by the pursuers following his death. S.19A provides aptly for the present action to proceed and I hold that is should be allowed to do so."

Statutory remedies

7.17 As previously indicated, some statutory provisions may ground an action at the instance of an employee injured at work.[74] However in the context of an examination of health and safety at work it is also necessary to consider the relationship between general employment statutory provisions and health and safety. Thus the general principles of unfair dismissal and discrimination law impact on health and safety particularly with regard to the introduction and enforcement of workplace rules which might cover a wide range of different matters, from a no-smoking policy to prevention of drug abuse or rules regarding hair length. It is beyond the scope of this work to consider the general principles of unfair dismissal or discrimination law, but in view of the relationship between these, and other areas of law and health and safety at work, this section attempts to place the special issues of health and safety in the perspective of these more general issues.[75]

Health and safety aspects of unfair dismissal

7.18 In accordance with their statutory and common law duties to take reasonable care for the safety of employees, employers frequently introduce policies and/or rules designed to ensure the performance of those duties and the maintenance of a safe working environment. The introduction and application of such policies and rules may bring into consideration issues like (a) the fairness of a decision to dismiss an employee who fails to observe health and safety rules, (b) whether the state of health of an employee supports a fair dismissal having regard to the creation of risks for his safety and that of others, (c) whether an employer's failure to operate a reasonably safe system of work or provide adequate clothing or equipment is a basis for a constructive dismissal claim and (f) ill-health dismissals *simpliciter*.

Breach of safety rules

7.19 It is clear that the dismissal of an employee for failure to observe a clearly-stated safety rule will be for a

---

[74] See Chap. 4, paras. 4.10 *et seq.*
[75] For coverage of the general principles of unfair dismissal and discrimination law, the reader is referred to V. Craig and K. Miller, *Employment Law in Scotland* (1991).

reason related to the conduct of the employee,[76] as will dismissal for conduct which poses a serious danger whether or not the precise conduct is covered by a particular safety rule. Thus in *Martin v. Galeshire Imperial Metals Ltd*[77] the reason for the dismissal of an employee who bypassed a safety device related to his conduct even although the nearest company rule merely provided that employees could be dismissed "for disorderly conduct likely to endanger the well-being or safety of other employees."[78] While generally an employer is entitled to promulgate and apply rules for the safe operation of the workplace it may be arguable that the introduction of a new rule or policy breaches an existing contractual right,[79] and an employer may elect to obtain the employee's express consent by incorporating the rule into the contract of employment.[80] Such a procedure would seem to avoid difficulties which arise from the method adopted for the introduction of the rule. Thus the dismissal of an employee for smoking in breach of a no-smoking rule which was inconsistently applied was held to be unfair where no warning had been given that the rule was now to be strictly applied.[81] Further, dismissal for breach of a rule prohibiting long hair which did not apply to women and was not specific was unfair,[82] while dismissal of a man for having hair which was 2½ feet long was fair where it followed several warnings and advice from the Factory Inspectorate.[83] Similarly even a clearly-stated and regularly-applied rule does not allow the employer fairly to dismiss an employee who deliberately defies the rule without allowing the employee to state his case, although the fact that a disciplinary procedure would have made

[76] EPCA, s. 57(2)(b); see *Ashworth v. John Needam & Sons*, 1978 H.S.I.B. 26.

[77] [1978] I.R.L.R. 440.

[78] And see *Frizzell v. Flanders*, 1979 H.S.I.B. 43 (fair dismissal for refusal to wear gas mask); *Singh v. J. Laing & Sons*, 1976 H.S.I.B. 10 (breach of rule regarding misusing toilet facility). Cf. *Mayhew v. Anderson (Stoke Newington)* [1978] I.R.L.R. 101 (unfair dismissal for refusal to wear cheap goggles which were uncomfortable).

[79] In *Dryden v. Greater Glasgow Health Board* [1992] I.R.L.R. 469 (EAT), it was argued, unsuccessfully, that the introduction of a no-smoking rule breached an implied term that the employee was entitled to have access to facilities for smoking during working hours.

[80] *Sutherland v. Sonat Offshore (UK) Inc*, 1993 H.S.I.B. 213 (EAT).

[81] *Bundall v. Paine and Betteridge*, [1973] I.R.L.R. 44.

[82] *Talbot v. Hugh M. Fulton Ltd* [1975] I.R.L.R. 52 (EAT).

[83] *Marsh v. Judge International Ltd*, 1977 H.S.I.B. 15.

no difference would be reflected in the remedy to be awarded by the industrial tribunal.[84]

Risks to employee and others

7.20 Where the health of an employee presents a risk to himself or others if he were to continue in employment the reason for his dismissal may be related to his capability.[85] However, the risk of illness cannot amount to grounds for a fair dismissal unless the nature of the employment is such that the risk is of such importance as to make it unsafe for the employee to continue in the job.[86] Thus the dismissal of an employee whose doctor could not give an assurance that there would be no recurrence of paranoid schizophrenia was held to be fair in light of the dangerous work taking place in a lead factory and that the job required such a high degree of concentration that a relapse could have had devastating effects.[87] However, the risks must be real and not merely imagined.[88] Where the risks could be reduced or eliminated by attendance at a training course it has been held to be fair to dismiss an employee who refused to attend.[89] Where employee and employer disagree over the nature of the risks and the employee is dismissed for refusing to continue working, whether the employer's response to the refusal fell within the band of reasonable responses is for the industrial tribunal to determine, with only limited scope for its decision to be challenged. Thus in *Lindsay v. Dunlop Ltd*[90] the Employment Appeal Tribunal refused to disturb an industrial tribunal's finding of a fair dismissal of an employee who refused to work in an atmosphere of

---

[84] *Wright v. Ladbrokes Ltd*, 1993 H.S.I.B. 211.

[85] EPCA, s. 57(2)(a); and see *Harper v. NCB* [1980] I.R.L.R. 260 (EAT).

[86] *Coverfoam (Darwen) Ltd v. Bell* [1981] I.R.L.R. 195 (EAT).

[87] *Singh-Den v. Chloride Metals Ltd* [1976] I.R.L.R. 56 (EAT). And see *Balogun v. Lucas Batteries Ltd*, 1979 H.S.I.B. 42 (continued employment with lead would have been harmful to employees with certain medical conditions); *Finch v. Betabake (Anglia) Ltd* [1977] I.R.L.R. 470 (motor mechanic with defective vision danger to himself and others).

[88] *Buck v. Letchworth Cinema*, 1988 (unreported) — dismissal of homosexual projectionist after objections from fellow employees who feared they might contract AIDS; and see R.A. Watt, "HIV Dismissals" (1992) 21 I.L.J. 280.

[89] *Minter v. Willingborough Foundries Ltd*, 1981 I.D.S. Brief 202.

[90] [1980] I.R.L.R. 93 (EAT).

hot rubber fumes in view of a report of the Health and Safety Executive on the carcinogenic properties of hot rubber fumes where the employer had agreed to deal with the fumes as quickly as possible and issued face masks as a temporary measure. Similarly in *Piggott Brothers & Co. Ltd v. Jackson*[91] the Court of Appeal, highlighting the dangers inherent in the approach advocated by another division of the same court,[92] restored the industrial tribunal's finding of unfair dismissal of employees who refused to work with materials which gave off unusual fumes after being certified unfit for work by their general practitioners. Neither the Health and Safety Executive nor the employers could identify the cause but the employers had not obtained a chemical analysis or a toxicological report and it could not be said that the industrial tribunal had misdirected itself in holding that the employers could reasonably have been expected to do more with a view to obtaining a definitive answer as to the cause of the employees' symptoms.

Constructive dismissal

7.21 Whether an employee is entitled to treat himself as constructively dismissed depends on whether the employer has repudiated the contract of employment,[93] and it is in the context of such a test that the contractual nature of the employer's duty of safety is of significance in that a failure to perform the duty in an important respect will allow the employee to leave and claim constructive dismissal. Thus a failure to provide safety equipment to the employee may justify rescission[94] and it may be necessary not merely to make safety equipment available but to provide each individual employee with the relevant item.[95] The employer's duty is not performed by

---

[91] [1991] I.R.L.R. 309.
[92] *Neale v. Hereford & Worcester County Council* [1986] I.R.L.R. 168 (C.A.) in which the "my goodness that was certainly wrong" approach to the test of perversity was commended.
[93] *Western Excavating (ECC) Ltd v. Sharp* [1978] I.R.L.R. 27 (C.A.), applied in *Greater Glasgow Health Board v. Pate*, 1983 S.L.T. 90.
[94] *British Aircraft Corporation v. Austin* [1978] I.R.L.R. 332 (EAT) (prolonged failure to provide safety glasses).
[95] *Crouch v. BREL* [1988] I.R.L.R. 404 (C.A.) (employer's duty was to provide goggles for employee to keep in tool kit — not reasonable to require employee to walk considerable distance each time he required to use them).

providing equipment or clothing which is inadequate,[96] and an employer will not act reasonably if he dismisses an employee to whom safety goggles costing 78p had been provided when she refused to wear them because they were uncomfortable and irritated her eyes without considering whether more expensive ones would have been acceptable to the employee.[97] Failures to provide security measures[98] and comfortable temperatures[99] have founded constructive dismissal claims, and the Scottish Employment Appeal Tribunal has recognised that there could be a constructive dismissal where an employee was required to work in intolerable conditions, for example where a serious danger to life was involved.[1] However, for a constructive dismissal case to succeed the employee has to show that it was the employer's breach of contract which led to him leaving,[2] and an employee who delays his decision to leave or give notice may be viewed as having accepted a variation of his contract.[3] Thus an employee who suffered a mental breakdown caused by allegations and complaints about her work failed to establish a constructive dismissal when she continued working for six months after her employer had taken remedial measures.[4] However, it has been held in Scotland that it is not open to an employee to affirm a contractual term which would undercut a minimum statutory wage,[5] and it would seem that the same reasoning would apply to an employee who continued working in the face of a contractual breach by the employer which was also the subject of a statutory provision like, for example, the Personal Protective Equipment at Work Regulations 1992 or the Provision and Use of Work Equipment Regulations 1992.

---

[96] *Kirkcaldy District Council v. Baxter,* 1978 E.A.T. 540/78 (binmen were entitled to refuse to work when waterproofs provided by employer were not adequate).
[97] *Mayhew v. Anderson (Stoke Newington)* [1978] I.R.L.R. 101 (I.T.).
[98] *Keys v. Shoefayre Ltd* [1978] I.R.L.R. 476 (I.T.).
[99] *Mariner v. Domestic and Industrial Polythene Ltd,* 1978 H.S.I.B. 26; *Graham Oxley Tool Steels Ltd v. Firth* [1980] I.R.L.R. 135 (EAT).
[1] *Knight v. Barra Shipping Ltd,* 1992 H.S.I.B. 203, 187/92; and see *Popeye of Scotland Ltd v. McLay,* 1976 E.A.T. 309/76 (driver entitled to refuse to drive suspected unroadworthy vehicle).
[2] *Walker v. Josiah Wedgwood & Sons Ltd* [1978] I.C.R. 744 (EAT).
[3] *Western Excavating (ECC) Ltd v. Sharp* [1978] I.C.R. 221 (C.A.). Cf. *Marriott v. Oxford Co-operative Society (No. 2)* [1970] 1 Q.B. 186; *W.E. Cox Toner v. Crook* [1981] I.C.R. 823 (EAT).
[4] *Wilton v. Cornwall & Isles of Scilly Health Authority,* 1993 H.S.I.B. 482 (C.A.).
[5] *Reid v. Comphill Engravers* [1990] I.C.R. 435 (EAT).

Dismissal for ill-health

7.22 One of the potentially fair reasons for dismissal is the capability of the employee, which is to be assessed by reference to, *inter alia* "health or any other physical or mental quality."[6] Thus, provided the reason for the dismissal related to the capability of the employee for performing work of the kind he was employed to do and the employer acted fairly in other respects, an employee dismissed on grounds of ill-health may have no claim against his employer and this is so even where it is the employer's conduct which has caused the illness which led to the dismissal.[6a] Unfair dismissal law in this respect seeks to hold a balance between the employer's need for the work to be done and the employee's need to be given time to recover from his illness.[7] For unfair dismissal law to be activated, however, there has first to be a dismissal. It follows therefore that in those cases where the ill-health is so serious that the contract is brought to an end by impossibility of performance or frustration there will be no dismissal. Where frustration truly operates the contract of employment is terminated by operation of law, and while an employer is always free to argue that termination has occurred by way of frustration it has to be noted (i) that the Employment Appeal Tribunal has cautioned industrial tribunals against too easy an approach to the question of frustration of the contract of employment,[8] and (ii) in the event of the employer's argument being unsuccessful it is unlikely that his pre-termination procedures will come near to satisfying the standards of reasonableness imposed by Employment Protection (Consolidation) Act 1978, s. 57(3). In the leading cases of *Marshall v. Harland & Wolff Ltd*[9] and *Egg Stores (Stamford Hill) Ltd v. Leibovici*[10] the following factors were stated to be amongst those requiring to be considered to determine whether a contract of employment had been frustrated: (a) terms of contract including provisions regarding sick

---

[6] EPCA, s. 57(2)(a), (4)(a).

[6a] *London Fire and Civil Defence Authority v. Betty* [1994] I.R.L.R. 384 (EAT).

[7] *Taylorplan Catering (Scotland) Ltd v. McInally* [1980] I.R.L.R. 53 (EAT); *East Lindsey District Council v. Daubney* [1977] I.R.L.R. 181 (EAT).

[8] *Williams v. Watson Luxury Coaches Ltd* [1990] I.R.L.R. 164 (EAT).

[9] [1972] 2 All E.R. 715 (NIRC).

[10] [1977] I.C.R. 260 (EAT).

pay, (b) likely duration of employment if no illness, (c) nature of employment and whether employee is "key" personnel, (d) nature of illness and prospects of recovery, (e) period of past employment, (f) need for the sick employee's work to be done, (g) risk to employer of acquiring statutory employment obligations to replacement employees, (h) continuation of wages, (i) actions of employer including dismissal or failure to dismiss.[11] Two contrasting decisions can be found in *Hebden v. Forsey & Sons*[12] and *Scarr v. Goodyear*.[13] In the former the contract was not frustrated principally because there was no reason why a surgical operation would not be successful, the employee had been kept on the employer's sick list and there had been no attempt to terminate his contract; in the latter the contract was frustrated because there was no prospect of the employee, whose work involved climbing ladders, being able to resume that work because of a heart condition.[14] However, whether a contract of employment is frustrated depends on the facts and circumstances of the case, and some earlier decisions which predate the caution advised by the Employment Appeal Tribunal in *Williams v. Watson Luxury Coaches Ltd*[15] should be treated with care: although the Employment Appeal Tribunal in *Harman v. Flexible Lamps Ltd*[16] was wrong to say that the doctrine of frustration was not applicable to contracts of employment which could be brought to an end by notice, nevertheless the Court of Appeal in *Notcutt v. Universal Equipment Co. (London) Ltd*[17] did accept that it was correct to be cautious about applying the doctrine to such contracts. Of course contracting parties may expressly provide that a particular event will not frustrate the contract,[18] and it would seem perfectly arguable that where a contract makes provision for sick pay that may be

---

[11] For a discussion of the issues involved see V. Craig "Frustration or Dismissal" (1985) 53 S.L.G. at p. 85.

[12] [1973] I.C.R. 607 (NIRC).

[13] [1975] I.R.L.R. 166.

[14] Other examples include *Hart v. Marshall & Sons (Bulwell) Ltd* [1977] I.R.L.R. 51 (EAT) (one of two employees who contracted dermatitis); *Harman v. Flexible Lamps Ltd* [1980] I.R.L.R. 418 (absences caused by depression and hospitalisation).

[15] [1990] I.R.L.R. 164 (EAT).

[16] [1980] I.R.L.R. 418 (EAT).

[17] [1986] I.C.R. 414 (C.A.).

[18] D. M. Walker, *Law of Contracts and Voluntary Obligations in Scotland* (2nd ed.) para. 31.53.

interpreted as an indication that in certain cases[19] the incapacity was anticipated by the contracting parties as one which would not frustrate the contract.[20]

7.23 Following the decision of the House of Lords in *Polkey v. A. E. Dayton Services*[21] it is clear that whether or not a dismissal is fair depends, in the normal case, ultimately on whether the employer acted reasonably in treating the reason as one sufficient for dismissing the employee; much attention is focused on the pre-dismissal procedures adopted by the employer and the statement by Lord Bridge of Harwich in *Polkey*[22] that in the great majority of cases an employer will not be acting reasonably unless and until he has taken the steps which are necessary to justify his course of action and "in the case of incapacity the employer will not normally act reasonably unless he gives the employee fair warning." In *A. Links & Co. Ltd v. Rose*[23] after an industrial tribunal had applied Lord Bridge's dictum literally and had concluded that the dismissal of an employee following two heart attacks was unfair because he had not been given any warning the Inner House reasserted that following *Polkey* there was no inconsistency between that case and authorities like *Taylorplan Catering (Scotland) Ltd v. McInally*,[24] which, while requiring consultation with a sick employee, indicated that warnings were inappropriate because while warnings were not generally applicable to ill-health of a more or less permanent character there might be a case for warnings where the employee's ill-health flowed directly from circumstances within his own control.[25] Following *Polkey* and in cases of intermittent absences while a

---

[19] Immediate, total and lasting incapacity is the obvious exception.
[20] See too the similar arguments canvassed in *F.C. Shepherd & Co. Ltd v. Jerrom* [1986] I.C.R. 414 (C.A.) regarding whether a contractual disciplinary procedure applying to misconduct might prevent frustration resulting from a sentence of imprisonment. And see *Jennison v. Airedale Health Authority* (1987, unreported, I.T.), in which it was accepted that sickness absences did not frustrate the contract in light of its provisions for sick pay.
[21] [1987] I.R.L.R. 503 (H.L.).
[22] *Ibid.*
[23] [1991] I.R.L.R. 353 (I.H.).
[24] [1980] I.R.L.R. 53.
[25] Lord McCluskey instanced cases of obesity which could be cured with reasonable dieting and remedying a physical incapacity by simple operation which the employee, for no apparent reason, was neglecting to take (*A. Links & Co. Ltd v. Rose* [1991] I.R.L.R. 353 at p. 356).

sympathetic approach has been recommended eventually it may be appropriate to caution the employee that his absences have reached a stage where it is impossible to continue with his employment.[26] Regarding consultation the industrial tribunal must determine as a matter of fact and judgment (a) what consultation, if any, was necessary in the known circumstances of the case, (b) what consultation took place and (c) whether it was adequate in all the circumstances.[27] Thus an industrial tribunal was entitled in the exceptional circumstances of the case to conclude that the dismissal of an employee — without any consultation — was fair because the director who took the decision not to engage in a face-to-face consultation did so to avoid the possibility of disclosing to an employee information about her health of which she was unaware.[28] While it is a management decision and not a medical one, it is a decision which has to be taken in the light of all the medical evidence.[29] Gathering the relevant information can be difficult although the employee may agree to his own doctor preparing a report for transmission to the employer. However the Access to Medical Reports Act 1988 permits an employee to agree to a report being prepared by his own general practitioner (or other doctor who has had responsibility for the employee's clinical care) subject to his right to see the report in advance of it being made available to the employer and even to refuse its disclosure.[30] The Act provides that a person (*i.e.* an employer) shall not apply to a medical practitioner for a medical report about an individual (*i.e.* an employee) to be supplied to him for employment purposes[31] unless (a) that person has notified in writing the individual that he intends to make the application and (b) the individual has notified in writing the applicant that he consents to the application[32] and because of the difficulties the 1988 Act has produced employers may wish to

---

[26] *Lynock v. Cereal Packaging Ltd* [1988] I.R.L.R. 510 (EAT).
[27] *Ibid.*
[28] *Eclipse Blinds Ltd v. Wright* [1992] I.R.L.R. 133 (I.H.).
[29] *East Lindsey District Council v. Daubney* [1977] I.R.L.R. 81 (EAT).
[30] Access to Medical Reports Act 1988, ss. 3, 4.
[31] "Employment purposes" are widely defined as the purposes in relation to any individual of any person by whom he is or has been, or is seeking to be, employed under a contract of service or otherwise (*ibid.*, s. 2(1)).
[32] *Ibid.*, s. 3(1); the notice to the individual must set out his rights to withhold or restrict his consent.

consider inserting a term into contracts of employment which requires employees to submit to medical examination by a doctor nominated by the employer whose report would be disclosed directly to the employer. Of course in the event that an employer proposed to dismiss an employee relying on such a report it would normally be necessary to make it available to the employee prior to taking the decision to dismiss[33] but an inadequate medical report instructed by an employer may result in the employer not having conducted a proper investigation.[34] Even where an employee has become incapable of performing the work he is contracted to do an employer will not act fairly if he does not at least consider alternative employment,[35] although there is no duty to create a special job for a sick employee.[36]

Special health and safety rights

Health and Safety representatives and other employees

7.24 Until the enactment of special provisions in 1993 employees who were dismissed for performing health and safety functions or for raising health and safety issues with their employer could rely only on the general rules of unfair dismissal with the effect that any employee with less than two years' continuous employment could generally[37] be dismissed with impunity. Particularly as a result of certain parts of the Cullen Report into the *Piper Alpha* oil platform disaster[38] it became clear that newly-appointed employees felt uneasy about raising health and safety concerns because of their insecure employment. To remedy the position and to implement EC Framework Directive 89/391, the Trade Union Reform and Employ-

---

[33] *Louis v. Coventry Hood and Seating Co. Ltd* [1990] I.R.L.R. 324 (EAT); *cf.* *Eclipse Blinds Ltd v. Wright* [1992] I.R.L.R. 133 (I.H.).

[34] *Ford Motor Co. Ltd v. Nawaz* [1987] I.R.L.R. 163.

[35] *Dick v. Boots The Chemist Ltd* (unreported), EAT, 68/91.

[36] *Merseyside and North Wales Electricity Board v. Taylor* [1975] I.R.L.R. 60 (EAT); *Carricks (Caterers) Ltd v. Nolan* [1980] I.R.L.R. 259 (EAT).

[37] In some cases, of course, it was possible to argue that the real reason was trade union membership and therefore automatically unfair (TULRCA, s. 152).

[38] Report of the Public Inquiry into the Piper Alpha Disaster (Cm. 1310); and see para. 6.46.

ment Rights Act 1993[39] confers on all employees, irrespective of their length of continuous employment,[40] protection against dismissal[41] in particular health and safety cases.[42] Thus the dismissal[43] is unfair if it was because:

(a) the employee having been designated by the employer to carry out activities in connection with preventing or reducing risks to health and safety carried out or proposed to carry out such activities,

(b) the employee, being a representative of workers on matters of health and safety at work or a member of a safety committee[44] performed or proposed to perform any functions as a representative or a member of the committee,

(c) the employee being employed at a place where (i) there was no representative or safety committee or (ii) where there was such a representative or committee but it was not reasonably practicable for the matter to be raised via such representative or committee, brought to his employer's attention by reasonable means circumstances which the employee reasonably believed were potentially harmful to health or safety,[44b]

(d) the employee, in circumstances of danger which he reasonably believed to be serious and imminent and which he could not reasonably be expected to avert, left, or proposed to leave, or (while the danger persisted) refused

---

[39] s.28; Sched. 5.

[40] EPCA, s. 64 as amended by TURERA, Sched. 5, para. 5.

[41] Similar protection is introduced against action short of dismissal by the insertion of new ss. 22A–22C into EPCA.

[42] EPCA, s. 57A as inserted by s. 28, Sched. 5 to TURERA.

[43] Selection for redundancy is also included (EPCA, s. 59 as amended by TURERA, Sched. 5, para. 4).

[44] For a fuller discussion of health and safety representatives and committees, see Chap. 5, paras. 5.16 *et seq.*

[44b] *Harris v. Select Timber Frame Ltd*, 1994 H.S.I.B. 222 (I.T.) (unfair dismissal following complaints about health and safety prompted by threat of prosecution).

to return to, his place of work or any dangerous part of his place of work[45] or

(e)   the employee, in circumstances of danger which he reasonably believed to be serious and imminent, took or proposed to take, appropriate steps to protect himself or other persons from the danger.

Because of the relationship between trade union membership and safety representatives and committees,[46] employees covered by paragraph (b) above could previously have acquired protection had they been able to demonstrate that the reason for their dismissal was truly a reason covered by section 152 of the Trade Union and Labour Relations (Consolidation) Act 1992 (dismissal on grounds related to union membership or activities); the addition of paragraphs (a) and (c)-(e), although peppered with judgmental issues like "reasonable means," "reasonable belief," "serious and imminent" and "appropriate steps" undoubtedly enhances the position of all employees who are driven to take action in the interests of health or safety. For the purpose of paragraph (e) the appropriateness of steps is to be judged having regard *inter alia* to the knowledge of the employee and the facilities and advice available to the employee at the time and a dismissal shall not be regarded as unfair if the employer can show that it would have been so negligent for the employee to take the steps he did take that a reasonable employer might have dismissed him for taking them.[47] The connection between trade union membership and paragraphs (a) and (b) above is confirmed by providing that dismissal for either of the reasons stated therein are to be "inadmissible" reasons giving access to a minimum basic award,[48] a special award[49] and the remedy of interim relief.[50] Where the reason for the dismissal falls into one of the paragraphs (c)-(e) the employee is entitled to the usual unfair dismissal remedies.

[45] Presumably this prevents the employer arguing that an employee who had left, or refused to return to, his place of work was taking part in a strike or other industrial action and whose dismissal was therefore covered by EPCA, ss. 62 or 62A. *Cf. Mariner v. Domestic and Industry Polythene Ltd,* 1978 H.S.I.B. 26.

[46] See Chap. 5, paras. 5.16 *et. seq.*

[47] EPCA, s. 57A (2), (3).

[48] EPCA, s. 73 (6A) as inserted by TURERA, Sched. 5, para. 8.

[49] EPCA, s. 72 as amended by TURERA, Sched. 5, paras. 7, 9.

[50] EPCA, ss. 77–79 as inserted by TURERA, Sched. 5, para. 10.

Pregnancy

7.25 EU Council Directive[51] on the introduction of measures to encourage improvements in the safety and health
of (a) pregnant workers, (b) workers who have recently
given birth or (c) who are breast feeding was adopted on
October 19, 1992, to be implemented by member states
within two years of that date. In part implementation of
the Directive, sections 23–25 of, and schedules 2 and 3 to,
the Trade Union Reform and Employment Rights Act
1993 were enacted and, by virtue of the Trade Union
Reform Employment Rights Act 1993 (Commencement
No. 3 and Transitional Provisions) Order 1994,[51a] these
provisions apply to any woman whose expected week of
childbirth (EWC) was on or after October 16, 1994
although since Maternity Leave Period (MLP) can commence up up to 11 weeks before childbirth it follows that
the new provisions have been effective since July 31,
1994. All women whose babies are due on or after
October 16, 1994 become entitled to 14 weeks' MLP
during which the woman is entitled to the benefit of the
terms of her contract of employment except remuneration.[51b] There are no qualifying conditions except various
notice requirements and it is generally for the woman to
decide, by giving her employer the appropriate notice,
when her MLP begins subject to the rules that (a) MLP
cannot begin earlier than the beginning of the 11th week
before the EWC, (b) MLP commences automatically if
childbirth occurs before the MLP would have begun, and
(c) MLP is automatically triggered by a day of absence
from work wholly or partly because of childbirth occurring after the beginning of the 6th week before EWC.[51c]
The MLP will last for 14 weeks or until the birth of the
child, if later, although it is provided that where a woman
is prohibited by any enactment (except one which gives
rise to a suspension on maternity grounds) from working,
her MLP is extended until the end of that prohibition and
MLP is ended by the dismissal of an employee.[51d] A
woman who is entitled to MLP is to work not be permitted to work during the two weeks beginning with child-

[51] Directive 92/85/EEC.
[51a] S.I. No. 1365.
[51b] EPCA, s. 33 as inserted by TURERA.
[51c] EPCA, ss. 34–36 as inserted by TURERA.
[51b] EPCA, s. 34 as inserted.

birth.[51cd] To perfect her right to MLP a woman must (unless not reasonably practicable) give at least 21 days before its commencement (a) written notice of pregnancy and her EWC, (b) if requested to do so a medical certificate of her EWC, and (c) notice (in writing if requested by employer) of (i) the date on which her MLP will begin or (ii) a day of absence because of pregnancy after the beginning of the 6th week before her EWC or (iii) childbirth[51e] and only if she intends to return to work before the expiry of the 14 week MLP is the woman required to give notice of her return; where she gives such notice (which must be at least 7 days) the employer can either (a) postpone (by notice apparently) her return to ensure he receives such notice provided her return is not postponed beyond the date on which the MLP would end or (b) withhold payment for days worked prior to the expiry of the 7 days.[51f]

Suspension from work on maternity grounds

7.25a An employee is to be suspended on maternity grounds where in consequence of a requirement imposed by a relevant provision of any enactment or code of practice approved under the Health and Safety at Work Act 1974 she is suspended by her employer on the ground that she is pregnant, has recently given birth or is breast feeding.[51g] A relevant provision is one which is specified as such by the Secretary of State and Regulations 13A and 13B[51gh] of the Management of Health and Safety at Work Regulations 1992[51h] have been so specified.[51i] The Management of Health and Safety at Work (Amendment) Regulations 1994 introduce into the Management of Health and Safety at Work Regulations 1992 an extension of the employer's general obligations to carry out a risk assess-

---

[51cd] Maternity (Compulsory Leave) Regulations 1994 (S.I. 1994 No. 2479) which give effect to Directive 92/85/EEC, Art. 8(2) which requires compulsory leave of at least 2 weeks either before or after childbirth.
[51e] EPCA, ss. 36, 37 as inserted.
[51f] EPCA, s. 37A as inserted.
[51g] EPCA, s. 45(1).
[51gh] Inserted by Management and Health and Safety at Work (Amendment) Regulations 1994 (S.I. 1994 No. 2865)
[51h] S.I. 1992 No. 2051.
[51i] Suspension from Work (on Maternity Grounds) Order 1994 (S.I. 1994 No. 2930).

ment so that where the employees include women of
child-bearing age and the work could involve a risk to the
health and safety of a new or expectant mother (or her
baby) from any substances, processes or working conditions (including but not only those specified in Annexes I
& II of Directive 92/85/EEC) the risk assessment shall
include an assessment of that particular risk. And it is
expressly provided that if complying with a statutory
provision would not avoid such a risk the employer shall,
if it is reasonable to do so (and it would avoid the risk),
alter the women's working hours or other conditions of
work[51k] and if the risk cannot be avoided by such an
alteration of conditions of employment the employee is
required, subject to Employment Protection (Consolidation) Act 1978, s.46 (the obligation to offer available
suitable alternative work), to be suspended on maternity
grounds.[51kl] However nothing in the regulations requires
an employer to take such steps in relation to an employee
until she has notified him in writing that she is pregnant,
has recently given birth, has miscarried or is breast
feeding[51l] although it has to be noted that the more
general duties of the Management Regulations and the
Health and Safety at Work Act itself would require
employers to take action to protect any worker they know
to be pregnant, or breast feeding. Regulation 13B requires
an employer — again subject to Employment Protection
(Consolidation) Act 1978, s.46 — to suspend a new or
expectant mother from night work (where she has a
medical certificate that it is necessary that she should not
work at night) for as long as is necessary for her health
and safety. Neither the Directive nor the Management
Regulations indicates what is meant by night work on the
view that that such a definition is unnecessary because
what has to be avoided is the exposure to risk and in the
meantime there is no evidence to show that the existence
or the quality of a risk is determined by the time at which
work is done.[52] Although the Management of Health and

[51k] Management of Health and Safety at Work Regulations 1992, reg.
13A(2).
[51kl] During suspension on maternity grounds a woman is entitled to her
remuneration (EPCA, s. 47, as inserted by TURERA).
[51l] Ibid., reg. 13C(1). And see reg. 13C(2) (relaxation of employer's duty
where no certificate of pregnancy produced etc.).
[52] See New and Expectant Mothers at Work—a guide for employers (HSE
Books, £6.95).

Safety at Work Regulations generally do not confer a right
of action in any civil proceedings that limitation is expressly revoked in respect of any duty imposed by the new
regulation 13A[53] so that an injury arising from a failure to
carry out the assessment required by regulation 13A(1)
would give rise to liability for breach of statutory duty.

Dismissal for pregnancy

7.25b These provisions are supplemented by the
Employment Protection Consolidation Act, s.60[54] which
extends the circumstances in which dismissal for pregnancy is unfair. No period of continuous employment is
required and a dismissal is unfair (a) if the reason for it is
pregnancy or a reason connected with it; (b) dismissal
ends her MLP and the reason is that the employee has
given birth to a child or any other reason connected
thereto; (c) the reason for the dismissal was that she
availed herself of the benefits of maternity leave; (d) she
was dismissed during the period of four weeks after the
end of her MLP while certified incapable of work and the
reason for the dismissal is that she has given birth or any
reason connected thereto; (e) the reason for her dismissal
is that the employer is required to suspend from work on
maternity grounds and (f) the employee's MLP is ended
by the dismissal because she is redundant and her
employer has not offered her a suitable available vacancy.

Medical suspension

7.25c A more general provision is found in the Employment Protection Consolidation Act, ss. 19–22, to the effect
that where an employee is suspended from work on
medical grounds in consequence of certain[55] provisions in
legislation or in a code of practice issued or approved
under the Health and Safety at Work Act 1974, he is
entitled to remuneration for up to 26 weeks.

---

[53] Management of Health and Safety at Work Regulations 1992, reg.
15(2).
[54] Inserted by TUREA, s.24.
[55] The provisions contained in EPCA, Sched. 1 (Control of Lead at Work
Regulations 1980, Ionising Radiations Regulations 1985, Control of
Substances Hazardous to Health Regulations 1988).

EMPLOYERS' LIABILITY INSURANCE

Introduction

7.26 As noted earlier,[56] the law imposes a wide variety of obligations designed to ensure the health and safety of people at work. Proper observance of these obligations is in many cases enforced by criminal sanction or the preventive Improvement or Prohibition Notices. Neither of these methods is principally[57] concerned with compensating a person injured at work, which is the province of the civil law. However, a sophisticated system of rules and obligations would be pointless if, having succeeded in establishing a case grounded either on the common law or a breach of statutory duty, a worker was confronted with a defender who was unable to pay the sum awarded in damages. To obviate such a result the Employers' Liability (Compulsory Insurance) Act 1969[58] requires every employer[59] who conducts business in Great Britain[60] to maintain approved insurance with an authorised insurer for liability for bodily injury[61] or disease sustained by an employee[62] arising out of and in the course of his employ-

[56] See Chap. 3.

[57] In some cases a Scottish court is empowered (subject to a statutory maximum) to require an offender to compensate a victim; while such a power is not restricted to cases in which a civil court could award damages as it may only be used where a person has suffered personal injury, loss or damage and it is intended to deal with simple cases in which the sum can be instantly calculated: Criminal Justice (Scotland) Act 1980, s. 58.

[58] The Act was conceived as a Private Member's Bill and although the government refused to sponsor the Bill it did assist the Bill's passage, prompted perhaps by the tragedy of the James Watt Street fire in which 22 employees died, in respect of whom there was no effective insurance although the General Accident Co. Ltd did offer *ex gratia* payments: see *The Scotsman*, Sept. 6, 1969; H.L. Deb., Vol. 304, col. 1391.

[59] Many public employers are exempt from the Act's provisions: Employers' Liability (Compulsory Insurance) Act 1969, s. 3; Employers' Liability (Compulsory Insurance) Exemption Regulations 1971 (S.I. 1971 No. 1933).

[60] Great Britain comprises England, Scotland and Wales: Interpretation Act 1978, s. 22(1).

[61] In England the Court of Appeal has held in a criminal case that as a person's body included his nervous system bodily injury might include injury to any of these parts of his body responsible for his mental and other faculties and that "actual bodily harm" could include psychiatric injury (*R. v. Chan-Fook, The Times*, Nov. 19, 1993 (C.A.)); and see para. 3.43 *ante*.

[62] An employee is narrowly defined to mean one who has a contract of service or apprenticeship with the employer: Employers' Liability (Compulsory Insurance) Act 1969, s. 2(1).

ment[63] in Great Britain. Thus, except insofar as specifically provided by regulations,[64] the legislation does not extend to injury or diseases suffered or contracted outside Great Britain,[65] and this when combined with a judicial reluctance to extend the duty of care to employees working abroad[66] dictates that employees who are dispatched abroad require to be satisfied in advance about the extent of their employers' liabilities and insurance therefor. Additionally it has to be emphasised that the 1969 Act merely requires the maintenance of approved insurance cover upon which the employer may call in the event of his liability for the employee's injury or disease being established in accordance with the rules discussed earlier.[67]

Approved policies

7.27 The policy or policies must provide cover of £2 million in respect of claims relating to any one or more of the employer's employees arising out of any one occurrence.[68] For a policy to be "approved" it must not contain any condition that there shall be no liability (on the part of the insurer) (a) in the event of some specified thing being done or omitted to be done after the happening of the event which gave rise to the claim; (b) unless the policy holder takes reasonable care to protect his employees against risk of bodily injury or disease in the course of their employment; (c) unless the policy holder complies with any enactment for the protection of employees against such a risk in the course of their employment; and (d) unless the policy holder keeps specified records or provides the insurer with certain information; however a term or condition which requires

---

[63] As to the scope of "arising out of and the course of employment" see paras. 3.44, 7.31.
[64] See Offshore Installations (Application of the Employers' Liability (Compulsory Insurance) Act 1969) Regulations 1975 (S.I. 1975 No. 1289).
[65] Employers' Liability (Compulsory Insurance) Act 1969, s. 1.
[66] See *Reid v. Rush & Tompkins Group plc* [1990] I.C.R. 61 (C.A.); *Square D Ltd v. Cook* [1992] I.R.L.R. 34 (C.A.).
[67] See in particular Chaps. 3 and 4. For a detailed critical analysis of the 1969 Act see R. Hasson, "The Employers' Liability (Compulsory Insurance) Act 1969 — A Broken Reed" (1974) 3 I.L.J. 79.
[68] Employers' Liability (Compulsory Insurance) General Regulations 1971 (S.I. 1971 No. 1117), reg. 3.

the policy holder to pay to the insurer sums the latter has, under the policy, paid out in respect of employees is permitted. Similarly, and rather oddly, there is nothing in the legislation to prevent an insurer inserting particular exclusions which may result in an injured employee's claim being excluded. Thus an approved policy may legitimately exclude cover for liability for silicosis, asbestosis and pneumoconiosis.[69] It has been suggested[70] that the effect of the legislation[71] is to permit an approved policy to contain terms which free the insurer of liability to indemnify the insured in the event of recklessness or gross negligence on the part of the insured or in the event of the insured failing to advise the insurers of an increase in risk. An approved policy is not required to be maintained in respect of certain relatives who are employees[72] or employees who are not ordinarily resident in Great Britain.[73]

Certificates and enforcement

7.28 By agreement with the Department of Employment the Health and Safety Commission has accepted responsibility for the enforcement of the 1969 Act.[74] Failure to effect and maintain insurance as required by the 1969 Act is itself a criminal offence punishable by a fine for each day of the failure.[75] Accordingly, since the contract of insurance is a contract based on the utmost good faith, where an employer misrepresents or fails to disclose a material fact when effecting or renewing a policy risk, not only does he risk the insurer reducing the contract but, if so, he will also be liable to a fine for failing to maintain an approved policy.[76] An insurer who enters into an

---

[69] *Ibid.*, reg. 2.
[70] See R. Hasson, *op cit.*
[71] Reg. 2(1) (b), (c).
[72] Employers' Liability (Compulsory Insurance) Act 1969, s. 2(2).
[73] However, such employees become covered by the 1969 Act if they are in Great Britain for a period of not less than 14 days: Employers' Liability (Compulsory Insurance) General Regulations 1971, reg. 4.
[74] See Chap. 2, para. 2.6.
[75] Employers' Liability (Compulsory Insurance) Act 1969, s. 5.
[76] Ironically the James Watt Street tragedy which acted as a catalyst for the 1969 Act would be dealt with no differently today; an insurer would still be able to reject claims on the grounds of misrepresentation or non-disclosure by the insured!

approved policy is required, within 30 days of commencement or renewal, to issue a certificate of insurance in
statutory form, and it is an offence for an employer to
whom such a certificate has been issued to fail to display
or produce it; similarly it is an offence for an employer
who has entered into a contract of insurance in accordance with the 1969 Act not to permit its inspection by an
inspector authorised by the Secretary of State.[77]

STATE INSURANCE

Introduction

7.29 Full treatment of the State system of insurance
benefits for industrial accident or disease (industrial injuries benefits) is outside the scope of this work which is
concerned primarily with the legal responsibilities of
employers.[78] Nevertheless it is necessary to give here a
general account of that system which, while hedged with
many statutory conditions, is not dependent on the
injured employee being able to establish legal liability
(personal or vicarious) on the part of the employer.
However the converse is not the case, in that in respect of
an accident or injury suffered on or after January 1, 1989
(or where a prescribed disease is concerned a person first
claimed benefit on or after that date) a person due to pay
compensation to the victim of the accident, injury or
disease (the compensator) may not make a payment[79]
before obtaining a certificate of total benefit from the
Secretary of State. The certificate requires the deduction
from the compensation otherwise payable of the amount
of the benefit paid or likely to be paid during the period
of five years from the date of the accident or injury (or in
the case of a disease the date of first claim).[80]

---

[77] Employers' Liability (Compulsory Insurance) Act 1969, s. 4,
Employers' Liability (Compulsory Insurance) General Regulations, regs.
5–8.
[78] For fuller treatment, reference may be made to R. Lewis, *Compensation
for Industrial Injury* (1987) or to A. Ogus and E. Basendt, *The Law of Social
Security* (3rd ed., 1988), Chap. 7.
[79] Certain compensation payments are exempt, *e.g.* under £2,500: Social
Security Act 1989, s. 22(4). And see para. 7.8 *ante*.
[80] Further details of the procedure may be obtained from the Compensation Recovery Unit, Department of Social Security, Hebburn, Tyne and
Wear, NE31 1XB.

Employed earner

7.30 A claim for industrial injuries benefits may only be made by an employed earner whose accident or disease was caused by employed earner's employment.[81] Broadly this embraces those who pay Class I National Insurance contributions and those employees whose earnings are below the contribution threshold. Apprentices and other special groups are deemed to be in employed earner's employment[82] but certain close relatives are excluded.[83] Although the Industrial Injuries Advisory Council (IIAC) has recommended that the self-employed in construction and agriculture be brought within the scheme, the government has not adopted it for reasons of principle and practice. Whether a person is an employed earner is a question reserved for decision by the Secretary of State,[84] who may also direct that where a contract of employment is void the employment is nevertheless to be treated as employed earner's employment for the purpose of industrial injuries benefits.[85]

Industrial accidents

7.31 The employed earner must have suffered "personal injury caused . . . by accident arising out of and in the course of his employment."[86] Personal injury is a "hurt to the body or mind"[87]: it therefore includes psychological injury and nervous disorders[88] and may include damage to a prosthesis or artificial limb[89] but not to spectacles, a hearing-aid or crutch.[90] The claimant/victim must prove that the personal injury was "caused by accident" but it is not necessary that the accident is the single cause of the

---

[81] Social Security Act 1975, ss. 50, 76.

[82] *e.g.* ministers of religion, lecturers and offshore workers (Social Security (Employed Earners' Employments for Industrial Injuries) Regulations 1975 (S.I. 1975 No. 467)).

[83] *Ibid.*

[84] Social Security Act 1975, s. 93.

[85] *Ibid.*, s. 156.

[86] Social Security Act 1975, s. 50 (1).

[87] *James v. Secretary of State for Social Services* [1972] A.C. 944 *per* Lord Simon at p. 1020.

[88] R(I) 22/59.

[89] Compare R(I) 7/56 with R(I) 8/81.

[90] R(I) 1/82.

injury; a contributory cause is sufficient provided it is a *causa causans* and not merely a *causa sine qua non*.[91] "Accident" has been said to denote "an unlooked-for mishap or an untoward event which is not expected or designed,"[92] but such a narrow understanding of "accident" has been superseded by decisions which recognise that injuries caused by (a) the deliberate and unlawful act of a third party[93] or (b) performing a heavy or dangerous job where accidents are common[94] are caused by accident. A more difficult issue arises in distinguishing an accident or "event" from a "process," only the former being covered by the scheme which is concerned with traumatic work injuries. The nature of the important distinction is best illustrated by observing that while the injury of an employed earner who suffered strain to his chest muscles by regular heavy lifting was the result of a process and not an event or accident[95] the injury of an employed earner who experienced pains in his chest when lifting a heavy weight on a particular day was caused by an event or accident.[96] In *Fraser v. Secretary of State for Social Services*[97] the Court of Session upheld the decision of a Social Security Commissioner refusing the claim of a civil servant who had developed an acute anxiety tension which was probably due to various strains and stress at work, namely, frustration over diminishing promotion prospects, anxiety over career prospects and transfers to departments for which he had no specialist skills. Commissioner Mitchell had stated that

> "in the present case I am unable to hold that the [claimant's] condition was attributable to one or more events capable of being recognised as constituting injury by accident if . . . the claimant's incapacity was due . . . to the effect of strains arising over a period from his working conditions the rele-

---

[91] R(I) 4/58 (burns which employed earner suffered when his clothing, soaked in flammable liquid in accident at work, caught fire while it came into contact with cigarette he was lighting at home held to have been caused by lighting of cigarette (*causa causans*) and not the accidental soaking of clothing).
[92] *Fenton v. J. Thorley Ltd* [1903] A.C. 443 *per* Lord Macnaghten at p. 448.
[93] *Trim Joint District School v. Kelly* [1914] A.C. 667.
[94] CI 4/49.
[95] R(I) 42/51.
[96] R(I) 54/53; and compare R(I) 43/55 with R(I) 32/60.
[97] 1986 S.L.T. 386 (I.H.).

> vant injury would . . . fall to be regarded as injury
> by 'process' rather than by accident . . . a change in
> the legislation would . . . be required before a nerv-
> ous disorder due to a period of strain arising from
> uncongenial working conditions could be recognised
> as personal injury by accident . . ."

More recently it has been held that injury by "passive" smoking may be caused by accident[98] but the facts there may be regarded as special in that the employed earner's evidence demonstrated she had inhaled considerable quantities of cigarette smoke on particularly identifiable occasions.

7.32 It is necessary that the accident arises out of and in the course of employment. Whether an employee is acting *in the course of his employment* has already been discussed in the context of personal and vicarious responsibility.[99] However for industrial injury it is also necessary that the accident arises *out of* the employed earner's employment. This additional requirement ensures that merely because an injury happens while a person is in the course of employed earner's employment is not sufficient to entitle a person to industrial injuries benefits. However, precisely how to formulate a test to separate accidents which do not arise out of employment from those which do has proved difficult.[1] In 1963 a Tribunal of Commissioners[2] stated that the critical issue is whether the claimant's own act creates a risk which is different from that created by the employment and in 1946 there was enacted a statutory presumption which now provides that an accident which arises in the course of an employed earner's employment shall be deemed in the absence of evidence to the contrary also to have arisen out of that employment.[3] However this helpful provision has been narrowly construed by the Commissioners, who have emphasised that the presumption is really only of much effect where there is no evidence to the contrary.[4] The result of the need for the accident to arise out of

---

[98] R(I) 6/91.
[99] See paras 3.10, 3.40.
[1] Consider R(I) 26/59, R(I) 2/63, R(I) 27/60.
[2] R(I) 2/63.
[3] Social Security Act 1975, s. 50(3).
[4] CI 3/49, CI 68/49. *Cf.* R(I) 1/64.

employment — even taking the presumption into account — is that an unexplained leg fracture while walking in the course of employment is not injury caused by accident arising out of employment[5] while slipping and fracturing the leg by falling to the ground is, even if you are susceptible to injury because of brittle bones.[6] Thus that the employment merely sets the scene for the accident has to be distinguished from it materially contributing to the risk.[7] Violence or misconduct occasioned to employed earners in the course of their employment by third parties, it was decided in 1958,[8] was not an accident arising out of employment. The result was to deny industrial injuries benefits to a bus conductor who was attacked while on duty. Subsequent legislation now enacts[9] that such an accident shall arise out of the employed earner's employment if it is caused by another person's misconduct, skylarking or negligence or by the behaviour or presence of a criminal or consists in the employed earner being struck by any object or by lightning, provided the employed earner did not directly or indirectly induce or contribute to the happening of the accident by his conduct outside employment or by any act not incidental to the employment. Where an employed earner responds to an emergency, an accident happening to him in or about any premises at which he is for the time being employed for the purpose of his employer's business is deemed to arise out of and in the course of his employment.[10]

Industrial diseases

7.33 The British system has opted to compensate occupational disease by creating a list of prescribed diseases which are known to be typical of certain specified activities and then requiring that a successful claimant demonstrate that he suffers from a prescribed disease as a

[5] R(I) 6/82.
[6] R(I) 12/52.
[7] R(I) 73/51.
[8] *R. v. National Insurance (Industrial Injuries) Commissioner, ex p. Richardson* [1958] 1 W.L.R. 851.
[9] Social Security Act 1975, s. 55(1).
[10] Social Security Act 1975, s. 54. And see R(I) 6/63 (injury to milkman who helped at house on fire to which he delivered milk).

result of working in an occupation prescribed for that disease. The disadvantages of this approach are that those who suffer from non-prescribed diseases are without a remedy and, arguably, the process of legislative prescription cannot match the speed with which new risks develop, while its advantages — encouragement of intensive study which leads to an improvement in prevention and rehabilitation — have little direct bearing on victims of occupational diseases. In 1981 the Industrial Injuries Advisory Council recommended that the system be amended to allow for individual victims to prove that although a disease was not prescribed nevertheless it was caused by their employment,[11] but even its modest proposals were not acceptable to the government.[12] The British system remains one of inclusion or prescription. Thus current legislation[13] provides that to become prescribed by the Secretary of State a disease ought to be treated in relation to particular employed earners as a risk of their occupations and not as a risk common to all persons and is such that, in the absence of special circumstances, the attribution of particular cases to the nature of the employment can be established with reasonable certainty. Although the Secretary of State has power to prescribe a disease without reference to the Industrial Injuries Advisory Committee (IIAC)[14] this power has never been exercised and the IIAC has been criticised for the time taken to make recommendations and that it has recommended the inclusion of too few diseases.[15] Thus between 1906 (when the scheme began) and 1948 the list of diseases grew from six to 41, with about 12 being added until 1988. Since then, however, avian and ovine chlamycliosis, Q fever, chronic bronchitis and emphysema in coal miners[16] and carpal tunnel syndrome for any

---

[11] *Report on Industrial Diseases* (Cmnd. 8393).

[12] 52 H.C. Official Report, Written Answer, Col. 327. But note that S.I. 1991 No. 1938 has enacted the recommendations of the IIAC in its reports on asthma (Cmnd. 1244) and zoonoses (Cmnd. 1243) by adding to the list of sensitising agents for asthma and introducing an open category thereby allowing for proof in an individual case.

[13] Social Security Act 1975, s. 76(2).

[14] Social Security Act 1975, s. 141; Social Security Act 1986, s. 61.

[15] Certain organisational changes have been made to ensure that the IIAC operates more efficiently. And see the interesting article tracing the prescription of PD D12 (Coal Miners' Chronic Bronchitis and Emphysema) by N. Wikeley (1994) 1 J.S.S.L. 23.

[16] But not for iron and steel workers.

occupation involving the use of hand-held vibrating tools[17] have been added to the list which now exceeds 60 prescribed diseases.[18] In Schedule 1 to the Social Security (Industrial Injuries) (Prescribed Diseases) Regulations 1985[19] diseases are arranged into four groups, each group being denoted by a capital letter which represents conditions of an anatomical or physical nature (A), biological (B), chemical (C) or general (D)[20] nature, with each disease being denoted by a number. Thus the denotation for coal miners' chronic bronchitis and emphysema is "P.D. D 12."

7.34 For a claim for industrial injuries benefits to be successful, an employed earner must therefore show that the disease from which he suffers is

(a) a prescribed disease (Schedule 1 to the 1995 Regulations lists the diseases which are prescribed);

(b) that disease is prescribed in relation to his occupation (Schedule 1 lists the occupations or types of activity for which a disease is prescribed)[21]; and

(c) a causal link between the occupation and the disease.

An initial decision is made by an Adjudication Officer or, on reference, an Adjudicating Medical Authority from whom an appeal lies to a Medical Appeal Tribunal; normally[22] it is presumed that the disease was due to the nature of the occupation if the claimant was employed in it at any time within one month preceding the date the

---

[17] Social Security (Industrial Injuries) (Prescribed Diseases) Regulations 1985 as amended by S.I. 1993 No. 862.

[18] See Sched. 1 to Social Security (Industrial Injuries) (Prescribed Diseases) Regulations 1985 (S.I. 1985 No. 967).

[19] S.I. 1985 No. 967.

[20] Appropriately but fortuitously most of the diseases in this group are in some respects caused by dust.

[21] The test is one of actuality rather than legality; a successful claimant must show that he actually did the type of work and not merely that he was legally bound to do so (R(I) 3/78; R(I) 2/77).

[22] Special rules operate regarding certain respiratory diseases and occupational deafness (S.I. 1985 No. 967), and in some cases the presumption does not apply at all (inflammation of nose, and non-infective dermatitis).

disease is treated as having developed.[23] The presumption is rebuttable by the Adjudication Officer adducing appropriate evidence; it is not necessary for the employment to be the sole cause of the disease, but it must be the real and substantial cause.[24]

Industrial injuries benefits

7.35 Since October 1, 1986 all industrial injuries benefits are paid in the form of a pension, lump-sum payments for disablement less than 20 per cent having been abolished by the Social Security Act 1986,[25] and are free of income tax.[26] The benefits are (a) disablement benefit, (b) reduced earnings allowance, (c) retirement allowance and (d) industrial death benefit. However, as reduced earnings allowance and retirement allowance are being phased out[27] and industrial death benefit has been abolished for deaths before April 11, 1988[28] only disablement benefit is dealt with here.[29]

Disablement and sickness benefits

7.36 To become entitled to disablement benefit a claimant must show[30] that he suffers, as a result of an accident or prescribed disease, from loss of physical or mental faculty[31] which has been described as "impairment of proper functioning of part of the body or mind"[32] and has been held to include the malfunctioning of a kidney[33]; by express statutory provision disfigurement is to be consid-

[23] S.I. 1985 No. 967.
[24] R(I) 10/53.
[25] The old rules still operate for assessments made on claims before Oct. 1, 1986 (Social Security Act 1986, Sched. 3, para. 3(3)).
[26] Income and Corporation Taxes Act 1988, s. 617.
[27] Social Security Act 1990, s. 3; no entitlement occurs where the onset of a prescribed disease or the accident occurs after Sept. 30, 1990.
[28] Social Security Act 1986, Sched. 3, paras. 8, 11.
[29] For a detailed account of reduced earnings allowance and retirement allowance, see A. Ogus and A. Barendt, *The Law of Social Security* (3rd ed., 1988).
[30] R(I) 1/62.
[31] Social Security Contributions and Benefits Act 1992, s. 103.
[32] *Jones v. Secretary of State for Social Services* [1972] A.C. 944, *per* Lord Simon at p. 1020.
[33] R(I) 14/16.

ered an actual loss of physical faculty.[34] While a loss of faculty does not have to be permanent it must have been present for some time, because disablement benefit is not available until after the expiry of 90 days beginning with the date of the accident or onset of the disease.[35] The extent to which the loss of faculty results in disablement is to be determined objectively without reference to the particular circumstances of the claimant except age, sex and physical and mental condition.[36] An important result of this is that the effect of a disablement on an individual's earning capacity is ignored.[37] For some conditions or injuries the degree of disablement is prescribed by regulation.[38] Thus loss of a hand or foot is regarded as 100 per cent disability while, at the other extreme, loss of part of a small toe but with some loss of bone is regarded as 1 per cent disability. However these are *prima facie* assessments and are subject to increase or reduction as may be reasonable in the circumstances by the medical authorities.[39] Where a condition is not prescribed by regulation, assessment is dependent on the facts and circumstances of each case and while the degree of disablement for prescribed conditions is relevant it is no more than a guide.[40] Since October 1, 1986 disablement benefit is paid only if the assessment of disablement is at least 14 per cent except in cases of pneumoniosis, byssinosis or diffuse mesothelioma for which benefit is payable where the assessment is at least 1 per cent.[41] Rates of benefit are adjusted regularly, but at the time of writing the weekly payment for a person over 18 who is assessed as 100 per cent disabled is £91.60 while a weekly payment for a person assessed between 1 per cent and 10 per cent disabled is £9.16.

7.37 Disablement benefit is therefore designed to compensate the person who is incapacitated as a result of an

---

[34] Social Security Contributions and Benefits Act 1992, s. 122(1).
[35] Social Security Contributions and Benefits Act 1992, s. 103(6). Regarding the time for claiming, see Social Security (Claims and Payments) Regulations 1979 (S.I. 1979 No. 628), reg. 14.
[36] Social Security Act 1975, Sched. 8, para. 1 (a), (c).
[37] R(I) 3/84.
[38] Social Security (General Benefit) Regulations 1982 (S.I. 1982 No. 1408), Sched. 2.
[39] *Ibid.*, reg.11(b).
[40] *R. v. Industrial Injuries Commissioner, ex p. Cable* [1968] 1 Q.B. 729.
[41] Social Security Contributions and Benefits Act 1992, s. 103; Social Security (Industrial Injuries) (Prescribed Diseases) Regulations 1985, reg. 20(1).

industrial accident or prescribed disease from working on a long-term basis. Since the abolition of the special injury benefit for those injured in the course of their employment or contracting a prescribed disease, for short-term incapacity statutory sick pay or sickness benefit is available. Sickness benefit is payable at a flat rate with increases for dependants but no earnings-related supplement, for any day on which the claimant is incapable of work by reason of some specific disease or bodily or mental disablement.[42] Unlike Disablement Benefit entitlement to Sickness Benefit, Invalidity Benefit or Statutory Sick Pay is not therefore dependent on the incapacity resulting from an industrial accident or prescribed disease. It is not paid for the first three days of a period of interruption of employment and extends for 28 weeks.[43] In fact since the extension in 1986 of statutory sick pay to 28 weeks the injured employee receives his short-term benefits from his own employer being required to claim from the Department of Social Security only if he is still incapacitated after 28 weeks except in the case of an employee who is not qualified to receive statutory sick pay from his employer.[44]

Incapacity benefit

7.37a With effect from April 13, 1995 Sickness and Invalidity Benefits will be replaced by a new benefit — Incapacity Benefit — which will re-focus on medical incapacity for work.[44a] Like Sickness and Invalidity Benefits entitlement is not dependent on the incapacity being the result of an industrial accident or prescribed disease. Detailed coverage of Incapacity Benefit falls within the province of social security law but the main import of the statutory provisions[44b] are described here. Whether or not

---

[42] Social Security Contributions and Benefits Act 1992, ss. 31, 57. Where the claimant is capable of work other than his normal work (*e.g.* "light work" or "work within certain limits") and is unable to find such work the claim should be for unemployment benefit.

[43] Social Security Contributions and Benefits Act 1992, s. 57(1)(d). At the end of the 28 weeks, invalidity benefit becomes available.

[44] Others who may claim sickness benefit are the self-employed.

[44a] The test of incapacity for work for Sickness and Invalidity Benefits had developed to allow all relevant personal circumstances (even of a non-medical nature like age, education etc.) to be taken into account (see R(S)11/51;, R(S)2/82).

[44b] Social Security (Incapacity for Work) Act 1994; Incapacity for Work Regulations 1994.

a person will be entitled to Incapacity Benefit depends on whether at the time of his claim he has been engaged in remunerative work for more than 8 weeks in the 21 weeks preceding the date of claim. If he was, he is entitled to benefit if he is "incapable by reason of some specific disease or bodily or mental disablement of doing work which he could reasonably be expected to do in the course of the occupation in which he is so engaged."[44c] Others, and those who are still in receipt of Incapacity Benefit after 196 days, must satisfy the "all work" test, namely a test — which refers only to medical matters — of the individual's incapacity by reason of some specific disease or bodily or mental disablement to perform prescribed activities.[44d] Benefit will be paid at two rates. Short-term Incapacity Benefit, payable at the same rate as Sickness Benefit, will be paid for the first 28 weeks and thereafter at a higher rate for the following 24 weeks. Long-term Incapacity Benefit will be paid from the 365th day of incapacity for those who meet the "all work" test or from the 197th day of incapacity for those who are terminally ill or entitled to the highest rate of the care component of Disability Living Allowance.[44e]

OTHER STATE HELP

Criminal Injuries Compensation Board Scheme

7.38 Since 1964 where a person suffers personal injury directly attributable to a crime of violence or while attempting to stop someone committing a crime or while apprehending a suspected criminal he is able to apply to the Criminal Injuries Compensation Board which may award a tax-free payment of compensation which is arrived at having regard to the principles applied by the civil courts.[45] There are some limitations to the scheme[46] in

[44c] Social Security Contributions and Benefits Act 1992, s. 171B as inserted by Social Security (Incapacity for Work) Act 1994, s. 5.
[44d] The activities are prescribed in the Schedule to the Incapacity for Work Regulations 1994.
[44e] Social Security Contributions and Benefits Act 1992, s. 390A as inserted by Social Security (Incapacity for Work) Act 1994.
[45] Where a person is killed an award may be claimed by a dependant who may elect a flat-rate bereavement award.
[46] The Criminal Justice Act 1988 would have placed the scheme on a statutory footing so that payments were no longer made *ex gratia*, however, the relevant part of the Act was never brought into force.

that no award is made if the loss is less than £750 nor if caused by a road traffic accident unless it involved a deliberate running down. Also it is important that a claimant notifies and co-operates with the police and that neither his own conduct not previous convictions justify withholding or reduction of an award. Nevertheless, as has been judicially noted[47] an employee who could not substantiate a claim against his employer may successfully claim an award from the Board.

7.38a However although the Criminal Justice Act 1988 sought to place the scheme on a statutory footing the relevant provisions of the Act were never brought into effect and in 1993 the government issued a White Paper which proposed to introduce a new scheme which, it is estimated, would save over £325 million over the next seven years and under which compensation for criminal injuries would be awarded on a tariff basis. The new scheme does not depend on any statutory provision but relies on the Home Secretary's common law prerogative powers and is not therefore subject to Parliamentary scrutiny. However, although at the time of writing an appeal to the House of Lords is pending, the Court of Appeal has held that the Home Secretary is under no duty to exercise the powers conferred on him by the 1988 Act for the purpose of introducing a new scheme but if he did not do so he was not permitted to introduce a radically different scheme under his prerogative powers so long as the relevant provision of the 1988 Act remained unrepealed.[47b]

7.38b One result of the new scheme being tariff-based is that no account is taken of individual matters as a result of which no compensation will be awarded for loss of earnings and earnings capacity which are likely to be important where the claim results from workplace violence; also the time limit for bringing claims will be reduced from three years to one year.

---

[47] *Charlton v. Forrest Printing Ink Co. Ltd* [1980] I.R.L.R. 331 (C.A.) *per* Lord Denning.
[47b] *R. v. Secretary of State for the Home Department, ex p. Fire Brigades Union, The Times,* November 10, 1994 (C.A.). Until the House of Lords has given its decision awards will continue to be made under the existing scheme.

Pneumoconiosis

7.39 By the Pneumoconiosis, etc. (Workers' Compensation) Act 1979 special provision is made for workers who are disabled as a result of pneumoconiosis, byssinosis or diffuse mesothelioma.[48] An applicant who satisfies the conditions is entitled to a lump-sum payment[49] from the Department of Employment.[50] At the time of writing[51] the maximum payment to a disabled applicant is £45,615 and to dependants[52] is £20,705. The conditions of entitlement are that (1) disablement benefit is payable to the applicant in respect of the disease, (2) every relevant employer[53] has ceased to carry on business, and (3) he has not brought an action or settled any claim for damages in respect of the disablement.[54] Generally, applications must be made within 12 months of the date disablement benefit was awarded or in the case of dependants, within 12 months of date of death.[55]

---

[48] The dependants of workers who have died while disabled by one of these diseases are also covered.

[49] The amount of the lump sum depends on the degree of disablement, assessed by a medical board, the period covered by the assessment and the applicant's age Pneumoconiosis, etc. (Workers Compensation) (Payment of Claims) Regulations 1985 (S.I. 1985 No. 2035).

[50] Pneumoconiosis, etc. (Workers' Compensation) Act 1979, s. 1.

[51] The figures are revised annually.

[52] Pneumoconiosis, etc. (Workers' Compensation) Act 1979, s. 3.

[53] Any person by whom the applicant was employed during the time he was developing the disease and against whom he might have had a claim for damages (*ibid.*, s. 2(3)).

[54] *Ibid.*, s. 2(2); for dependants the conditions are slightly different.

[55] Pneumoconiosis, etc. (Workers' Compensation) (Determination of Claims) Regulations 1979 (S.I. 1979 No. 727).

APPENDIX I

HSE ORGANISATION
Responsible to the Health and Safety Commission, under the authority of the Employment Department (London).

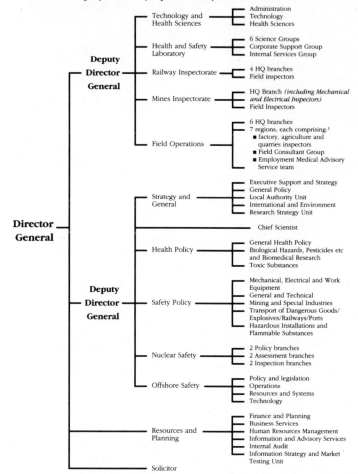

Director General

Deputy Director General

- Technology and Health Sciences
  - Administration
  - Technology
  - Health Sciences
- Health and Safety Laboratory
  - 6 Science Groups
  - Corporate Support Group
  - Internal Services Group
- Railway Inspectorate
  - 4 HQ branches
  - Field inspectors
- Mines Inspectorate
  - HQ Branch *(including Mechanical and Electrical Inspectors)*
  - Field Inspectors
- Field Operations
  - 6 HQ branches
  - 7 regions, each comprising:[1]
    - factory, agriculture and quarries inspectors
    - Field Consultant Group
    - Employment Medical Advisory Service team

Deputy Director General

- Strategy and General
  - Executive Support and Strategy
  - General Policy
  - Local Authority Unit
  - International and Environment
  - Research Strategy Unit
- Chief Scientist
- Health Policy
  - General Health Policy
  - Biological Hazards, Pesticides etc and Biomedical Research
  - Toxic Substances
- Safety Policy
  - Mechanical, Electrical and Work Equipment
  - General and Technical
  - Mining and Special Industries
  - Transport of Dangerous Goods/ Explosives/Railways/Ports
  - Hazardous Installations and Flammable Substances
- Nuclear Safety
  - 2 Policy branches
  - 2 Assessment branches
  - 2 Inspection branches
- Offshore Safety
  - Policy and legislation
  - Operations
  - Resources and Systems
  - Technology
- Resources and Planning
  - Finance and Planning
  - Business Services
  - Human Resources Management
  - Information and Advisory Services
  - Internal Audit
  - Information Strategy and Market Testing Unit
- Solicitor

Reproduced from Health & Safety Commission Annual Report 1993/94

[1] Note: H.M. Industrial Pollution Inspectorate for Scotland is a separate body from HSE responsible to the Scottish Office (Edinburgh). HSE Field Ops. division (Scotland region) liaises with HMIPI on environmental matters in accordance with legislative requirements and a memorandum of understanding.

INDEX